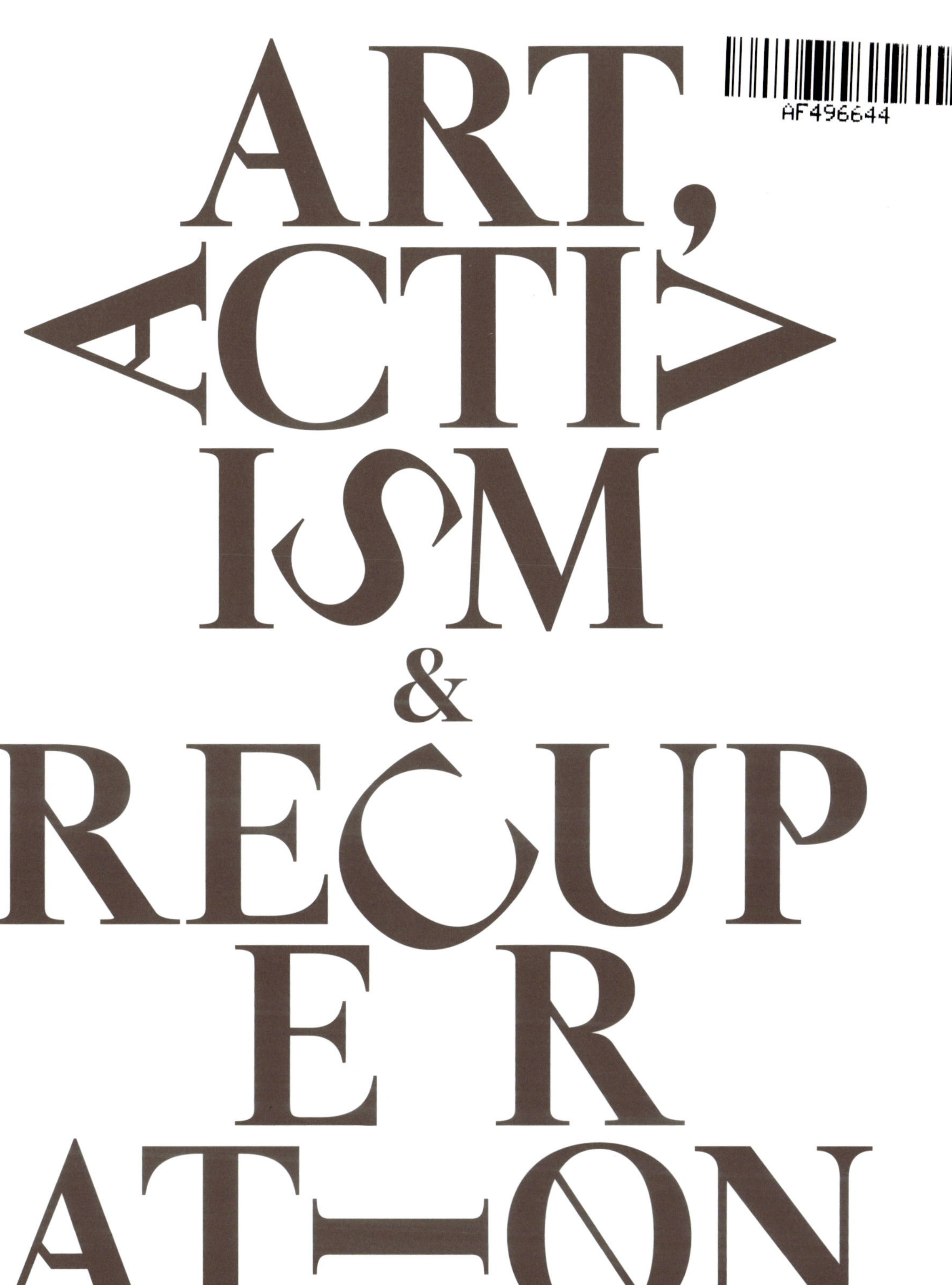

What are the power relations between art, activists and cultural institutions? Who ultimately benefits from these relationships? What critical role can art and/or activism really have in a situation where any form of critique is automatically recuperated and neutralised by the mainstream? Under such conditions, what are effective strategies of opposition? What is to be done (with art)?

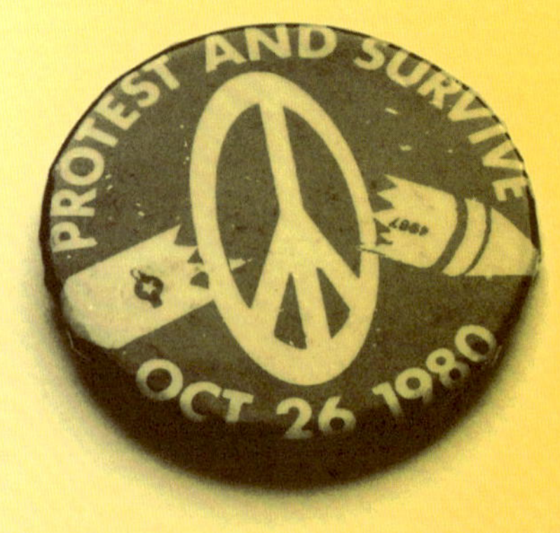

Protest and Survive, 1980
Courtesy Rob Webster
Photograph Carl Newland

What school did you go to ?

Mark Wallinger, 2010
www.makeamark.org.uk

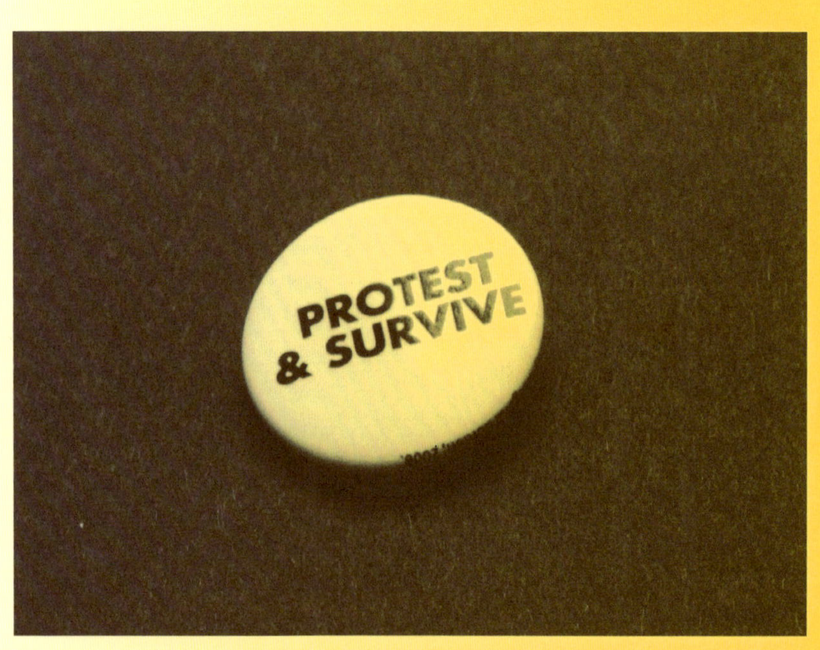

Protest & Survive 20000
Whitechapel Gallery Inaugural
Exhibition, 2009
Photograph Carl Newland

Who can afford to go private

?

Mark Wallinger, 2010
www.makeamark.org.uk

GLOSSARY

ACTIVIST: Not necessarily one of those people who wears a Che Guevara T-shirt in an un-ironic way. Activists are those involved in action looking to create social, political, economic, or environmental change. The action is either in support of, or opposition to, one side of an often controversial argument, thus habitually adopting a binary/oppositional stance. Some forms of activism do not necessarily involve direct protest, but look to change the behaviour of individuals rather than directly focusing on power.

APPARATUS: Apparatus (or dispositif in French) is both a ubiquitous and nebulous concept in Foucault's later thinking, according to Agamben's essay 'What is an Apparatus?' (2009). Agamben's essay tries to clarify things: "I will call an apparatus literally anything that has in some way the capacity to capture, orient, determine, intercept, model, control, or secure the gestures, behaviors, opinions, or discourses of living beings". Seen from this perspective, Agamben's work, like Foucault's, may be described as the identification and investigation of apparatuses, together with incessant attempts to find new ways to dismantle them. An apparatus is a kind of network between elements; it acts within relations, mechanisms and plays of power – bound to processes of subjectification. Agamben says: "It would probably not be wrong to define the extreme phase of capitalist development in which we live as a massive accumulation and proliferation of apparatuses."

THE ART STRIKE: Alain Jouffroy first suggested an art strike in 1968 to "not to end the rule of production, but to change the most adventurous part of 'artistic' production into the production of revolutionary ideas, forms and techniques" ('What's to be done about art?'). In 1974, Gustav Metzger called upon artists to support a three-year Art Strike between 1977 and 1980, to protest against the relationship between art, the State and capitalism in methods of production, distribution and consumption. Metzger looked to bring down the art system through a total withdrawal of labour, where artists would refuse to produce, sell or let work go on exhibition, and refuse any collaboration with the art world. He was unable to gather support from other artists however, and the strike was unsuccessful. Stewart Home and others took part in an Art Strike from 1990–1993 in opposition to neo-liberal EU policies, moving beyond the gallery system to question artistic production and the role of the artist. More recently, Redas Dirzys and a Temporary Art Strike Committee called for a strike in response to Vilnius becoming a European Capital of Culture for 2009; and in Eastern Europe, there have been successful actions by artists including a strike in Poland where artists refused to exhibit work in State galleries.

ARTIVIST: An activist looking to create change using the medium and resources of art.

COMMONS: The idea of the 'commons' is generally taken as an antonym of private property. The enclosure movement, at the end of the 18th Century in the UK, demonstrates how common land was fenced off and entitled to private owners. Landowners used the legislative framework at the time to appropriate common land for private profit, and the landless working classes became the labour force of the industrial revolution. In other words, what was inherently held in common (common-wealth) was stolen. As property rights have been extended from land to capital to information, clear parallels exist to how issues of class and property flow from the commodification of information. Nowadays the term is often used in relation to intellectual property, the 'intellectual commons', and its meaning comes close to the public domain. Behind this is the identification of common assets, and the ways these are organised, governed, used in practice, and become part of particular ownership regimes (Copyright or GNU General Public License, for instance). The importance of a discussion of the intellectual commons lies in emphasising that this is not simply a legal issue but one that necessitates political action to protect the commons from privateers. Closely related is the term 'commons-based peer production' as an alternative form of organisation of productive activity. Peer production suggests that the commons is good for innovation outside of the capitalistic relation of property.

COPYLEFT: Copyleft is an ethical, philosophical, and political movement that seeks to free ideas from the constraints of intellectual property law. According to the proponents of copyleft, duplication is part of the very essence of what it means to have an idea and to share it. They say, "sharing is the nature of creation". The earliest example of a copyleft license is the GPL written in 1989 (see GPL below). In his essay 'Copyfarleft and Copyjustright' Dmytri Kleiner takes the concept further by linking it to waged labour and thus arguing for licenses with different rules for different classes.

GPL: The GNU General Public License, is intended to guarantee a producer's freedom to share and change free software. By free software, the qualification is important that free refers to freedom as in speech not price. The Free Software Foundation explain: "Free software is a matter of liberty, not price. To understand the concept, you should think of 'free' as in 'free speech', not as in 'free beer'" (http://www.gnu.org/philosophy/free-sw.html). To be free software, the human-readable form of the program (the source code) must be released fully into the public domain. But this goes further than 'open source' because it emphasises the ideological aspect of freedom. There are broader social implications too, in making comparisons with other examples of multiple production and rethinking the concept of the public. Arguably new forms of creative and political practices emerge from such principles alongside new social and subject formations.

GREEN IMPERIALISM: A form of hypocrisy from the Western privileged classes. For example, the case of rich countries running polluting industries with cheap labour in places like China, whilst simultaneously pointing the finger at them for climate change. Or post-reproductive, wealthy, white men (such as Optimum Population Trust members like James Lovelock and David Attenborough) blaming the population growth of the rural poor in developing countries for global warming. In the arts, Green Imperialism can be seen in the practice of 'activist-artists', who are very often, again, from the privileged classes, telling audiences how to live their lives, whilst consistently taking no regard for the energy, resources and funding streams required in producing an exhibition about such an issue.

IDEOLOGY: Even the denial of ideology is an ideological issue in itself (to paraphrase Slavoj Žižek).

INFORMATIONAL CAPITALISM: Informationalism is the result of the restructuring of capitalism's mode of production to a mode of information; from a mode of development focused on economic growth and surplus-value (industrialism) to one based on the pursuit of knowledge and increased levels of complexity of information (informationalism). Networked technologies have enhanced the effectiveness of global capitalism, enabling it to become more flexible, adaptable, faster, efficient and pervasive. To a large extent, in the 'over-developed world', the assembly lines have been replaced by the network as the organisational model and metaphor for production of all kinds. Industrial production is superseded by information, and capital is regenerated in a new form suitable to the general state of science and progress of technology and to maintain its logic. New forms remain instruments of domination but also they present new opportunities for resistance leading to an alternative vision of communication and the commons.

ISAs: The 'ideological State apparatuses' (ISAs), that include the family, schools, church, legal apparatus, political system, trade unions, communications media, arts and culture, and so on, are distinct from the 'repressive State apparatuses', the government, army, police, courts, prisons, and so on. Both function through repression and ideology but the essential difference is that rather than predominantly acting by repression or violence, ISAs function through ideology and do so more covertly. State power is thus maintained by the State apparatus that includes institutions that represent the repressive apparatus and the ideological apparatus. This is not a new phenomena. In pre-industrial times, the ideological State apparatus worked through the Church predominantly, controlling other apparatuses like education, communications and culture. Writing in 1969, Louis Althusser, in 'Ideology and Ideological State Apparatuses: Notes Toward an Investigation', thinks this central position has been taken by the education apparatus in capitalist social formations, and the contemporary conception of cognitive capitalism would appear to confirm this idea. In education, there is a captive and free audience for the reproduction of the capitalist social formation: "the relations of exploited to exploiters and exploiters to exploited, are largely reproduced" as he puts it. The ideas of a human subject are "material actions inserted into material practices governed by material rituals which are themselves defined by the material ideological apparatus from which derive the ideas of that subject".

NEW INTERNATIONAL DIVISION OF LABOUR: The New International Division of Labour (NIDL) is an outcome of globalisation and processes of production driven by trade liberalisation, technological change and economic reform. Developments in transportation and communication have enabled companies to search for the cheapest places to manufacture and assemble components, and from the early 1950s to late 1990s, there has been a global shift in manufacturing processes from developed to developing countries where costs are substantially lower.

POLITICAL AESTHETICS: Rather the politics of aesthetics than the aesthetics of politics, to use Benjamin's formulation.

POVERTY JOURNALISM: A journalistic activity based on capturing images of extreme poverty, usually in the developing world, through the work of lens-based media (photography and video) practitioners. Most often, the imagery is created by and for the Western news media. A certain lack of reflexivity often exists towards poverty journalism from 'politically-engaged' artists using the documentary style to depict scenes of exploitation and poverty, raising ethical questions of their own gaze.

REFUSAL: Refusing to work follows the logic that capitalism is an irrational system that cannot be replaced by anything through better planning or anything that employs its logic. It derives from Mario Tronti's essay 'The Strategy of Refusal' of 1965, pointing out that capital uses workers' antagonistic opposition for its own development. The mistake in Classical Marxism had been to simply see the working class as the antagonistic subject of capitalism, and therefore the advocated alternative to break free of exploitative conditions is for work itself to be transformed through self-determination and made more autonomous (sometimes referred to as 'self-valorisation'). Creative labour can re-appropriate the instruments that are part of its very domination in the 'cycle of struggle' between labour and Capital.

RECESSIONAL AESTHETICS: A term coined by art historians Hal Foster and David Joselit presented in a talk entitled 'Recessional Aesthetics: New Publics or Business as Usual' in New York in 2009, at the height of the global recession. Initially looking to propose a series of questions to address the condition of contemporary art in a recession era, Foster eventually conceded "David and I know more about receding hairlines than we do about recessional aesthetics."

RECUPERATION: Recuperation is a sociological term, first proposed by Guy Debord of the Situationist movement. It is the process by which ideas and actions deemed 'radical' or oppositional become commodified or absorbed into mainstream society and culture.

SEMIOCAPITALISM: Semiocapitalism is the term Franco Berardi gives to the current system where informational capitalism incorporates linguistic labour (he combines semiotics – the science of signs, and capitalism – the social system founded on the exploitation of labour and the accumulation of capital). The term emphasises how language has become fully integrated into the valorisation process effecting both the economic and linguistic fields, thus contributing to the crisis of value. The Marxist theory of value is seen to be inadequate because of the difficulty in calculating working time related to signification as opposed to the relative ease of calculating working time against making traditional objects. Similarly there are effects on language production as it becomes increasingly economised: supply and demand correspond to an excess of signs and levels of social attention (the so-called attention economy). Berardi sees added consequences in terms of the psyche, as language acts on the construction of subjectivity itself.

WHAT IS TO BE DONE?: 'What is to be Done?' is the title of a famous essay by Vladimir Ilyich Lenin, written in 1901. It addresses key 'burning' questions of tactics, party organisation, and terror, arguing for the positive role of intellectuals to direct the efforts of the working class to reach full socialism, and questioning the liberal notion of freedom. See also 'What is to be Done (with Lenin)?' by Slavoj Žižek from 2004. In 2007, *Documenta 12* also asked 'What is to be done?' – with art.

WHO'S RECUPERATING WHO?

TOM TREVOR

In recent times there has been a string of high profile 'political' artworks supported by mainstream art institutions, which have featured heavily in the media. Anti-war protest art such as Mark Wallinger's ***State Britain*** (2007), an exact replica of Brian Haw's one-man peace camp re-located from Parliament Square to Tate Britain, or Jeremy Deller's ***It is what it is*** (2009), which took the wreckage of a car destroyed by a bomb in Baghdad on a tour of art museums across the USA, have been widely fêted by the cultural establishment – both artists mentioned have been awarded the Turner Prize, for example. But what is it that public-funded institutions find so appealing about art that purports to be political, especially as such works would seem to directly criticise the policies of the very state that funds them? Or perhaps the question should be turned around to ask, what does it mean for the political efficacy of the artworks to be so whole-heartedly embraced by the cultural institutions of the State?

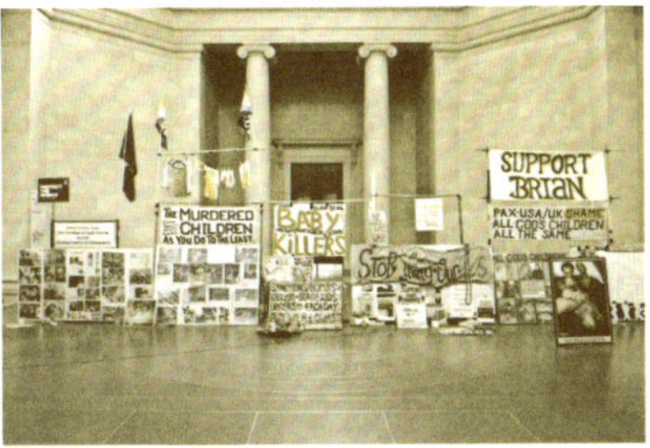

State Britain, Mark Wallinger, 2007
Installation at Tate Britain
Courtesy the artist, and Anthony Reynolds Gallery London
Photograph Dave Morgan

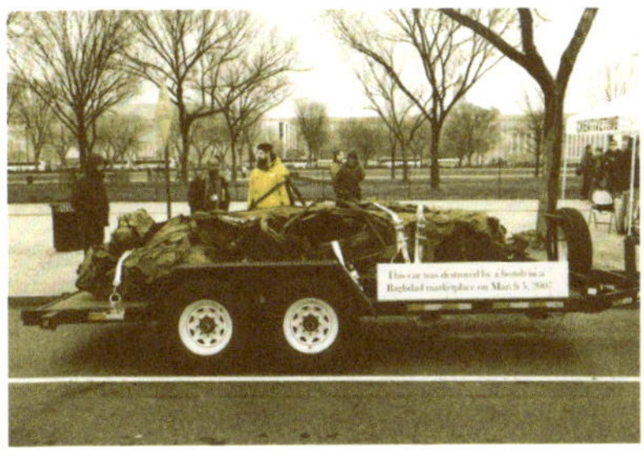

It Is What It Is, Jeremy Deller, 2009
Courtesy Creative Time, New York
Photograph David B. Smith

There is, of course, a long tradition of artist/activists in contemporary art, from Joseph Beuys to the Artist Placement Group, the feminist art movement of the 1970s to the environmental activist groups of today. Reflecting upon one's own individual relationship to social conventions, or how 'my' experience is translated and represented in the wider world, is inherently political, inevitably bound up with an awareness of the distribution of power in society. However, as soon as this process of reflexive inquiry becomes involved with the institutional structures of art, the focus of the questions must inevitably shift away from a straight forward critique of the politics of representation, to the more introspective issues of recuperation and one's own implication in the processes of absorption and neutralisation by the mainstream.

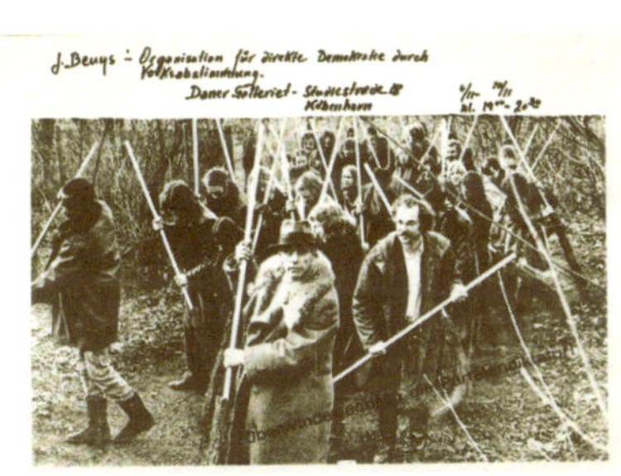

Overcome Party Dictatorship Now,
Joseph Beuys, 1971
Courtesy Tate, London

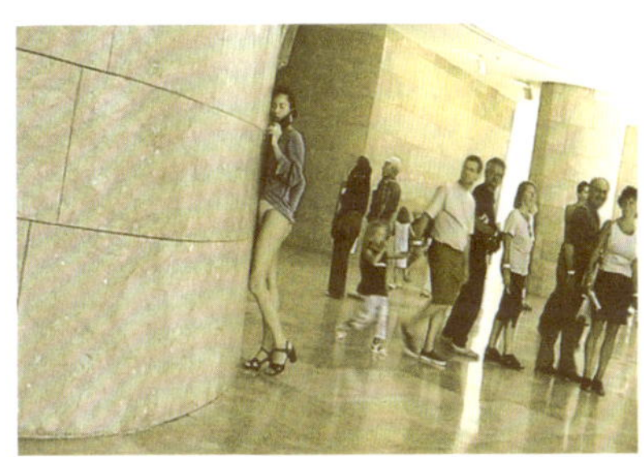

Little Frank and His Carp,
Andrea Fraser, 2001
Performance at Guggenheim Bilbao
Courtesy Friedrich Petzel Gallery, New York

Since the 1960s many artists, from Hans Haacke to Michael Asher, Fred Wilson to Andrea Fraser, have made work which specifically takes as its subject a critique of the institution that houses art, and the structures – financial and ideological – that support them. However critical such art may itself be, paradoxically, it also serves to highlight the institution's liberalism by allowing it to be there in the first place. Inevitably such inclusiveness defuses the very criticism being offered. It is as if the critique has been turned into a form of validation; as if the act of 'dissent' has been drained of its power to effect change and turned instead into a hollow signifier of liberal democracy in action. Thus, despite an individual's best intentions, as soon as they partake in the public discourse of contemporary art they are inevitably implicated in a process of recuperation.

Guy Debord, who co-founded the Situationist International in 1957, described recuperation in a sociological sense, as the procedure by which the mainstream takes a radical idea and repackages it as a safe commodity for consumer society. According to Debord, recuperation is a process by which "avant-garde innovations might be recovered for use by the reigning social order, that revolutionary negativity might be recouped to strengthen bourgeois affirmation." The mainstream apparatus actually feeds off the energy of dissent and gains strength from it. As such, the Situationist notion of recuperation was a development on from Antonio Gramsci's concept of 'hegemony', which theorised the ways in which one set of bourgeois values are normalised as everyday 'common sense' by allowing space for dissent.

Of course such an idea is immediately in danger of recuperation itself. Debord's strategy therefore, was to employ the language of consumerism but to turn its back upon itself. In *The Society of the Spectacle*, he defines the principle of 'détournement' as using mainstream communication but including an element of self-critique within it in order to turn the attention of passive consumers of spectacle culture back towards the material considerations of everyday life and historical struggle. As capitalism has fetishised the 'sign' (the seductive images of consumerism), Debord argued that by adopting the language of spectacle culture, but including a reflexive critique within it, the underlying contradictions would be revealed.

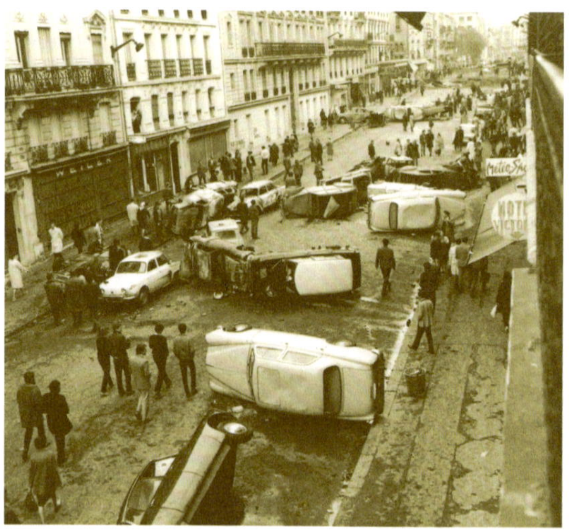

Rioting students block Gay Lussac Street,
Paris, 11th May 1968
Courtesy TopFoto

Situationism came to the peak of its influence in the protests of May 1968 in France. It was decided to bring the group to an end in 1972 as, according to Debord, they wanted "to destroy the revolutionary commodity it had become", saying "the more our theses become famous, we ourselves will become even more inaccessible, even more clandestine". Ironically, the shock tactics and mocking, cynical stance of disengagement put forward by the Situationists went on to spawn punk in the late 1970s in the UK, which started out as a radical style of refusal but very rapidly became sanitised and re-packaged as mainstream popular culture. The resistant attitude of Situationist ideology was thus itself commodified and recuperated by the market, leaving the likes of Joe Strummer to sing in vain about "turning rebellion into money" (in The Clash's best-selling record *White Man In Hammersmith Palais*), while fashion entrepreneurs Malcolm McLaren and Vivienne Westwood cashed in on the new-found marketing potential of rebellion.

Daily Mirror
BRITAIN'S BIGGEST DAILY SALE
6p Thursday, December 2, 1976 No. 22,658

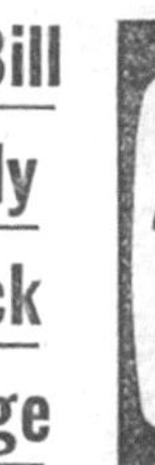

TV's Bill Grundy in rock outrage

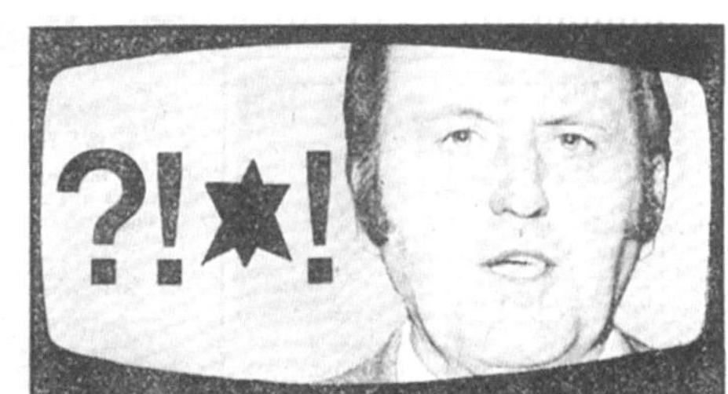

THE FILTH AND THE FURY!

Judge in 'murder' pardon shocker

By ARNOT McWHINNIE

A JUDGE made an astonishing attack yesterday on the way a man convicted of murder was given a royal pardon.

He told a jury: "You may well have come to the clear conclusion that he was rightly convicted."

The man at the centre of the storm is 48-year-old Patrick Meehan, who was freed from jail in May after serving nearly seven years.

The judge, Lord Robertson, said: "There is no legal justification whatsoever for saying that Meehan was wrongly convicted."

He went on to suggest that Meehan's conviction for killing elderly Mrs.

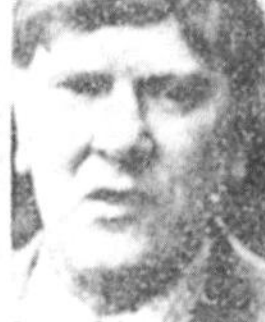

Meehan yesterday

Rachel Ross still stood, despite the pardon.

The judge spoke out at the end of a second trial over the same murder.

This time, 38-year-old Ian Waddell was in the dock. He was a prosecution witness when Meehan got a life sentence in 1969.

Yesterday, the jury acquitted Waddell of murder—and also cleared him of giving false evidence at Meehan's trial.

During the judge's summing up, Meehan stormed angrily from the public gallery at Edinburgh High Court.

He said outside: "I might as well tear up my royal pardon. It's a worthless piece of paper. It seems I am still convicted."

The judge said of the pardon: "In the ordinary use of language if you pardon someone you pardon them for something they have done—not for something they haven't done.

"It certainly doesn't quash the conviction."

● Who killed Rachel Ross?—Centre Pages.

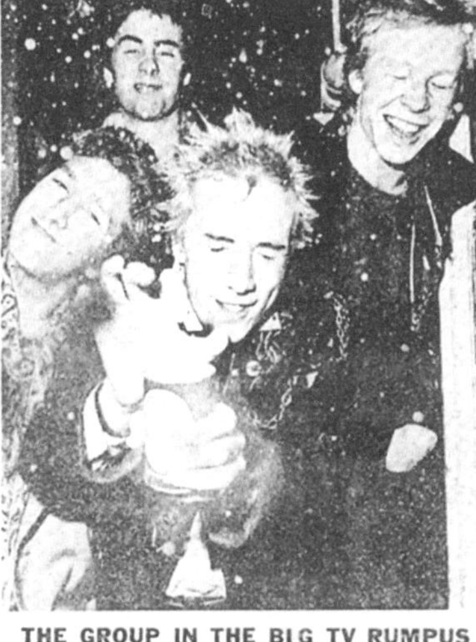

THE GROUP IN THE BIG TV RUMPUS

Johnny Rotten, leader of the Sex Pistols, opens a can of beer. Last night their language made TV viewers froth.

When the air turned blue..

INTERVIEWER Bill Grundy introduced the Sex Pistols to viewers with the comment: "Words actually fail me about the next guests on tonight's show."

The group sang a number — and the amazing interview got under way.

GRUNDY: I am told you have received £40,000 from a record company. Doesn't that seem to be slightly opposed to an anti-materialistic way of life.
PISTOL: The more the merrier.
GRUNDY: Really.
PISTOL: Yea, yea.
GRUNDY: Tell me more then.
PISTOL. F——ing spent it, didn't we.
GRUNDY: You are serious?
PISTOL: Mmmm.
GRUNDY: Beethoven, Mozart, Bach?
PISTOL: They're wonderful people.
GRUNDY: Are they?
PISTOL: Yes they really turn us on. They do.
GRUNDY: Suppose they turn other people on?
PISTOL, (in a whisper): That's just their tough s——.
GRUNDY: It's what?
PISTOL: Nothing—a rude word. Next question.
GRUNDY: No, no. What was the rude word?
PISTOL: S——.
GRUNDY: Was it really? Good heavens. What about you girls behind? Are you married or just enjoying yourself?
GIRL: I've always wanted to meet you.
GRUNDY: Did you really? We'll meet afterwards, shall we?
PISTOL: You dirty old man. You dirty old man.
GRUNDY: Go on, you've got a long time yet. You've got another five seconds. Say something outrageous.
PISTOL: You dirty sod. You dirty bastard.
GRUNDY: Go on. Again.
PISTOL: You dirty f——er.
GRUNDY: What?
PISTOL: What a f——ing rotter.
GRUNDY: Well, that's it for tonight . . . I'll be seeing you soon. I hope I'm not seeing YOU again. Goodnight.

A POP group shocked millions of viewers last night with the filthiest language heard on British television.

The Sex Pistols, leaders of the new "punk rock" cult, hurled a string of four-letter obscenities at interviewer Bill Grundy on Thames TV's family teatime programme "Today."

The Thames switchboard was flooded with protests.

Nearly 200 angry viewers telephoned the Mirror. One man was so furious that he kicked in the screen of his £380 colour TV.

Grundy was immediately carpeted by his boss and will apologise in tonight's programme.

Shocker

A Thames spokesman said: "Because the programme was live, we could not foresee the language which would be used. We apologise to all viewers."

The show, screened at peak children's viewing time, turned into a shocker when Grundy asked about £40,000 that the Sex Pistols received

By STUART GREIG, MICHAEL McCARTHY and JOHN PEACOCK

from their record company.

One member of the group said: "F---ing spent it, didn't we?"

Then when Grundy asked about people who preferred Beethoven, Mozart and Bach, another Sex Pistol remarked: "That's just their tough s---."

Later Grundy told the group: "Say something outrageous."

A punk rocker replied: "You dirty sod. You dirty bastard."

"Go on. Again," said Grundy.

"*You dirty f---er.*"

"What?"

Uproar as viewers jam phones

"*What a f---ing rotter.*"

As the Thames switchboard became jammed, viewers rang the Mirror to voice their complaints.

Lorry driver James Holmes, 47, was outraged that his eight-year-old son Lee heard the swearing . . . and kicked in the screen of his TV.

"It blew up and I was knocked backwards," he said. "But I was so angry and disgusted with this filth that I took a swing with my boot.

"I can swear as well as anyone, but I don't want this sort of muck coming into my home at teatime."

Mr. Holmes, of Beechfield Walk, Waltham Abbey, Essex, added: "I am not a violent person, but I would like to have got hold of Grundy.

"He should be sacked for encouraging this sort of disgusting behaviour."

WHO ARE THESE PUNKS? PAGE NINE

Daily Mirror,
Thursday 2 December 1976
Courtesy Mirrorpix

Whilst punk would undoubtedly not have had such a far-reaching impact if it were not for McLaren's instinct for hype and the intelligence with which he played the media at its own game, it is also undeniable that, in the years since, the market has made full use of the consumer appetite for shock and the re-packaged signifiers of so-called 'counter-culture'. Indeed, in his book *Hello I'm Special*, Hal Niedzviecki describes the post-punk model of rebellion as the 'new conformism', where we are all "invited, urged and commanded to rebel against the system to gain access to the system". It could be argued that the true inheritors of the Situationist tools of détournement are the advertising executives and media spin doctors of the last decade or, in respect of the art market, Banksy, Damien Hirst and Tracey Emin.

So, what is to be done? If every action one takes to try to change society is simply turned into so much fuel to sustain the prevailing order, would it not be better just to do nothing? While reflexivity enables an understanding of one's own implication in the processes of recuperation, such self-consciousness can lead to a kind of paralysis and ultimately become an obstacle to change in itself. 'Institutional critique', for example, has become a standard strategy for contemporary art within the museum, so much so that it appears like an orthodoxy that stifles any other form of critique, effectively marginalising more direct artist/activist practices in a wider social context. Under such conditions, what are effective strategies of opposition?

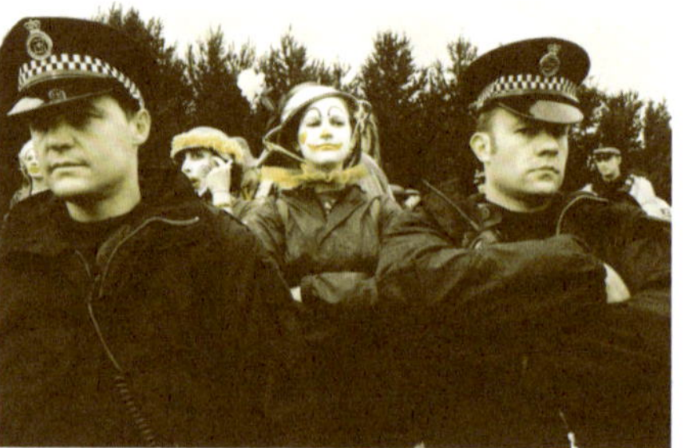

Cops and Clown, Clown Army, 2009
Courtesy Creative Time
Photograph David B. Smith

The maxim (generally attributed to Gramsci), "pessimism of the intellect, optimism of the will", deftly sets out the challenge of nurturing a self-critical yet constructive scepticism that still does not fall prey to cynicism or passive resignation in the face of seemingly overwhelming forces. 'Pessimism of the intellect' is only constructive if, while remaining sceptical in the best Enlightenment tradition, it avoids the cynicism that can undermine 'optimism of the will'. Thus, whilst the pessimist's analysis might be that hegemony feeds off dissent, it does not mean that one should not continue to voice that dissent, in full knowledge of its imminent recuperation, and so pursue change, teetering on the edge between activism and absorption.

In terms of the institutions of art, parallel to the increasing corporatisation of larger museums and cultural spaces that has been taking place since the 1990s, new forms of more flexible institutions have emerged in close alliance with artists' critique. Whereas in the 1960s critique was directed against the institution from the 'outside', more recently this reflexive principle has been internalised by the institutions themselves as a kind of auto-critique so as to effect change from within. What is fundamental to the new concepts of the more progressive institutions is a radically different understanding of the public sphere and thus the structure of public spaces. Rather than conceiving of a singular, homogenised and essentially passive public, which demands a populist programme of mass appeal, the so called New Institutionalism seeks to actively 'produce' multiple and diverse communities of interest as co-generators. The public sphere is considered as a space structured by diversity, in which different conflicting interests exist in parallel. With the recognition of dissonance as a productive force, the more progressive art institutions therefore seek to create "a democratic space of polyvocality", as Nina Möntmann describes it, in which the public takes an active role as producer, and from which new social and artistic structures can emerge within civil society. Thus the institution becomes a means for involving art in democratic processes, a means for re-politicising art.

Through the mediation of progressive institutions, art is therefore able to introduce subjectivity back into the democratic process or, as Lars Bang Larsen has written, "introduce levels of desire into political concepts". Post-1968, Michel Foucault fundamentally re-shaped an understanding of the relationship between institutions and subjectivity, and their relation to the idea of hegemony. The asylum, the prison, the school, all of those institutional bodies that form the disciplinary matrix of modern society were now analysed as mechanisms of discipline, and the kind of subjectivities they produced as modes of subjection. Foucault characterised his work as a 'genealogy of the modern subject': a history of how people are constructed as different types of subjects, whether as delinquents, homosexuals, mentally ill, or, through such exclusions as 'normal' and 'healthy'. By focusing on the 'histories of the present', such as the history of sexuality, madness or criminality, Foucault aimed to show how our subjective conceptions of reality and social relations are entirely relative, shaped by "a precarious and fragile history". It is only by studying how we have become what we are, that we can begin to imagine becoming something else. Thus Foucault's archaeologies and genealogies are explicit efforts to re-think the subject, so as to enable the transformation of society.

Contemporary art has always been a space for re-thinking subjectivity. The order of the day then becomes to forge new modes of subjectivity and to re-shape the 'economy of desire', as described by Gilles Deleuze and Félix Guattari, redefining desire as a form of productivity rather than a manifestation of lack, and thus as an instrument of liberation. In his late work *The Three Ecologies*, Guattari extended the definition of ecology to encompass social relations and human subjectivity, as well as the environmental context, as the inter-connected sites for the transformation of society. He argued that just as nature is threatened by the forces of globalisation, so is society and our own mental health. It is within this framework, and through the mediation of its more self-critical institutions, that contemporary art can begin to produce a space of democratic multiplicity that enables an exploration of the relationship between subjectivity and hegemony, ever mindful of the thin line that exists between activism and recuperation.

Tom Trevor is Director of Arnolfini.

RECUPERATOR/ RECUPERATED

For this issue of Concept Store, a selection of artists and curators were invited to respond to the following question: As an artist/artists' group/curator, you are known for work that problematises power relations both within the art establishment and in a wider social context. To what extent do you feel that the system has effectively 'recuperated' the oppositional aspects of your work? Reflecting upon your own implication in these processes of absorption and neutralisation, how can you avoid becoming an agent of recuperation yourself? In other words, are you 'recuperated' or 'recuperator'?

Recuperator/Recuperated 1: PLATFORM
Recuperator/Recuperated 2: Thomas Hirschhorn
Recuperator/Recuperated 3: The Institute for the Art and Practice of Dissent at Home
Recuperator/Recuperated 4: Sarat Maharaj
Recuperator/Recuperated 5: FREEE
Recuperator/Recuperated 6: Piratbyrån

RECUPERATOR/ RECUPERATED 1 PLATFORM

What are the power relations between art, activists and cultural institutions?

Working definitions: in these responses, 'cultural institutions' is taken to mean mainstream organs run by the dominant culture; 'activism', from PLATFORM's perspective, is vision, collaboration, and action towards social and environmental justice; 'art' is an imaginative, sensual, skilled, social and powerful practice with impacts beyond rational explanation, that can happen anywhere and which belongs to everyone. Activists can be artists, artists can be activists, and activists can be found within cultural institutions.

In a healthy democratic society, power relations between these three areas are productively tense, constantly challenging, full of potential and very fluid. In a repressive society, relations are aggressive, embattled, manipulative and desperate.

Who ultimately benefits from these relationships?

In a healthy society, everyone. In a repressive society, it's a struggle - often literally - to the death.

What critical role can art and/or activism really have in a situation where any form of critique is automatically recuperated and neutralised by the mainstream?

In late capitalism, every interesting, imaginative, rebellious idea is fodder for market or state appropriation. However, the strategic aim of activism can often be precisely to use this fact to make a new idea mainstream, to stigmatise a previously accepted norm so that it becomes unbelievable that it ever was considered normal, to create new realities. The constant danger is of pick-and-mix: that only part of the thinking or new vision is acceptable and made mainstream, and that systemic change is left off, or contorted. Activists have to keep vigilant, keep upping the stakes.

Usually, everything is happening at once: artist-activists or activist-artists are at one and the same time way out in advance, while being appropriated (whether intentionally or not), while also heavily critiquing dominant forces, including their own practices. This work may at times have to take place underground, sometimes for long periods, but it is irrepressible.

Under such conditions, what are effective strategies of opposition?

It's impossible to be totally recuperated or neutralised, unless you give your consent. Activist art is viral as are all cultures of resistance, protest, and vision. It's like a critical relay. As such, even if there are signs of consent, defeat, or cooption, somewhere else there will be people jumping up to point this out and grab the baton. Strong cultures of activism are centred on solidarity, networks, and building resilience. These cultures grow sophisticated early warning systems and healthy support mechanisms, while always building towards the society they want.

And above all - what is to be done (with art)?

There's nothing to be done apart from the core work: constantly and publicly to ask the question: "Who speaks, under what conditions, on behalf of whom?" (Henry Giroux)

To what extent do you feel that the system has effectively recuperated the oppositional aspects of your work?

The key is to have a vibrant internal critique, incisively planning for where recuperation might happen; cross-examining risks, looking for intentional or unintentional recuperation or neutralisation. Firstly, you have to know who, or what values, you are in solidarity with, to whom or to what you are ultimately accountable in terms of the issues core to your work. If this is clear, then it's possible to be honest and clever about recuperation. Sometimes a bit of seeming or actual recuperation is a good tactic for a wider goal. 'Playing the game' can get you into certain places which might be very useful. The main thing is to identify the risks, listening carefully to what allies have to say, and plan for the exit, or for when you are spat out. And do this together. Every group, every project is corruptible by ideological rifts, egos out of control, financial pressures, political seductions, let alone recuperations, so it's important to take the risks together. Build in a shared understanding of the conditions under which you would pull the plug, to "sink the project for a principle".

Reflecting on your own implication in these processes of absorption and neutralisation, how can you avoid becoming and agent of recuperation yourself? In other words, are you 'recuperated' or 'recuperator'?

See above. There's always the possibility of abuse of power in all directions. PLATFORM is not exempt from this.

Finally to return to the point that it's impossible to be totally recuperated or neutralised, unless you give your consent, we're put in mind of Osip Mandelstam who wrote the poem below in response to his imprisonment under Stalin:

You took away all the oceans and all the room.
You gave me my shoe-size in earth with bars around it.
Where did it get you? Nowhere.
You left me my lips, and they shape words, even in silence.

PLATFORM is a group of environmental and human rights artists, activists, campaigners and researchers. Jane Trowell & James Marriott.

RADICAL ARTISTS & MAINSTREAM INSTITUTIONS / A MARRIAGE MADE IN INCREASINGLY HOT TEMPERATURES

BRIAN HOLMES

Where are we, and where are we going now? It's a quest. I want to begin by looking back to a time about 6 years ago, when I wrote a text called 'Liar's Poker'. The motivation for writing this text was just after the Strasbourg No Border Camp, a week long direct action on the issues of open borders in Europe held in the centre in Strasbourg where the Schengen Information System is based. Following the camp, I went to *Documenta 11* and looked around at all the works. Every work it seemed was about the problems of migration, situations of people being subject to the power of the State, the ravages created by the capitalists and an already neo-liberal all-guard South American self. I thought – fantastic, here I am at this big museum after this direct action border camp, and I see the same things everywhere.

Outside the museum door, there was a partly-public, static caravan that had also been at the border camp; a sort of mobile theatre structure initiated by an interventionist art activist group who had suffered imprisonment only a year before. The next thing that I knew, the security team of Documenta was descending on the bus, causing and enforcing its departure. So I wrote a text called 'Liar's Poker' and it starts like this,

> Basically, what I have to say here is simple: when people talk about politics in an artistic frame, they are lying. Indeed, the lies they tell are often painfully obvious and worse is the moment when you realise that some will go forever unchallenged and take on, not the semblance of truth, but the reliability of convention. In a period like ours when the relationship to politics is one of the legitimating arguments for the very existence of public art, the tissue of lies that surrounds one when entering a museum can become so dense that its like falling into an ancient cellar full of spider webs and choking on them as you struggle to breathe. Now, the mere mention of this reality will make even my friends and allies in the artistic establishment rather nervous, but it is a reality nonetheless. And like most of the political realities in our democratic age, it has directly to do with the question of representation.

The basic idea of 'Liar's Poker' was that activism in the museum is a kind of game. The game works like this, there are actually two ways of playing it: the usual way of playing Liar's Poker is that the artist who claims to hold the great legitimate winning card in the game – the Ace of Politics – is bluffing. The artist really has no real connection to any kind of social unit and what is more, his or her bluffing will never be called because everyone is very comfortable for the artist and the artwork to live like a king inside the white cube. The other way of playing the game is to bluff that you are bluffing, to pretend that you are only pretending and occupy the museum, or engage in a process in the public institution, just up to that point where you must in fact play the Ace of Politics. This is the very point at which you then withdraw whatever resources you have been able to gather, and leave or are rejected from the institution.

Now you can ask – where are we now, am I bluffing? Or have times changed, is it that I would like to maybe get a job, buy a new house, become a university professor or perhaps be a curator. I think that times have changed. I think that times have been changing slowly for a long time and what is happening now is quite an acceleration of that. The question that I will go on to talk about changes in a moment. The overall question is whether we can really succeed or not in changing this artistic frame, which is essentially the frame of hypocrisy. This frame allows the representation of problems and efforts to change them, but only their representation; which allows for the common play of the image of social and political action, but not the real unfolding of the necessarily antagonistic process. Politics itself, in Western societies at least, is antagonistic and involves risking something essential.

So the question: whether it is really possible that we change the artistic frame and to eliminate hypocrisy. The reason that times have changed I think, is that increasing numbers of people know that the way we live really will change in our lifetime. Our lifestyles are on the way to becoming necessarily different to the ones we have known up to now. What we have now is an explicit situation of triple crisis: economic crisis, ecological crisis and security or military crisis. We have an economic melt-down, we have the precipitous melting of polar ice caps, and we have two blazing wars going on (in which the UK is involved).

These crises have finally come into the Western European and North American parliaments after an entire neo-liberal period marked by crisis all around the globe. In a recent article Alex Foti notes that climate change means an increased consciousness of precarity for the simple reason that it is a carelessness of life, and it touches people who are less fortunate in situations more immediately. We see this very clearly in the United States with Hurricane Katrina, and events in Britain such as floodings which are certain to continue, growing more intense, and highlighting this relationship between climate change and a precarious existence.

Something real, which may or may not become clear, is that climate change also brings a new kind of fascist. In fairly large areas of the world – in particular, low-lying cities, but also areas subject to desertification, areas subject perhaps to new kinds of storms that will cause people to flee uninhabitable areas – there is no way to avoid the rising conflicts associated with this environmental decay. I think that we are already in this period. There is already an emphasis on security and border closures, on the homogenisation and purification of national identity, on the biometric identification of individuals. All these things are the elements of new kind of authoritarian society, which we already have experience of, particularly in the United States, in the UK, and the regimes approaching Iraq. This is not science fiction, this is something that already exists and is shown to grow.

So, under these conditions: the awareness that people have, the kinds of political engagement without a misplaced fanaticism, or a misplaced utopianism, and an awareness of the different types of critiques that have been levelled with anti-capitalist movements for years. That kind of critique is now dissipating as an awareness of the triple crisis that we're involved in grows, the question is of how to respond to this? Changes which are incremental cannot simply be a dramatic single response to such changes; there could only be a rather deep process-based social response that involves the taking of many, many, many different positions by a vast range of individuals and with groups of institutions and organisations in society, at all different levels of society.

There are many ways that those kinds of conditions have been taken already, and those kinds of processes are being launched. We here are even one of them with the attempt to bring the critiques embodied by direct action movements, embodied by non-governmental organisations, embodied also by figures of public intellectuals, into an institution that is no longer a classic institution, but a neo-liberal institution in the ultimate neo-liberal state that we live in. Obviously there are going to be problems with this and these problems are something that we should think about and work on, because in a way we have no time, and in another way we have: this is the time that we have, this is the time to be doing this, and there is no other time to be doing this.

So the questions that I see are: how to create sites where highly differentiated groups become not only visible to each other, but capable of collaborating with each

other, or at least knowing that they are working in parallel? This is something that you can do with an institution like a museum, which is all about showing, telling and discussing.

How do you legitimate these kinds of projects so that they don't come under attack, either for not being art – that is the classic old refusal from the art establishment that we know very well, there are many forms of this attack based in various environments and conditions, or for not being neutral – a great demand of classical institutions, for not being entertainment which is the great demand for the neo-liberal institutions, for not being bipartisan, which is the great demand in America with anything public that goes for and against the republic? How to legitimate this kind of problem is a major question.

Another question, how do we avoid getting lost in the complexity of what is now world society and world politics? How do we avoid the contrary dilemma of getting lost in the passion of politics and the passion of what becomes a sort of extreme version of political commitment?

Another question: how to make the new perception of the world and the new imaginary of what the world could become into subjective forms, forms that are not simply confined either to their representation in the museum or to the actions that people take, but into subjective forms to conceit into daily life and instruct a change in expectations that people have towards their daily life?

So, how to ensure the transformation of the artistic frame to make the museum a very different kind of platform for middle- and long-term activism, without cutting off the possibility of revolution? The only way to sustain a critique like this is to realise that fundamentally it is a critique of capitalism and therefore it is a revolutionary idea. I don't think that there is any other way to sustain critique than realising that the entirety of the system is what has produced the triple crisis.

I have maintained this very intense relationship with the official institutions throughout the last few years but I have also had these ideas of transformations, so I want to go back a little further to a text I wrote in the year 2000 called 'Reflecting Museums'.

> Writing in 1986, the German sociologist Ulrich Beck showed how impossible it is for modern democratic governments and administrations to carry out a critique of the major orientations of society ("progress"). Faced with the risks of techno-economic development, embodied at the time by the nuclear industry, such a critique appeared extremely urgent: modernity had to learn to reflect on its own priorities. Beck predicted the growing importance of social movements as the 'sub-political' agents of this critique; he also pointed to the importance of ethical stances within the professional disciplines.

I think that this is very interesting; the conjunction, or at least the parallel, between the socially operated, outside the established institutions and frameworks, and on the other side, the ethical commitments that professionals who are bound by the obligations that they have to mandate the institution, but at the same time have an ethical sense which gives them the power, the courage really, to take certain kinds of stance where of course their professional career is placed at risk. The understanding that there are two very different kinds of input into this sort of reflective process is very important.

> Can the museum become a site for artistic demonstrations of this social reflexivity? Can it become a social laboratory, redefining the meaning of progress? With the intensifying grip of the informational economy on all aspects of human communication, we reach one of those moments "when knowing if one can think differently and perceive differently than one sees, is absolutely necessary if one

> is to go on looking and reflecting at all." To bring about this shift in perception and thought, one would first have to dispel the postmodern enchantment, and cease to believe that culture, politics and the economy are always inseparable, caught in a system of reciprocally produced effects with no exit. Concretely, for an artistic institution, that would mean seeking other publics, outside the flows of international tourism, outside the productive loops of immaterial labour.

The museum has to open its doors, or better, shift these resources, toward the sources of a healthy alienation located in social and psychic spaces within the distance of dominant systems, or in direct opposition to them. This is extremely difficult for museums to do, not only must they invent new processes for working with their publics – at risk of upsetting the internal hierarchies of the institution; they must also legitimate results before funding bodies and trustee boards without help from the usual criteria. I would like to say that over the last decade this has really been key. It is not at all the case. It will not be the case until the financial casino is transformed into centres of ecological sensibility, where people learn about different aspects of life, and different relationships within society. To get there it would involve all kinds of direct action, conscientious objection, ethical stances, social movements, educational processes – all sorts of things which can represent the principal of hope in society. There would need to be some kind of generosity in a social condition which we now know will change. Where we can become the agents of our healthy change by maintaining a dialect between, on one side, a sort of refusal – the position of radicality, and on the other, willingness to work.

This is the basic outline of what I would like to bring up here. I think that the notion, one of the key notions that is being developed here, that is being denounced here, and also maybe where an alternative is being suggested, is the notion of desk murder: a kind of harm and aggression and an actual force of destruction that is exerted at a distance essentially for money. These processes of remote control face what money does. Money controls people, it dictates our actions. There's a real resistance happening here and also an attempt to open up a sensible space where we can feel things differently, we can imagine things differently and from there you can go out in front of the world.

Brian Holmes is a theorist, writer and translator living in Chicago.

This text is the edited transcript of a talk given by Brian Holmes at the symposium 'Who's Recuperting Who?' at Arnolfini, 26 November 2009.

THE ARTS COUNCIL OF GREAT BRITAIN

105 Piccadilly, London, W1V 0AU

TELEPHONE: 01-629 9495 TELEGRAMS: AMEC, LONDON, W.1

CHAIRMAN: THE LORD GOODMAN
SECRETARY-GENERAL: HUGH WILLATT

26 April 1972

Dear Will:

Many thanks for your letter of 21st April. There are indeed problems over the APG grant from the Council. Our Advisory Panel has now taken the view that APG is more concerned with social engineering than with straight art, and that while they have done some useful work in this area, there have not been quite enough tangible advantages to artists to justify our continued support on the former scale.

I can well understand your support since the fellowship given to Garth Evans by the Steel Corporation was exactly the kind of result we were hoping to see from APG's activities.

Yours,

Robin Campbell
Director of Art

William Camp, Esq
100 Wigmore Street
London W 1

Letter from The Arts Council of Great Britain to the Artist Placement Group, 1972
Courtesy Tate

RECUPERATOR/ RECUPERATED 2 THOMAS HIRSCHHORN

As an artist, you are known for work that problematises power relations both within the art establishment and in a wider social context. To what extent do you feel that the system has effectively 'recuperated' the oppositional aspects of your work?

Nobody and no one 'recuperates' my work. I never think of or about this. To think of this is a defeatist attitude and a loss of energy. To believe that art can be 'recuperated' is faithless to me, it's an opinion, it's journalism, it's an evaluation and it's a complete weakness. I am for the weak and I am often weak - but I am fighting against weakness and I am fighting my own weakness. Furthermore I am against cultivating weakness. I never give a thought for concerns about 'being recuperated' or to 'recuperate' because I have my work to do! I have work and I want to work! There is no 'oppositional aspect' in my work. There is no more of an 'oppositional aspect' in my work than in any other artwork! Because all art - is opposition. Art is opposition to culture, to tradition, to un-freedom, to exclusion, to calculation, to education, to sentimentalism, to control, to fear, to security, to harmony, to consumption, to capitalisation, to correctness, to the past.

However I have faith in art. I have faith in the autonomy of art, in the universality of art and in art as resistance. Not resistance against something or resistance against someone or against 'the system'. No, art as such is resistance! That is perhaps the misunderstanding about the faithless concern for 'recuperation'? Today, the terms 'political art' and 'political artist' are used too often as simplifications, abbreviations and cheap, lazy classifications. I am only interested in what is really political, the political that implicates: Where do I stand? Where does the Other stand? What do I want? What does the Other want? The politics of opinions, of comments and of commonly accepted views, does not and has never interested me. I am concerned with doing my art politically - I am not, and was never, concerned with making political art. To me, doing art politically means deciding in favour of something, for something, towards something - it's never 'recuperating' something! My decision is to position my work in the realms of love, politics, philosophy and aesthetics. One of these realms is politics. To choose politics means that I always want to ask: What do you want? Where do you stand? This also means that I always want to ask myself: What do I want? Where do I stand? I am aware that politics - just as the field of aesthetics - could be interpreted negatively. But the point is to never exclude or reject the negative, it is precisely about confronting the negative, also and involving oneself in it. It is always a matter of not being negative oneself. Through my work, I want to create a new truth beyond negativity, beyond current issues, beyond commentaries, beyond opinions and beyond evaluations.

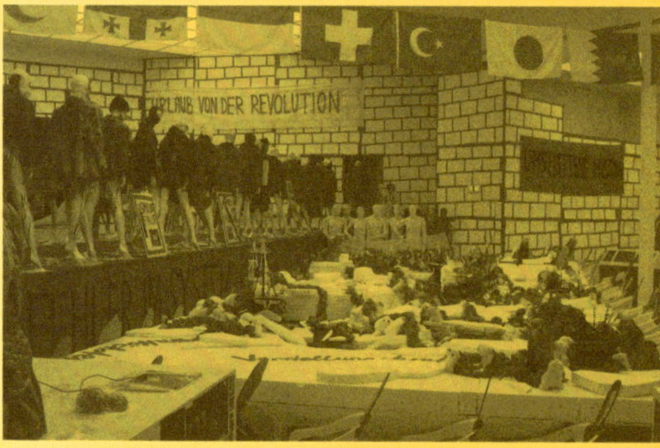

Das Auge, Thomas Hirschhorn, 2008
Secession, Vienna
Courtesy Arndt & Partner Galerie, Berlin

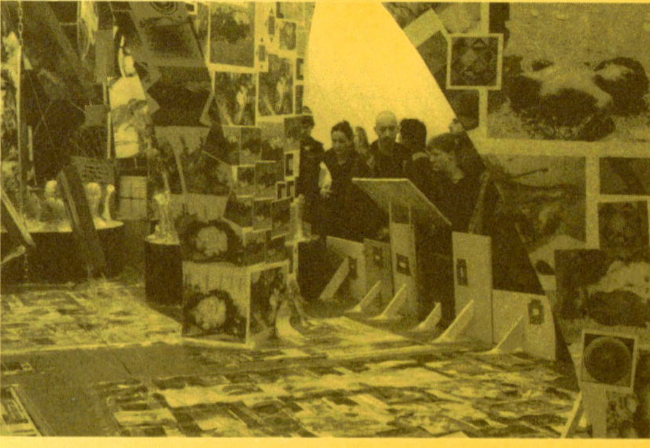

Superficial Engagement, Thomas Hirschhorn, 2006
Gladstone Gallery, New York
Courtesy Gladstone Gallery, New York

Reflecting upon your own implication in these processes of absorption and neutralisation, how can you avoid becoming an agent of recuperation yourself?

I am not trying to avoid becoming this or that, nor trying not to be an agent of this and that. I am trying to work hard and I am trying to use art as a tool! I understand art as a tool to encounter the world. I understand art as a tool to confront reality. And I understand art as a tool to live within the time in which I am living. I always ask myself: Does my work have the ability to generate an event? Can I encounter someone with my work? Am I trying to touch somebody through my work? Can something be touched through my work? I want to consider the work that I am doing today - in my milieu, in my history - as work which aims to reach out of my milieu - beyond my history. I want to address and confront universal concerns. Without being afraid of what you call 'absorption' or 'neutralisation' or 'being an agent'! Therefore I must work with what surrounds me, with what I know, with what I love and with what affects me. I must not give in to the temptation of the particular, but on the contrary, try to touch universality. The particular, which always excludes, must be resisted. For me this means that I want to do my work, the work that I am doing here and now, as a universal work. The essential question to me as an artist is: does my work have the power to implicate a non-exclusive audience?

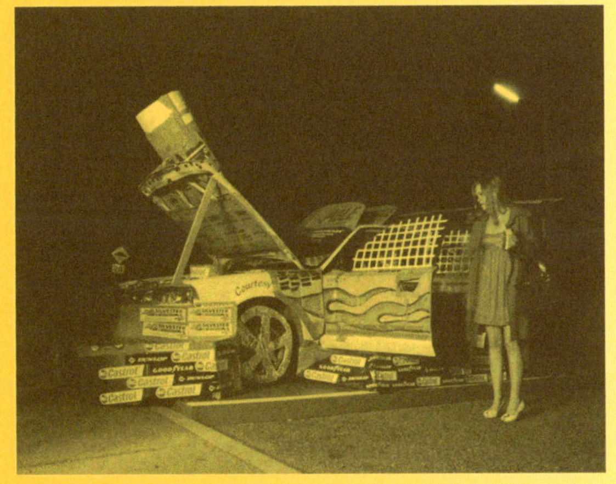

Poor-Racer, Thomas Hirschhorn, 2009
Exhibition *One-day Sculpture*, Christchurch, New Zealand

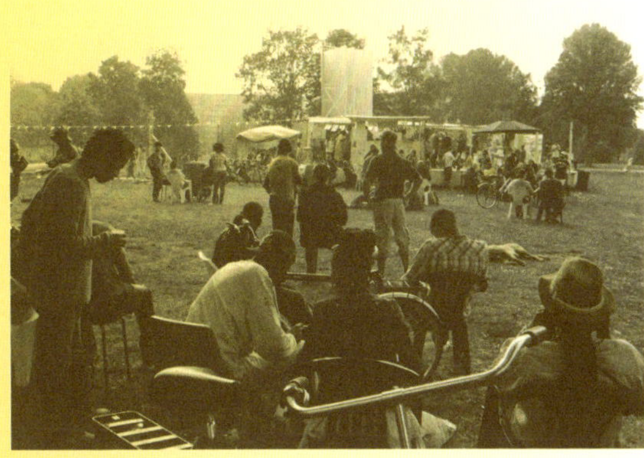

The Bijlmer Spinoza-Festival, Thomas Hirschhorn, 2009
Courtesy the artist
Photograph Vittoria Martini

In other words, are you 'recuperated' or 'recuperator'?

Neither. Why should I be one of them? Why should I take things on these terms? I never use these terms myself? As an artist, shouldn't my work consist in creating new terms, new notions? Yes, I am an artist with the ambition to create a new term for art - with my work! I want to create something new. Not more and not less. I want to work ahead towards something - I do not want to look back. But I am convinced that I can only create or fulfil something new if I address reality positively, even the hard core of reality. It is a matter of never allowing the pleasure, the happiness, the enjoyment of work, the positive in creation, the beauty of working, to be asphyxiated by criticism. I do not want to work with the fear of being 'recuperated'. This means to be active always. Art is always action, Art is never reaction. Art is never merely a reaction or a critique. It doesn't mean being uncritical or not making a critique - it means being positive despite the sharpest critique, despite uncompromising rejection and despite unconditional resistance. It means not to deny oneself passion, hope and dream. Creating something means to risk oneself and I can only do that if I work without simultaneously analysing what I am making. To take the risk, to have joy in working, to be positive, are the preconditions for making art. Only in being positive, can I create something that comes from myself. I want to be positive, even within the negative. But if I want to be positive, I must gather the courage to touch also the negative - that is where I see the challenge, the problem and the hardcore. I want to be critical, but I do not want to let myself be neutralised by being critical.

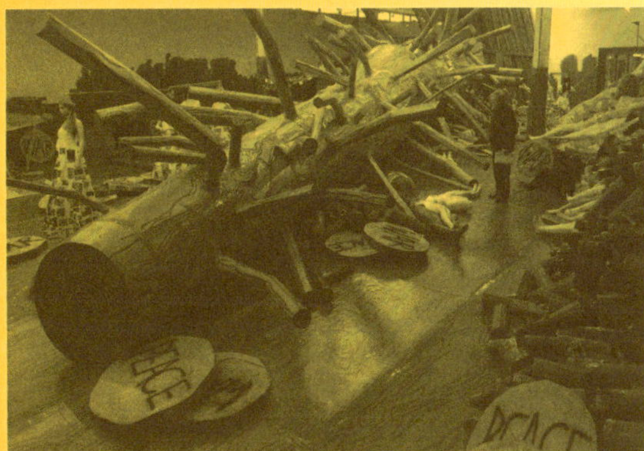

It's burning everywhere, Thomas Hirschhorn, 2009
Dundee Contemporary Arts (DCA) Dundee

And above all - What is to be done (with art)?

I can only speak for myself and say what I have to do, what I want to do and what is a pleasure and joy to do: it's to work! To work for a non-exclusive audience! I want to give form and I want to build a platform with my work. Not making a form - but giving form. A form which comes from me and can only come from me because I see it that way, I understand it that way and am the only one to know that form. To give form, as opposed to making a form, means to be one with it. I must stand alone with this form. This means raising the form, asserting this form and defending it against everything and everyone. It means confronting the great artistic challenge: How can I create a form that takes a position? How can I create a form that resists facts? I want to understand the question of form as the most important question for an artist. What I want is to build a platform with my work. Creating a platform enables others to come in contact with the work. I want all my works to be understood as a surface or a field. This surface must be a locus for dialogue or for confrontation. I think that art has the power and capacity to create the conditions for a dialogue or a confrontation, one-to-one, without communication, without mediation, without moderation. I always want to ask myself: Does my work possess the dynamic for a breakthrough? Is there an opening, is there a path into my work? Does my work resist the tendency toward the hermetic? My work must create an opening; it must be a door, a window or even a hole - a hole carved into today's reality. The notions I am concerned with today are: Precariousness, Presence and Production! I want to make my artwork with the will to create a breakthrough. The question to me is: Can I - with and through my work - contribute to the construction of a 'critical corpus'?

Thomas Hirschhorn is an artist based in Paris.

THE JURY STAYS OUT

/

ART ACTIVISM & ART'S NEW NORMATIVITY

LARS BANG LARSEN

In the past decade, we have witnessed how governments have phased out democratic and cultural institutions. At the same time, art has become norm as an asset in creative industries and the experience economy. In the so-called creative city, talent, invention and desire became normative and prescriptive for work, for the building of the economy and for the production of subjectivities. In this way, aesthetic modalities have become instruments for State and commerce to re-organise the workplace and to re-enchant markets. Such mechanisms lie in continuation of those of the culture industry, but they also go beyond this logic. Analyses of the culture industry have typically revolved around a critique of the mass-consumption and mass-mediation of art, and not about the production of subjectivity, the marketing of cities or the reinvention of work.

Art was also normative and prescriptive in the 19th and 20th Centuries to be sure, but today it is so in a specific sense that is relatively independent of what art meant within the cultural order of the bourgeoisie. In this way the question of how one makes, consumes and engages with art when art is a norm, a must, a mechanism of control, urgently reasserts itself.[1] From the point of view of artistic production, a not unusual response to art's new normativity is to engage with forms of activism. Through direct action, art activism makes art re-appear on a political stage in a de-hierarchised form. However if the historical avant-gardes reflected a limit between political representation and artistic representation, art activism is often less certain what to do with the artistic side of this question; while the creative industries and the experience economy are now putting pressure on the art concept, we can ask if art activism – from a quite different angle – may in fact be doing the same. The following is a generalising deliberation of art activism and its relationship to the art concept that I hope can serve to continue a discussion on this subject and break open up new questions. I should also mention that I am writing from the point of view of art history and critical theory, and not as someone with activist experience; just like I would write about art without being an artist.

We cannot pretend to fully know what we talk about when we say 'art activism', and thus be pulled into a categorical piousness or ontological showdown.[2] Perhaps because it is a critically-charged practice, important aspects of which are to explicitly address urgencies, support and negate, construct and start over; or insofar as it operates with binaries such as inside and outside the institution and subversion of pre-existing repression, art activism both employs and provokes judgment. The last thing we need today, in debates concerned with art activism and its connections to aesthetics and democratic debate at large, is to reinforce judgment. The jury stays out. I will argue that a deferral of judgment (in favour of knowledge production, scepticism and speculation) is not inimical to activist art forms; at least I wish to emphasise other aspects in order to confront paradoxes that manifest themselves in art activist practices that see art as a problem-solving device.

ACTION, ETHICS, GESTURE

The hybrid term 'art activism' was coined in the 1970s, the counter-cultures and student revolts of the late 1960s having paved the way for it. These movements "posed questions to politics without themselves being reinscribed in a political theory", as Michel Foucault put it, and thus often developed anti-authoritarian practices through aesthetic tropes of play and creativity.[3] However it was not uncommon that happening inspired protest, street theatre and artistic behaviour transferred onto social process developed into

explicitly anti-artistic forms post-1968. At this point many activists dropped symbolic production altogether in order to engage with forms of direct action that were perceived to be more real such as squatting, solidarity work, urban activism and production communes.[4] After the 'festival of life' of the late 1960s, came a hardening of the attitudes upon which the concept of art activism recuperated artistic agency, after militant stances had eclipsed art.[5]

However if post-1968 militancy negated art, art activism tended to negate the entire question of art versus anti-art by exceeding and replacing the art concept with terms such as 'cultural democracy' (Lucy Lippard), or by responding like Nina Felshin:

[activist artists] are creatively expanding art's boundaries and audience and are redefining the role of the artist. In the process, they seem to suggest that the proper answer to the question 'But is it Art?' is: 'But does it matter?'[6]

This appears to be the right question: only for a retrograde, segregating interrogation, or for the capitalisation of such clear-cut differences, would it be relevant whether something can be unequivocally called art, while other events and objects are discarded. On the other hand such a position doesn't necessarily encourage an integrated analysis of the work or event that takes into account a multiplicity of (linguistic, affective, sociological, epistemological, scientific, etc.) perspectives necessitated by a contemporary concept of art. As long as agents prefix their work with the term 'art', and as long as there exist such things as the art institution and a domain of aesthetic thinking, aesthetic discussion remains relevant. Moreover, since art activism tends to circulate within the art system, its relation to the art institution, beyond that of a tactical use of the latter's resources and infrastructures, should be analysed. Lastly, in Felshin's assertion, there is a modernist remainder of the idea that an art that sublates itself into the life world, through a rejection of the bourgeois concept of art as the ultimate art form. This is the avantgardistic *Aufhebung* of art; to realise something through a negation that is capable of abolishing and maintaining it at the same time.[7]

Just as it can be conservative or unproductive to insist on categorical stability, the refusal to reflect on concepts depletes critical insight as well as experience. Hence the consideration of whether or not a phenomenon falls within the theoretical and linguistic domain of aesthetics, is not the same as a traditionalist re-territorialisation of art. In fact, art activist resistance to such a discussion is often informed by a quasi-modernist concept of art that doesn't take into account the integrated analyses that contemporary art calls for. Art is based on the concept of art and on ways in which culture and individual subjects re-imagine that concept – as it must always be re-imagined.

Art activism resolves aesthetic problems in social space. This is an idea it shares with artistic strategies since the 1990s that revolve around participation and collaboration. Art historian Claire Bishop sees a tendency in "socially ameliorative art", and critical discourses around it to equate social labour with artistic success.[8] Her criticism of an 'ethical turn' in art focuses on socially collaborative practices in which the good collaboration becomes the good art work. These are set to work to heal (through empathy, recognition of difference, empowerment), and may even operate with more or less transcendent modalities (happiness, consensus), under which Bishop detects unarticulated religious sentiment. In this way, she asserts, we tend to judge such art for its artistic intentionality rather than for how it produces aesthetic reflection and affect.

A debate between 'activism' and the 'properly artistic' is often marked by refrains and mutual blindness to heterogeneous concatenations of politics, affect and aesthetics. Beyond that a criticism of work that engages with art's social forms must obviously be historically informed; we can look behind the 1990s to projects such as Group Material, whose 'cultural activism' was socially collaborative without falling into traps of intentionality. Ethics, however, is indeed a panic of signification that reinstates judgment and, in aesthetic work, risks collapsing in an evangelical common sense. When art resorts to ethics, disagreement and thinking – that is, politics as an experimental and open-ended, interpretive process – is trumped; in activism by the reappearance of the Kantian Judge in the garb of the street fighter, educator or labour organiser who delivers a critique of the status quo through demands to truth expressed in transparent forms. One can further argue that when it is the case that art activists predicate their work on the good act – on what must be done – they take a *super*-ethical stance, in which they overrule as insufficient the way existing social institutions represent citizens, and instead take democratic representation in their own hands. Any normative art revolves around the conversion of art into value: not only into economic and cultural values, but also apodictic 'human' and 'social' values. It is impossible to rely on the good act for a subversion of normativity as such, insofar as one wishes to maintain an art concept that is more than merely instrumental.

Giorgio Agamben writes how Aristotle's *Nicomachean Ethics* distinguishes between production and action: "Action *[praxis]* and production *[poiesis]* are generically different. For production aims at an end other than itself; but this is impossible in the case of action, because the end is merely to do what is right."[9] The good act doesn't have to await interpretation, analysis or meditation the way the art work does, and hence the good act sacks artistic parameters. This may matter little to art activists who work from an instrumentalised or sociological interpretation of art. However one may take note of the fact that according to the Aristotelian definition (and this is ironic vis-a-vis art activism since it is explicitly heteronomous), action, by being in itself an end, relies on autonomy as much as the art concept does, or did. What should matter to activists is the fact that action is not (the same as) production. Action is a supplement. This reveals a vacuum at the heart of agency which must be qualified if it isn't to remain self-fulfilling; and it cannot be qualified by way of art, if art is repressed or sublated in the process.

If producing is a means in view of an end and praxis is an end without means, Agamben sees the gesture as that which breaks "the false alternative between ends and means that paralyses morality and presents means which, *as such*, are removed from the sphere of mediation without thereby becoming ends".[10] The gesture is "undertaking and supporting", Agamben says, and therefore "opens up the sphere of *ethos* as the most fitting sphere of the human."[11] Today, much art activism is gestural. In our era of desktop publishing and immediate access to the internet as a global medium, it isn't enough to take over means of production that are accessible anyway. Instead activists create effects through enterprising and effective gestures; the media freaking of the Yes Men is a famous example. However the gesture – hovering between action and production – is a highly ambiguous concept that differs from structural and analytical efforts; just like it brings aesthetics back into play and hence displaces the essentialism of the good act and artistic intentionality. In the context of the media happening however, it is difficult to see how gesture escapes mediation, understood as a condition that can no longer be a choice for contemporary agency and production.[12] Put differently in the words of Henri Bergson, the gesture is profoundly different from action because it is an automatism, "a mental state that expresses itself (...) from no other cause than an inner itching".[13] He considered the gesture as "something explosive" that disturbs or arouses us and "prevents our taking matters seriously." Accordingly, one can polemicise media happenings by characterising them as socio-cultural tics. The fact that a protest reaches hearts and minds doesn't change the way that the matrix of mass media society replaces the event; it reaffirms this matrix, prevents us from taking it seriously. The gesture is then a recording of a loss rather than the re-appropriation of what we have lost. Such a strategy arguably had greater impact and reason in the 1960s when the focused unseriousness of the Yippies, for example, was pitted against bourgeois culture. Today there is a fine line between media-freaking and the effervescent imagery that spin doctors plough into the collective memory.[14]

Thus agency can be problematised from the point of view of gesture, of how it differs from production, and of how it necessitates an aesthetic and linguistic analysis supplemented by the sociological insight of how mediation has eclipsed production in the info-society.

RECONSTRUCTION, STRUCTURAL AGENCY AND AFFECT

When one begins to problematise normative power, laborious processes of reconstruction are needed. These processes may be of a semiotic kind or the kind that art activists often take it upon themselves to undertake through self-organised, collective practices. In both cases, it is about developing new sites from which to speak, and thus self-organisational and self-institutionalising processes are an important, structural form of action. They also embody the particular time-space of art activism; the slowness that is a result of the group author as an explicitly produced space of production that is intrinsically opposed to the desire for immediate effect, when such a time-space is characterised by collective processes that are painfully democratic. Such a slow temporality, such a tarrying militancy, is in itself a valuable asset of art activism that knows how to make its own time through self-organisation, and does not buy into the proliferation of pretexts to make art. Art activism must be credited for such attempts, within any multitude, at providing conditions of possibility for articulations that recompose social corporeality.

However one cannot stop at reconstruction. An aesthetic event is indeed in excess of the sociological analysis that will have lead to the conclusion that reconstruction is required. At the same time, the reconstructive process is an inextricable part of the artistic enuncitation: it will always mumble along, the way the ideological setting of the *salon des refusés* informs readings of the work of Pissarro or Manet.[15]

Art activism typically has aspects of functionalism in so far as it has a pronounced therapeutical, ameliorative or enlightening purpose. It is meant to work within the direct mode of address that underlies a politics of visibility.[16] Such an operationality revolves around the possible from the point of view of critical organisation. It typically takes place in 'the outside world' – outside the studio, gallery or institution – in protest against market and professional exclusion, and in order to include marginalised subjects. Where this is the case, the production of space is of special interest; the self-organised space, the counter-public sphere, alternative networks of distribution, and so on. In this way the *plaisir* of interpretation, that informed so much post-structuralist theory, is supplemented by parameters such as use value, social value and political effect (or it is, in some cases, annulled altogether).

But while art activism often foregrounds instrumental reason, it is not entirely based in rationalism. Brian Holmes writes in his 'Affectivist Manifesto',

> Expression unleashes affect, and affect is what touches ... An artistic event does not need an objective judge. You know it has happened when you can bring something else into existence in its wake. Artistic activism is affectivism, it opens up expanding territoriums.[17]

Somewhat counter-intuitively, Holmes defines strategies for social change in terms of an interiority, namely intimacy; art activism does indeed operate with a concept of desire, then. In this way it can neither claim, nor be taken to task for, an exclusively sociological reading of art. But Holmes' concept of affect is affirmative and hence one, I would argue, that again passes artistic parameters by. As he sums up, "I am interested in art that goes outside of art".[18] Because of its focus on what we can call sociological outsides, art activism is often insensitive to the vague and indefinite perception and signification; outside of any instrumentalised production of space whether governmental, corporate or anti-authoritarian.

One artistic parameter that could be used to put an affirmative concept of affect into perspective is Antonin Artaud's concept of cruelty, with which he coupled agency with theatre. When Artaud in the early 1930s wrote that "everything that acts is cruelty", he couched cruelty in terms of "diligence, unrelenting decisiveness, irreversible and absolute determination."[19] As a Nietzschean concept it had little to do with blood and sadism, but touched instead on something that also activists can subscribe to; something "very lucid, a kind of strict control and submission to necessity."[20] There is, in this sense, cruelty in decision-making, in making visible, in stirring up affect, in social relations, in language itself. An activist's discipline in the face of the chaos they take upon themselves is cruel; it is always easier to play the game. So why does much activism only have an affirmative language for this? Artaud's theatre of cruelty is of course a hyperbolic, modernist position, but one that can be used to stir up transparent public ideals.

One may replace art activism's positive intensities (intimacy, recognition, togetherness, 'shared heartbeats'), with a register of ambiguous and negative ones that come with an avant-garde pedigree (provocation, shock, absurdity, pleasure).[21] However even if such ambiguities may be better equipped at opening up to artistic experiment and self-reflexivity there is, in late capitalism, no such thing as uncontaminated tropes. Indeed, one must struggle to regain and rearticulate a concept such as 'pleasure' from the abuse it has suffered, not to mention shock and provocation. In this way, one cannot replace affects for structural work; one remains on the level of intensities and strategic calculations of their effects. If the revolution that ushered in the modern subject in 1789 was an appeal to democratic reason, then it can in fact be claimed that much post-1968 activism has appealed to life through (a departure from) art. Such a position is not only aesthetically ambiguous, but also politically unreconstructed when notions of affect are in themselves no longer transgressive, but have been transformed to the very infrastructure of cognitive capital.

The above remarks may hopefully serve as a few starting points for a discussion about art activism's relationship to aesthetic processes. Beyond that one can also consider the larger relationship of activism and democracy. The fact that anti-democratic political movements such as fascism also appear in activist forms annuls an inherent relation between activism and democratic reason. In contemporary society, we can also take note of another development. We are used to thinking of activism as pre-institutional, either according to the demands for rights claimed by a marginalised collectivity, or in a broader sense in terms of Marx's description the bourgeoisie as the first ruling class whose authority was based not on who their ancestors were, but on what they themselves actually did; their purposefulness, organisational abilities and production of visions as an 'activist' class.[22] But if we take into account how militancy has risen in the wake of the onslaught on cultural and democratic institutions – from anti-global resistance to the Tea Party movement in the US – we can also consider it a post-institutional and post-political phenomenon that defies governmental representation.

If democratic reason is a measure for forms of activism, it is more unpredictable than ever how the latter relate to it. What do such departures from parliamentary politics entail for the ways in which we reimagine society in the 21st Century? And how does aesthetics factor into this, as one of the spaces still available to us for democratic deliberation?

1. In my pamphlets 'Kunst er Norm', 'Organisationsformer' and 'Spredt væren' ('Art is Norm', 'Forms of Organisation' and 'Dissipated being', published by the Art Academy of Jutland, 2008–2010), I discuss art's new normativity.
2. Julie Ault sums up various definitions of the notion of an activist art: "Vanalyne Green and Margia Kramer, for example, described activist art as an art of 'unique, compressed, intense, visual constructs of experience, information and material' that responds to specific social needs, an art distinguished form 'fetishized consumer commodity art' ... Lucy Lippard, for her part, characterised activist art as a paradigm for the practice of contemporary political art wherein 'some element of the art takes place in the 'outside world', including some teaching and media practice as well as community and labor organising, public political work and organizing within the artist's community ... Greg Sholette further refined the term as 'the opposite of those aesthetic practices that, however well-intentioned or overtly political in content, remain dependent on the space of the museum for their meaning.'" (Ault, J. *Alternative Art New York, 1965–1985.* Minneapolis: Minnesota University Press, 2002. 339.)
3. Foucault, M. *The Foucault Reader.* Ed. Paul Rabinow. Pairs: Pantheon, 1984. 34.
4. See for example my book *Palle Nielsen: The Model. A Model for a Qualitative Society (1968).* Barcelona: MACBA, 2010.
5. 'Festival of life' is the term Abbie Hoffman uses in *Revolution for the Hell of it – by Free.* New York: Pocket Books, 1970.
6. *But Is It Art? The Spirit Of Art As Activism.* Ed. Nina Felshin. Seattle: Bay Press, 1995. 13. Commensurately, the New York City radicals Black Mask wrote in the late 1960s, "We are neither artists nor anti-artists. We are creative and revolutionary men." (My translation from *Motherfuckers! De los veranos del amor al amor armado.* Madrid: La Fulgueta, 2009. 110.)
7. Miwon Kwon writes about community-based activism that while it understands itself as heir to the historical avant-gardes, it in fact reverses their project. The avant-gardes saw it as their mission to provoke and disturb with inorganic (explicitly produced) art, while activism focuses on healing communities and reintroducing an organic social bond: "A culturally fortified subject, rendered whole and unalienated from or through an encounter or involvement with an art work, is imagined to be a *politically* empowered social subject with opportunity (afforded by the art project) and capacity (understood as innate) for artistic self-representation (= political self-representation). It is, I would argue, the production of such 'empowered' subjects, a reversal of the aesthetically politicised subjects of the traditional avant-garde, that is the underlying goal of much community-based, site-specific public art today." Kwon, M. *One Place After Another. Site-Specific Art and Locational Identity.* Massachusetts: MIT Press, 2004. 97.
8. Bishop claims in 'The Social Turn: Collaboration and its Discontents' (*Artforum*, February 2006) that there "can be no failed, unsuccessful, unresolved, or boring works of collaborative art because all are equally essential to the task of strengthening the social bond."
9. See Agamben, G. "Notes on Gesture." *Infancy and History. On the Destruction of Experience.* London: Verso, 2007. 154. Italics as in original. I am grateful to Niels Henriksen for this reference.
10. Ibid.
11. Ibid. 154.
12. Franco 'Bifo' Berardi puts it succinctly, stating that we now live in a milieu where "mediatization prevails over any other form of relation with the human body." Berardi, F. *The Soul at Work: From Alienation to Autonomy.* New York: Semiotext(e), 2009. 114.
13. I am relying on Scott Lash and Celia Lury's discussion of Bergson's text 'Laughter. An Essay on the Meaning of the Comic' (1911) in their *Global Culture Industry.* London: Polity Press, 2007. 92–3.

14. I am paraphrasing Michael Taussig here: "What is 'spin' if not the intoxicating and unstable mix of power and fear bound to effervescent imagery plowed into collective memory so as to change the future?" (Taussig, M. *My Cocaine Museum*. Chicago: Chicago University Press, 2004. 235.)
15. Bishop doesn't take into account such a politics of enunciation; to me, this is a sociological and aesthetic blind spot in her reading that revindicates the individual author and that disregards parameters of the particular kind of institutional critique that self-institutionalising art projects embody. It also exacerbates the rift between 'mainstream' and 'alternative' art that is so apparent in the U.S. Bishop pits 'socially ameliorative art' against what she sees as more complex artistic takes on collaboration, exemplified by works by Jeremy Deller, Artur Żmijewski, Phil Collins, Carsten Höller and Thomas Hirschhorn. Their many qualities notwithstanding, none of these projects operate on the levels of self-institutionalisation and integrated collective authorship; while this is perhaps a point in itself for Bishop, it comes across as conventional that none of these artists are women or non-European. Furthermore, where it is no doubt necessary to consider how rhetorics deployed by New Labour are "almost identical to the practitioners of socially engaged art in order to justify public spending on the arts" (Bishop, ibid.), we cannot isolate the problem to cultural policies, but need to address the fact that cognitive capitalism in general colonises aesthetic tropes. Seeing how contemporary biopolitical regimes are linking up life, work and social imagination, the instrumentalisation of art is much more viral than that.
16. Peggy Phelan writes about visibility politics, "Visibility politics are additive rather than transformational (to say nothing of revolutionary). They lead to a stultifying 'me-ism' to which realist representation is always vulnerable. ... Visibility politics are compatible with capitalism's relentless appetite for new markets and with the he most self-satisfying ideologies of the United States: you are welcome here as long as you are productive. The production and reproduction of visibility are part of the labor of the reproduction of capitalism." Phelan, P. *Unmarked. The Politics of Performance*. London and New York: Rotuledge, 2006. 11.
17. Holmes, B. "The Affectivist Manifesto. Artistic Critique in the 21st Century." 2008 < http://brianholmes.wordpress.com/2008/11/16/the-affectivist-manifesto/>.
18. Brian Holmes in a talk at Platform Garanti, Istanbul, for the launch of his book *Escape the Overcode. Activist Art in the Control Society* (Eindhoven: Van Abbemuseum/Zagreb: WHW, 2009), in connection with the opening of the *11th Istanbul Biennial*, 13 September 2009.
19. Artaud, A. *The Theatre and its Double*. London: Calder, 1999 (1933). 65 and 79.
20. Ibid. 80.
21. Claire Bishop writes, "By contrast, I argue that shock, discomfort, or frustration – along with absurdity, eccentricity, doubt or sheer pleasure – are crucial to a work's aesthetic and political impact." (Ibid.)
22. Engels, F. and Marx, K. "The Communist Manifesto." *The Marx-Engels Reader*. Ed. Robert C. Tucker. New York: Norton, 1978. 473–83.

Lars Bang Larsen is an independent writer and curator based in Bilbao and Copenhagen.

Banksy vs Bristol Museum

The exhibition *Banksy vs Bristol Museum* was presented at Bristol's City Museum and Art Gallery from 13 June–31 August, 2009. The following facts and figures evaluating the exhibition were compiled by Destination Bristol and provided by the museum.

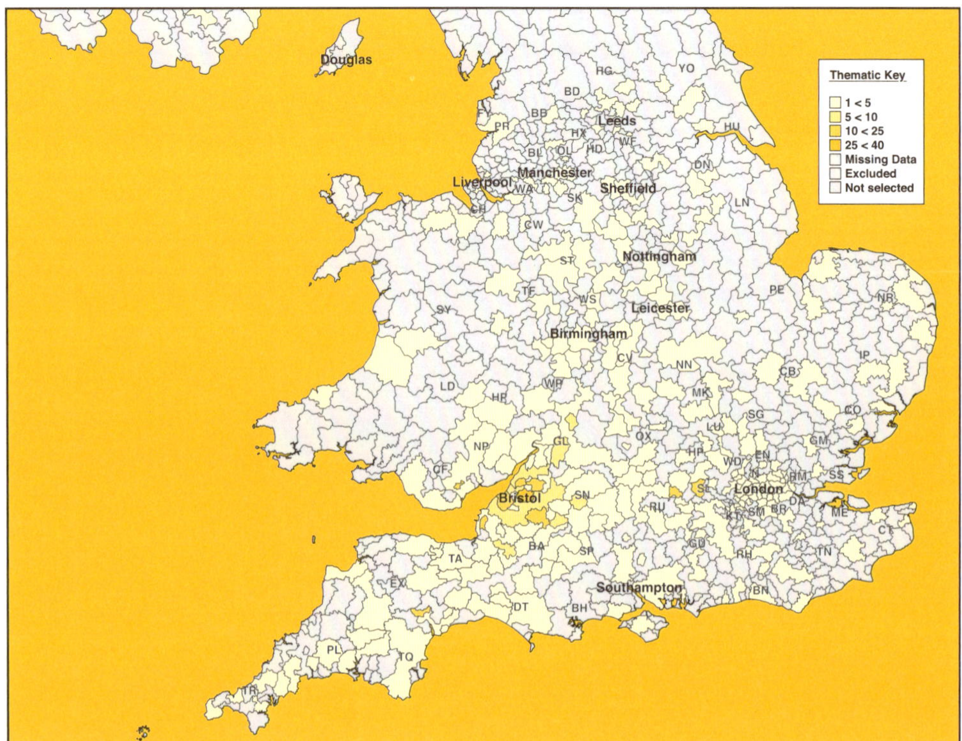

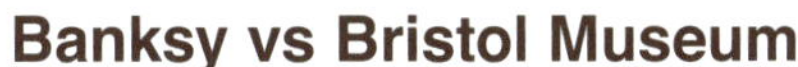

Banksy vs Bristol Museum

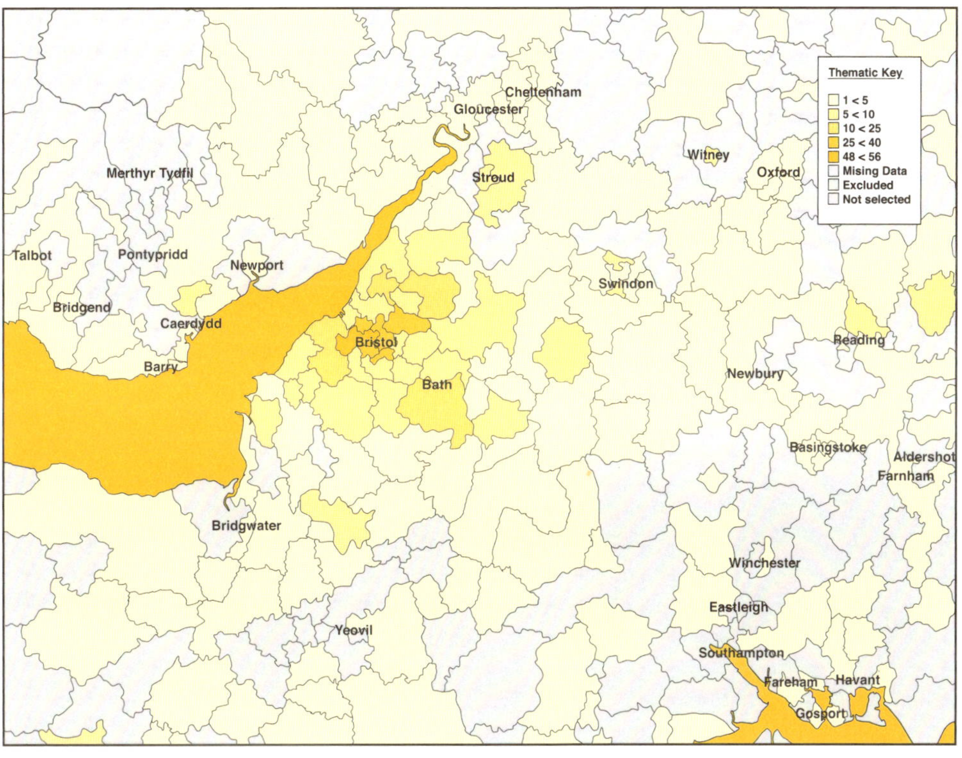

Banksy vs Bristol Museum

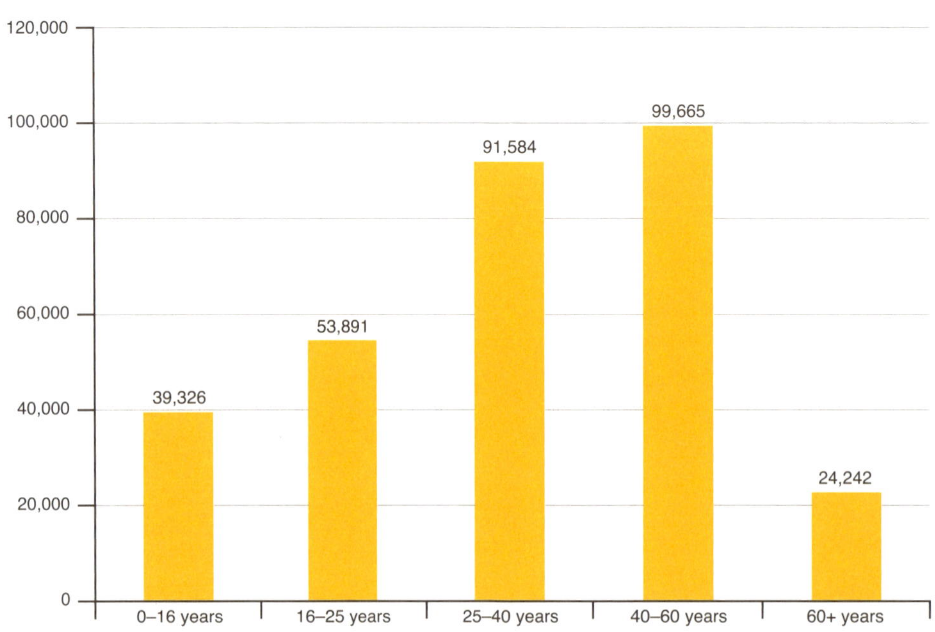

Banksy vs Bristol Museum

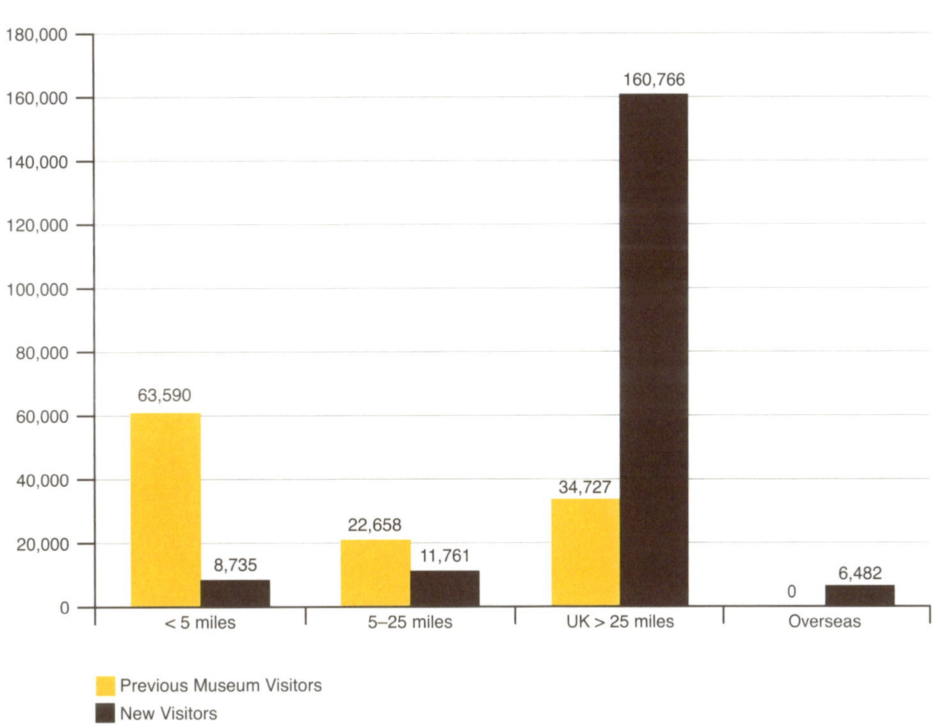

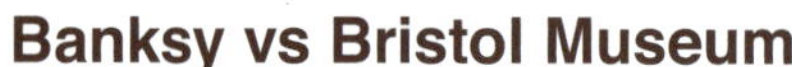
Banksy vs Bristol Museum

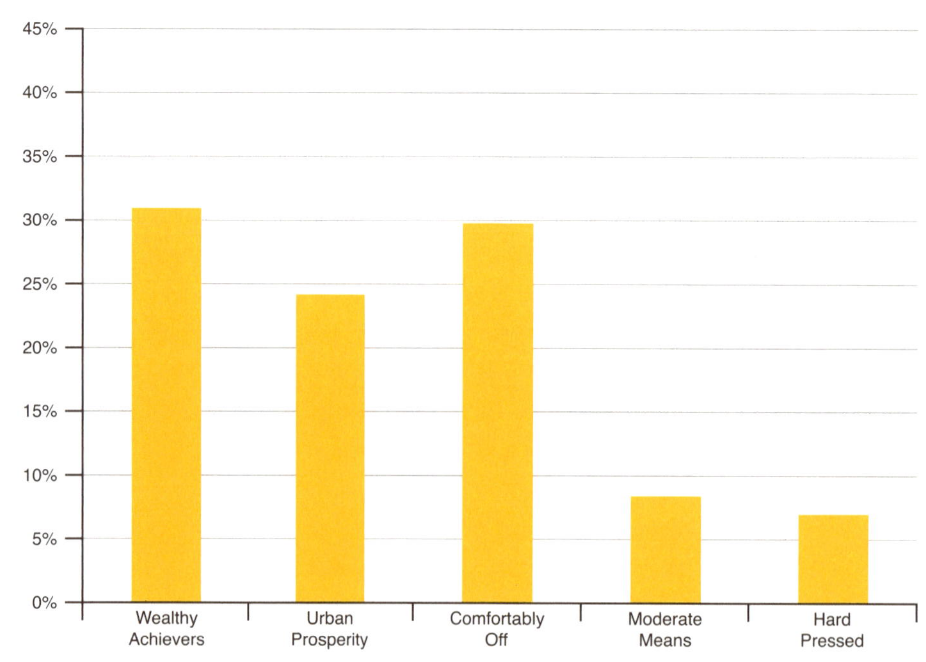
ACORN CLASSIFICATION
ALL VISITORS
45%
40%
35%
30%
25%
20%
15%
10%
5%
0%
Wealthy Achievers
Urban Prosperity
Comfortably Off
Moderate Means
Hard Pressed

Banksy vs Bristol Museum

Headlines:

- A total of 308,719 people attended the exhibition
- 106,744 visitors lived within 25 miles and 201,975 lived further away
- 6,482 overseas residents viewed the exhibition
- 97.8% of non-local visitors (197,531) had prior knowledge of the exhibition, the rest found out about it after their arrival in the city
- 69.4% of all non-local trips were motivated by the exhibition – that is if the exhibition had not been on, these people would not have visited the city. The exhibition therefore generated a total of 140,170 additional trips to Bristol by non-local people
- Of these additional trips, 88,307 were day visits and 51,863 were staying trips, (averaging 1.51 nights per trip)
- Non-local visitors spent:
  23,612 nights in friends and relatives homes,
  50,165 nights in hotels, and
  4,792 nights in other accommodation
- Spending generated by non-local visitors whose trips were solely motivated by the Banksy exhibition was:
  £6,169,610 by staying visitors
  £4,238,736 by day visitors

Banksy is a graffiti artist from Bristol.

ART, ACTIVISM, RECUPERATION

ALANA JELINEK

This publication asks, what are the power relations between art, activism and the institution? What is the role of a critical art practice that is immediately recuperated by the mainstream? In this relatively short essay I have less than 2000 words to describe two changes that have developed but gone largely unnoticed by the artworld. Both of these changes are complex and have implications for the questions posed by this publication. The first of these two changes is in how art has been defined 'institutionally' in recent years, going from a wholesale exclusion of activism as legitimate art practice, to a recent re-emergence of activist art or activism as art within the institution. The second change is broader than the milieu of the artworld. It is in the understanding of the role of culture within bourgeois society, which could be described as the shift from Gramsci to Foucault (described later in this text). Because these changes have gone largely unmarked, questions of recuperation and opposition, market versus state, left versus right, continue to be asked within the artworld and not just by this publication. I believe there are more generative lines of enquiry, which might reflect a more nuanced understanding of the state of culture and society today, if we acknowledge these changes instead of harking back to 20th Century frames of reference.

My perspective comes from a somewhat 'sociological' or outside view of the artworld despite the fact that I am an insider. By this I mean that I am interested in how the artworld operates within society; I am interested in its normative structures, how it self-regulates and also how the artworld works within wider bourgeois society. Both my artwork and my writing explore the individual relationship with a system, be it a microcosm or wider society. It is the characteristics of this relationship that fascinate me. First I will try to describe the shifts briefly, though I am aware that any in-depth description or analysis chafes at the word count.

I'll begin with a description of the Institutional Theory of Art. Its most famous proponent is Arthur C. Danto who, in 1964, when confronted with the philosophical shock of Andy Warhol's *Brillo Box*, concluded that "To see something as art requires something the eye cannot descry – an atmosphere of artistic theory, a knowledge of the history of art: an artworld."[1] The paradox that Danto describes is when two sets of materially indistinguishable objects – a grocer's brillo boxes and Warhol's *Brillo Box* – are exactly the same, and yet only one is art. Danto concludes that it is criticism, philosophy and theory that make one art and the other not-art. In other words, it is the artworld that makes art. There is no quality, be it aesthetic or anything else, that necessarily makes one thing art and another not-art. This was a great shift from previous theories of art which were based on beauty or other transcendent or universal values, as described by Kant, among others. Philosopher, George Dickie takes the institutional definition seriously concluding the following:

> A work of art is an artifact of a kind created to be presented to an artworld public.
> An artist is a person who participates with understanding in the making of a work of art.
> A public is a set of persons the members of which are prepared in some degree to understand an object which is presented to them.
> The artworld is the totality of all artworld systems.
> An artworld system is a framework for the presentation of a work of art by an artist to an artworld public.[2]

In other words, anything the artworld says is art, is art. There is no criteria other than artworld consensus. The making of art may therefore be understood as a highly social-political act. This is especially so given Pierre Bourdieu's observations about art, class and value. Because, according to Bourdieu, art carries markers of social distinction,

it has 'cultural capital' which has a fungible value. Art has cultural capital that may be exchanged for large sums of money proportionate with its cultural capital.[3]

It is important to understand this relationship because we realise through the institutional theory of art that the category of art therefore rests on numerous exclusions. One of the little acknowledged jobs of the artworld is to police the boundary of art; to determine what is and is not art. Generally an artworld assumption is that the definition of art is always an expanding, progressive one, going from exclusion to inclusion. The artworld is generally proud of art's ability to shock whenever there are new, highly visible inclusions in the definition of art. We can think of a parade of shocking incursions into the definition by Marcel Duchamp, Andy Warhol, Carl Andre, Martin Creed and Tracey Emin; but this belies a historical reality of constant flux. Since Danto's 1964 text, the definition of art has accommodated and expelled a variety of practices including both the highly commercial and the highly political. The definition of art has both expanded and contracted over time. It is only recently that the political or activist has been reintroduced as a legitimate art practice in the UK. (The notable exception during the 1990s was artists whose backgrounds were expected to be 'political', like those from Latin America, China and Russia.[4]) That decade saw the highly commercially orientated becoming legitimate art practice for the first time since the late 19th Century. The fall in Warhol's artworld credibility in the 1970–80s and then his reinstatement as an artworld great in the 1990s is one example of this trend. In the 1970s and 80s in Britain and USA, it was a politicised art production that was de rigueur, while in the 1990s that same mode of practice became marginalised or invisible as Martha Rosler bemoans in *Interventions and Provocation: Conversations on Art, Culture and Resistance*.[5] We see a waxing and a waning of both the commercially orientated and the political as legitimate art practice within the institutional definition of art during the post-war period of the 20th Century. Far from a story of growing inclusion, what counts instead as legitimate art practice is specific to its moment in time and space and is perhaps somewhat arbitrary. Thinking about Danto, we could say that by the late 1990s and early 2000s the likes of Claire Bishop, Nicolas Bourriaud, Jane Rendell and Grant Kester (to name but a few writers on a politicised art practice) almost follow his dictum in their creation of a space for this type of practice through the creation of a legitimating artworld discourse. It should be no surprise that activism is back in the institution by the early 2000s.

What I am saying is that the questions of power and recuperation asked here are basically irrelevant if we consider the history of art as seen through the prism of the institutional definition of art. Together, artist, institution, critic, historian, dealer, (et al) comprise the artworld and therefore create art. Instead of talking about recuperation, we could ask which type of art practice is legitimated as art at any given moment and why that particular type of art is deemed to be art as a more interesting line of enquiry, but this is a question for another essay. I want now to describe the relationship of culture, specifically the artworld, to bourgeois society as this shift too has not quite sunk in.

Though many in the artworld have been quoting Foucault for decades, it seems hearts still lie in the oppositional politics of Gramsci or even the Frankfurt School, judging by the questions raised by this publication and elsewhere. I am not going to argue that these theorists have no relevance for the contemporary moment (and here I'm thinking in particular of Adorno as well as Gramsci), just that it is no longer accurate to describe the cultural milieu of the UK in terms of dichotomy. Foucault's description of power in liberal democracies is far more nuanced and more accurate – where each

of us is our own agent of power, self-managing as good citizens and helping others also to act as the good citizen of a liberal market democracy. Each of us embody and enact the values of society and each of us help to acculturate ourselves and others through discourse. Tony Bennett uses both Gramsci and Foucault to describe and analyse how culture, including museum culture, is implicated in this process. He asks:

> Are museums not still concerned to beam their improving messages of cultural tolerance and diversity as deeply into civil society as they can reach in order to carry that message to those whom the museum can only hope to address as citizens, publics and audiences? ... If this is so, however, we shall have to see these contact zones as both the sites and artefacts of government and, as such, tethered to the civic programs which put them – and intellectuals who work within and criticise them – at work in the world.[6]

It is also worth remembering that since the 1990s, centre-left governments of the UK and USA entrenched economic policies which leave the notion of separate public and private spheres in tatters. There is now little grounds for imagining socio-politics in bipolar terms of left/right, public/private, market/state.[7] Gramsci wrote from a time when political dichotomies prevailed and so describes the State as an 'educator' where the State is "the entire complex of practical and theoretical activities with which the ruling class not only justifies and maintains its dominance, but manages to win the active consent of those over whom it rules."[8] While his analysis has certain components which help us today understand how the State does in fact create consensus in its citizenry through its various educative outlets, like museums and culture, it is also predicated on an idea of a dialectic – a push and pull between two opposing forces, the working class and the ruling class. Foucault instead describes how each and every one of us order and shape power relations. For Bennett, the site of a politicised engagement therefore must not be understood as an outmoded dialectic but in the 'politics of detail' that entails ways of addressing and acting effectively in relation to the governmental programmes through which particular fields of conduct are organised and regulated.[9] In other words, it can no longer be understood as helpful to use the old dichotomies, the old binaries, when understanding the artist's role or the institution's role within society. We are each of us constitutive of the various worlds we operate in and a politics of engagement must start from that understanding. This essay aims at shifting our perception of that engagement and our participation in it in the hope that the questions we ask in the future take us forward in a generative, relevant way.

1. Danto, A. "The Artworld." *The Journal of Philosophy* 15 Oct. 1964: 571–84.
2. Dickie, G. *Art Circle: A Theory of Art.* Chicago: Spectrum Press, 1997.
3. Bourdieu, P. *The Production of Belief.* Cambridge: Polity, 1983.
4. See Julian Stallabrass on this point in *Art Incorporated*, 2004.
5. Martha Rosler interviewed by Robert Fichter and Paul Rutkovsy. *Interventions and Provocation: Conversations on Art, Culture and Resistance.* Ed. G. Harper. New York: State University of New York Press, 1998. 13.
6. Bennett, T. *Culture: A Reformer's Science.* London: Sage Publications, 1999. 213.
7. As Anthony Giddens remarks in *The Third Way*, 1999, these were the neoliberal policies of right wing governments which the left adopted for various reasons.
8. Gramsci, A. *The Prison Notebooks.* New York: International Publishers, 1971. 258–260.
9. Bennett, T. *Culture: A Reformer's Science.* London: Sage Publications, 1999. 83.

Alana Jelinek is an artist, curator and writer, and is currently AHRC Creative Fellow at Cambridge University Museum of Anthropology and Archeaology.

RECUPERATOR/ RECUPERATED 3 IAPDH

As an artists' group, you are known for work that problematises power relations both within the art establishment and in a wider social context. To what extent do you feel that the system has effectively 'recuperated' the oppositional aspects of your work? Reflecting upon your own implication in these processes of absorption and neutralisation, how can you avoid becoming an agent of recuperation yourself? In other words, are you 'recuperated' or 'recuperator'?

Dear Tom,

In answer to your email questions we are sending you an image, a budget and this email.

It is important for us to say two things by way of introduction. First, what it means for us to be asked to participate in this debate, and second, we want to critically contextualise the image and the budget we've sent you.

We think the first point is very important to discuss because it is so easy to ignore. You have selected us for a contribution. Already there is a lot to talk about in terms of power relations and how they operate between us and you, Tom Trevor, Director of the Arnolfini, and the cultural institution(s) that you and we work for. It strikes us that 90% of what could be said in these pages has already been said by accepting the invitation to contribute. We are now, already, participating in a set of complex relations - sometimes referred to as the culture industry - something that, for whichever reason, tends to maintain political and social inequalities both within the gallery system and in wider society. What we now choose to say from this platform is largely, almost entirely, irrelevant. That's the 10% that's left for the artist (or whoever) to play with. We have noted that usually the most instructive feature of artists' participation in the culture industry is the silence they maintain about their own participation. Most artists, and you can't blame them, see the opportunity to present work in a gallery (or in this journal) as a chance to express or explore something dear to them. In our experience it is rare that artists or groups of artists want to look critically at their own positions within the processes of production, both within the gallery and in wider society. And who can blame them, it sounds really boring, doesn't it?

Of course we can feel proud to have been invited, even seduced by the idea that other important artists may be contributing alongside us. We all have egos and enjoy the recognition, but if we are really honest with ourselves we can't ignore the 90% to 10% ratio this platform offers. In other words we are doomed from the start if we believe that by participating in the culture industry we can say something very important to the rest of world. At most, and if we're very lucky, our 10% may encourage a connection made subsequently with others. Our email, image and budget is our 10%. We suppose there's always hope.

The image is our promise that our artist's fee of £2000 from the taxpayer for our commissioned work with PLATFORM for C Words: Carbon, Climate, Capital, Culture (Arnolfini, 2009) will fund our activism at the Copenhagen Climate Change Summit (COP15), December 2009. The budget that we have sent you is a breakdown of what we spent the money on.

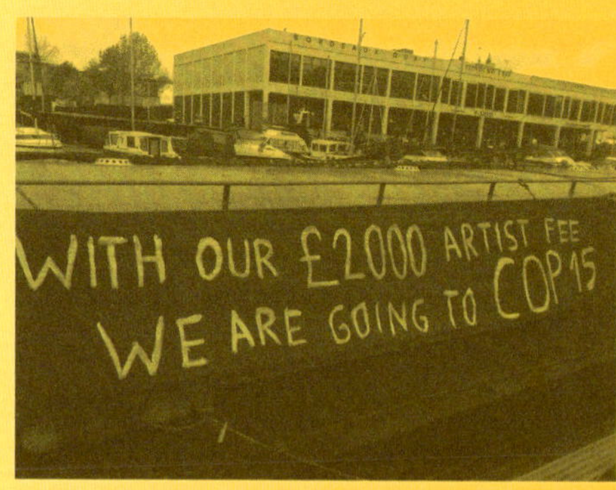

Red Banner on Canal Barge, The Institute for the Art and Practice of Dissent at Home, Arnolfini, 2009

We believe that exposing our positions in the processes of production within the gallery system is worthwhile. The hope is that this invites in others, whilst nurturing in ourselves, a deeply critical sensibility. One of our methods for doing this is refusing to remain silent about the nature of our participation by providing a degree of financial transparency about our funding. That in itself isn't going to change the world but it might help some of us reflect on our conservative positions regarding art's function in the world. So, we are not being oppositional as such, to you or the culture industry or Concept Store, but positional in relation to it. Exposing the machinations of the culture industry is a form of opposition to it, but getting strapped to the 'us' and 'them' see-saw is something we haven't yet dedicated our energies to. We are part of the problem.

The Institute for the Art and Practice of Dissent at Home is a home-run initiative, run out of the spare room of a council house in Liverpool. It is run by a family of two adults and three kids, collectively, twoaddthree (Gary, Lena, Neal, Gabriel and Sid). www.twoaddthree.org

The Institute for the Art and Practice of Dissent at Home Budget Breakdown

With Our £2000 Artist Fee We Are Going to COP 15

EXPENDITURE	£2000		RUBBISH
Harwich - Esbjerg Ferry Return Ticket	£332.10	£1667.90	A4 receipt
Liverpool - Harwich Train Return Ticket	£142.80	£1525.10	tickets
3 croissants Delicie de France @ Euston	£4.05	£1521.05	Delicie de France bag + napkins
3 baguettes 2 waters @ Upper Crust	£13.97	£1507.08	Upper Crust bags + napkins + 2 bottles of Buxton water
Harwich International Terminal Cafe	£8.65	£1498.43	3 Ribena juices, straws, plastic, 3 Walkers crisps, 2 polystyrene cups with lids
Ferry Food: Dinner and Breakfast	£100.80	£1397.63	some food waste + napkins
Ulla Present: L'Oreal and Glenlivet	£53.15	£1344.48	packaging for makeup and whiskey - to be dealt with by Ulla
3 bottles of wine and bottle opener Shop	£43.35	£1301.13	3 bottles, packaging for wine opener, 2 plastic bags from Duty Free
Virgin Mobile Top Up for L&G	£20.00	£1281.13	
Extra in £ on Carmel's dog & wine	£4.65	£1276.48	
M&S Food @ Euston for train journey	£20.90	£1255.58	3 drinks carton, 1 water bottle, 4 banana skins + packaging around them, 5 packs of crisps, 3 plastic boxes for ham, 1 plastic box for cheese, 3 plastic small wraps for cheese, chocolate chip cookies wrap, chocolate raisins bag, 2 plastic bags
Wizz Kidz donation @ Euston	£1.00	£1254.58	
Two Virgin train teas	£3.20	£1251.38	packaging from two teas, 2 cups, 2 paper bags
Taxi home	£5	£1246.38	
3 LFC scarfs - present for Ulla and kids	£17.97	£1228.41	
postage includng envelope	£5.59	£1222.82	
Cash Book	£0.65	£1222.17	
Esbjerg - Copenhagen Train	DKK 608	...	train tickets
4 hot dogs and waters	DKK 124	...	hot dog
tissue/bags 4 plastic bottles, 1 given back to the shop for	DKK 1	...	
chocolates	DKK 51	...	chocolate wrappers
crisps and teas on train	DKK 72	...	crisps packets, 2 teacups, 2 bags of tea, more napkins which are used as tissues
bus tickets in Copenhagen	DKK 42	...	bus tickets
2 pints and 3 juices near Ulla's	DKK 140	...	3 bottles from juice but café will deal with it
8 beers and 5 juices from shop	DKK 195	...	8 cans of beer + 5 bottles of juice - will be recycled, says Ulla
3 sweatshirts Climate Justice	DKK 600	...	
pastries near Christiania	DKK 106	...	2 bags+ napkins from pastries
Nemoland café food, juices and teas	DKK 100	...	2 plastic cups + 2 wooden sticks
bus tickets in Copenhagen	DKK 42	...	bus tickets
butchers - mince beef for Shep Pie	DKK 62	...	packaging from food shopping, from meat, carrots…
corner shop veg + stuff for Shep Pie	DKK 176	...	tomatoes, peas, potatoes, peppers, cheese
corner shop veg + stuff for Shep Pie	DKK 151	...	
wine and cheese	DKK 200	...	1 wine box
metro ticket for 10 rides	DKK 130	...	1 metro ticket for 10 rides
pizzeria near Reclaim Power march	DKK 255	...	6 plastic cups, 2 pizza boxes, 1 plastic bag, 1 bottle of lemonade, napkins
given to Ulla for hot chocolate	DKK 100	...	
butchers - leg of lamb, Louise dinner	DKK 237	...	meat packaging - some paper
rosemary	DKK 40	...	
potatoes and parsnip	DKK 30	...	veg packaging
given to Ulla for beef soup-dinner club	DKK 500	...	
ice skating	DKK 115	...	
muffins, coffees, hot juices	DKK 155	...	stuff around muffin, juice bottles that café deals with 4 falafels +
lemonades	DKK 200	...	foil in which falafels were wrapped, one plastic bag, lots of napkins, 4 cans
wine and beer	DKK 250	...	cans of beer - not sure how many, lots; box of wine
Copenhagen - Esbjerg train	DKK 775	...	
bowling next to Klima Forum	DKK 175	...	
sandwiches at Klima Forum	DKK 100	...	4 sandwich wrappers
teas and juices at Klima Forum	DKK 55	...	3 plastic cups, 2 teabags, 2 paper cups, 1 wooden stick
cakes at Klima Forum	DKK 60	...	2 paper plates, 4 serviettes for cakes
bread at Netto	DKK 33	...	2 bags of bread packaging, also eggs cartoon
tooth fairy	DKK 50	...	
food for train journey	DKK 227	...	5 banana skins, 1 plastic bag, packages from 4 sandwiches, 4 plastic bottles from apple juices
one cup of tea on train	DKK 18	...	1 paper cup
toilet on Esbjerg train station	DKK 2	...	
Carmel's present: beer, sausage, chocolate	DKK 300	...	1 plastic bag
Carmel's present: dog + wine on ferry	DKK 450	...	3 bottles of wine
dinner on ferry	DKK 796	...	minimal food waste, 2 toothpicks
breakfast on ferry	DKK 327	...	some blue napkins
	DKK 8049		
	£ 974.06	£248.11	
			recipts in general
			26 nappies out of which 14 were soiled
			45 wipes, two of which were randomly used, one was bloodied
			1 nappy bag
			8 cosmetic pads
			Klima forum magazine
			packaging from Ali Kazam and 2 Jack the Pirate costumes
Art not Oil Diaries	£50.00	£198.11	

£198.11 is the left over money that we are sending to vacuum cleaner in Stanley Picker gallery in a package. We will deduct p&p expenses.

AN INTRODUCTION TO THERAPOETRY

/

THE VOICE AGAINST THE IMAGE/ POETRY AGAINST SEMIOCAPITAL

FRANCO BERARDI (BIFO)

Does art have something to do with the creation of subjective autonomy in the sphere of immaterial production and Semiocapitalism? In order to answer this question I'll briefly explain what Semiocapitalism is. In the classical form of manufacturing capitalism; price, wages and profit fluctuations were based on the relationship between necessary labour time and the determination of value. Following the introduction of microelectronic technologies and the resulting intellectualisation of productive labour, the relationship between different magnitudes and different productive forces entered a period of indeterminacy. Deregulation marked the end of the law of value and turned its demise into a political economy. In his main work, *L'échange symbolique et la mort [Symbolic Exchange and Death]*, Jean Baudrillard intuitively infers the overall direction of the development of the end of the millennium: "The principle of reality coincided with a certain stage of the law of value. Today, the whole system has precipitated into indeterminacy and reality has been absorbed by the hyper-reality of the code of simulation."[1]

The whole system precipitates into indeterminacy as all correspondences between symbol and referent, simulation and event, value and labour time no longer hold.

Isn't this also what the avant-garde aspired to? Did not the experimental art of the XX Century wish to sever the link between symbol and referent? In saying this, I am not accusing the avant-garde of being the cause of neo-liberal economic deregulation. Rather, I am suggesting that the anarchic utopia of the avant-garde was actualised and turned into its opposite when society internalised rules and capital was able to abdicate both juridical law and political rationality to abandon itself to the seeming anarchy of internalised automatisms, which is actually the most rigid form of totalitarianism. As industrial discipline dwindled, individuals found themselves in a state of formal freedom. No law forced them to put up with duties and dependence. Obligations became internalised and social control was exercised through a voluntary albeit inevitable subjugation to chains of automatisms.

In a regime of aleatory and fluctuating values, precariousness became the generalised form of social relations, which deeply affected the social composition and the psychic, relational and linguistic character of a new generation as it entered the labour market. Rather than a particular form of productive relations, precariousness is the dark soul of the productive process. An uninterrupted flow of fractal and recombined info-labour circulates in the global web as the agent of universal valorisation, yet its value is indeterminable. Connectivity and precariousness are two sides of the same coin: the flow of semio-capitalist production captures and connects cellularised fragments of de-personalised time; capital purchases fractals of human time and recombines them on the web. From the standpoint of capitalist valorisation, this uninterrupted flow is undifferentiated and finds its unity only in the resultant value: Semiocapital. However, from the standpoint of cognitive precarious workers the supply of labour is fragmented: fractals of time and pulsating cells of labour are switched on and off in the large control room of global production. Therefore the supply of labour time can be disconnected from the physical and juridical subjectivity of the worker. Social labour time becomes an ocean of valorising cells that can be summoned and recombined in accordance with the needs of capital.

When industrial capitalism transposed into the new form of Semiocapitalism, it first and foremost mobilised the psychic energy of society to bend it to the drive of competition and cognitive productivity. The 'new economy' of the 1990s was essentially a 'Prozac-economy', both neuro-mobilisation and compulsory creativity. Art, in this situation, far from being a factor of autonomy and self-empowerment, becomes an element of aestheticisation and mobilisation of everyday life. The same word 'activism' is undergoing a similar destiny. Art and activism are united under the sign of the mobilisation of nervous energies. Should we not free ourselves from the thirst for activism that fed the 20th Century to the point of catastrophe and war? Should we not set ourselves free from the repeated and failed attempt to act for the liberation of human energies from the rule of capital? Is not the path towards the autonomy of the social from economic and military mobilisation only possible through a withdrawal into inactivity, silence, and passive sabotage?

By the beginning of the 21st Century the long history of the artistic avant-garde was over. Beginning with Wagner's *Gesamtkunstwerk* and resulting in the Dadaist cry to "Abolish art, abolish everyday life, abolish the separation between art and everyday life", the history of the avant-garde culminates in the gesture of 9/11. Stockhausen had the courage to say this, whilst many of us were thinking the same: terrorising suicide is the *Gesamtkunstwerk*, the total work of art of the century with no future. The fusion of art and life (or death, what difference does it make?) is clearly visible in the form of action that we might call 'terrorising suicide'. Let us take Pekka Auvinen as an example. The Finnish youngster turned up to his class at school with a machine gun, killing eight people, himself included. Printed on his T-shirt was the sentence: "Humanity is overrated". Was not his gesture pregnant with signs typical of the communicative action of the arts?

At this point I want to oppose the concept of poetry to the concept of art. The realm of sensibility is involved in this ongoing process of cognitive reformatting that is implied in the Semiocapitalist mutation. Central to this mutation is the insertion of the electronic into the organic, the proliferation of artificial devices in the organic universe, in the body, in communication and in society. Therefore, the relationship between consciousness and sensibility is transformed and the exchange of signs undergoes a process of increasing desensitisation. The digitalisation of social communication leads on the one hand to a sort of desensitisation to the voice, to the caressing power of words, to the continuous flows of slow becoming, and on the other, it leads to a 'becoming sensitive' of code: sensitisation to sudden changes of states and to the sequence of discrete signs. This mutation produces painful effects in the conscious organism that we read through the categories of psychopathology: dyslexia, anxiety and apathy, panic, depression and a sort of suicidal epidemic.

Aesthetic perception – here properly conceived of as the realm of sensibility and aesthesia – is directly involved in this transformation – in its attempt to efficiently interface with the connective environment, the conscious organism appears to increasingly inhibit what we call sensibility. By sensibility, I mean the faculty that enables human beings to interpret signs that are not verbal nor can be made so or the ability to understand what cannot be expressed in forms that have a finite syntax. This faculty reveals itself to be useless and even damaging in an integrated connective system. Sensibility slows down processes of interpretation and renders them aleatory and ambiguous, thus reducing the competitive efficiency of the semiotic agent.

Let's think of the relation between image and sensibility. Let's think of *youporn.com* as Art. *Youporn* is the final realisation of art because life is in the image, and the image is

in the media, and the media are into life. Here the circle of *Gesamtkunstwerk* and of Dada is fulfilled. Hyper-speed optic fibre circulation of the image is producing an effect of *mise en abyme* of desire, an effect of hyper-stimulation and perpetual postponement of pleasure. Pleasure becomes asynthotic, in the kingdom of dromocracy and image pervasion.[2]
The sensuous body is simultaneously provoked and deceived, and at the end it is erased. More sex-images, less time for caresses. This is the final realisation of art in the sphere of Semiocapitalist acceleration.

> **Once upon a time pleasure was repressed by power. Now it is evoked and promised, and finally deceived. Pleasure is shown and simultaneously dissolved. This is the pornographic feature of Semioproduction in the sphere of the market. The eye has taken the central place of human sensory life, but the eye's domination is the domination of merchandise as a promise never fulfilled and always postponed. Acceleration is the beginning of panic and panic is the beginning of depression. The voice is forgotten, erased and cancelled in the erotic domain of Semiocapitalism. The voice and the words are forgotten. Sex has no more words and no more voice, when it becomes marketing overload, when the education of a new generation of humans happens in an environment where the body of the mother is replaced by display machines. When sex loses its voice and its words, it becomes a desert with no pleasure. Desire becomes frenzy: lost is the time of caresses when lost is the time for words.**
> **The voice is the gate of poetry.**
> **Poetry is the gate of self-therapy.**
> **Therapy is the gate of pleasure.**
> **And pleasure, the gate of autonomy.**

When I say therapy, I do not mean normalisation at all, I do not mean restoration of the working self either. Rather, I mean the ability to listen to the voice, the ability to understand words. This is why I want to oppose the voice to images, and poetry to art.

> **This is why I think that the way toward social recomposition and autonomy necessitates the de-visualisation of imagination, and the therapeutic action of the voice.**

1. Baudrillard, J. *Symbolic Exchange and Death.* Paris: Gallimard, 1976. 12.

Franco Berardi (Bifo) is a writer, media-theorist and media-activist, and Professor of Social History of Communication at the Academy of Fine Arts in Milan.

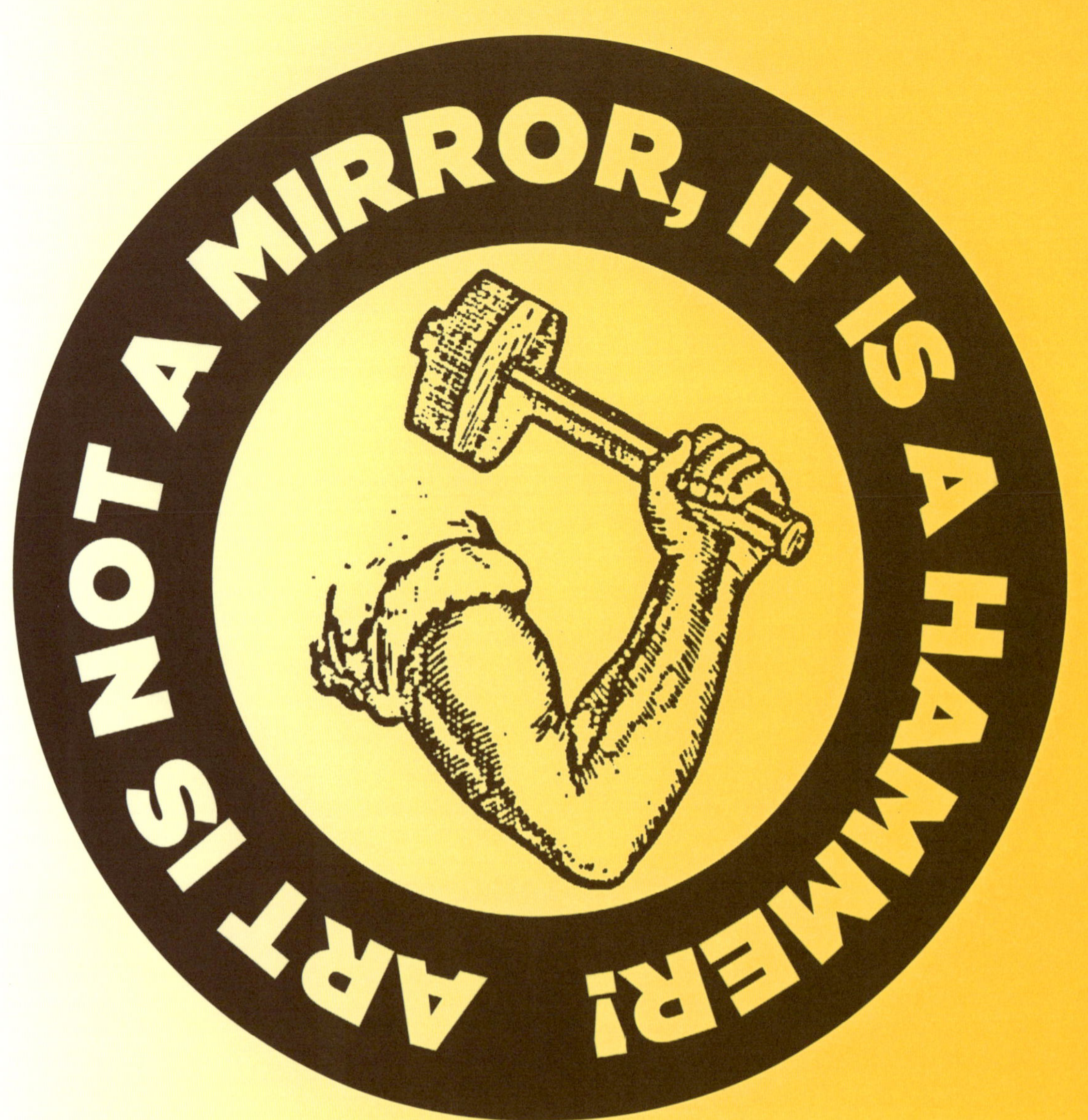

Art & Hammer, Dejan Kršić
Courtesy WHW/What, How & for Whom

RECUPERATOR/ RECUPERATED 4 SARAT MAHARAJ

Almost everything is 'taken for granted' in the art world as 'oppositional and radical'. Theory, above all – even though it seems to have become increasingly the central 'spectacle' in art fairs and biennales (its original point was to query 'spectacle').

Also, we appear to have forgotten the pointed link Adorno drew between the museum/gallery and the mausoleum - that art only gets to the former to be 'interred'.

There is a tendency to focus on 'de-territorialising', without enough attention to what comes in its wake – 're-territorialising' (recuperation). Deleuze tended to give equal importance to both processes. To the latter, not so much a 'shock horror' or 'scandal' or 'sell out' but as a part of the ongoing force of creation, the solidifying and dissolution of mental and emotional territories and fields of action.

Sarat Maharaj is a curator and writer. He is a research professor at Goldsmiths' College, London, and is currently Professor of Visual Art at Malmö Art Academy, Sweden.

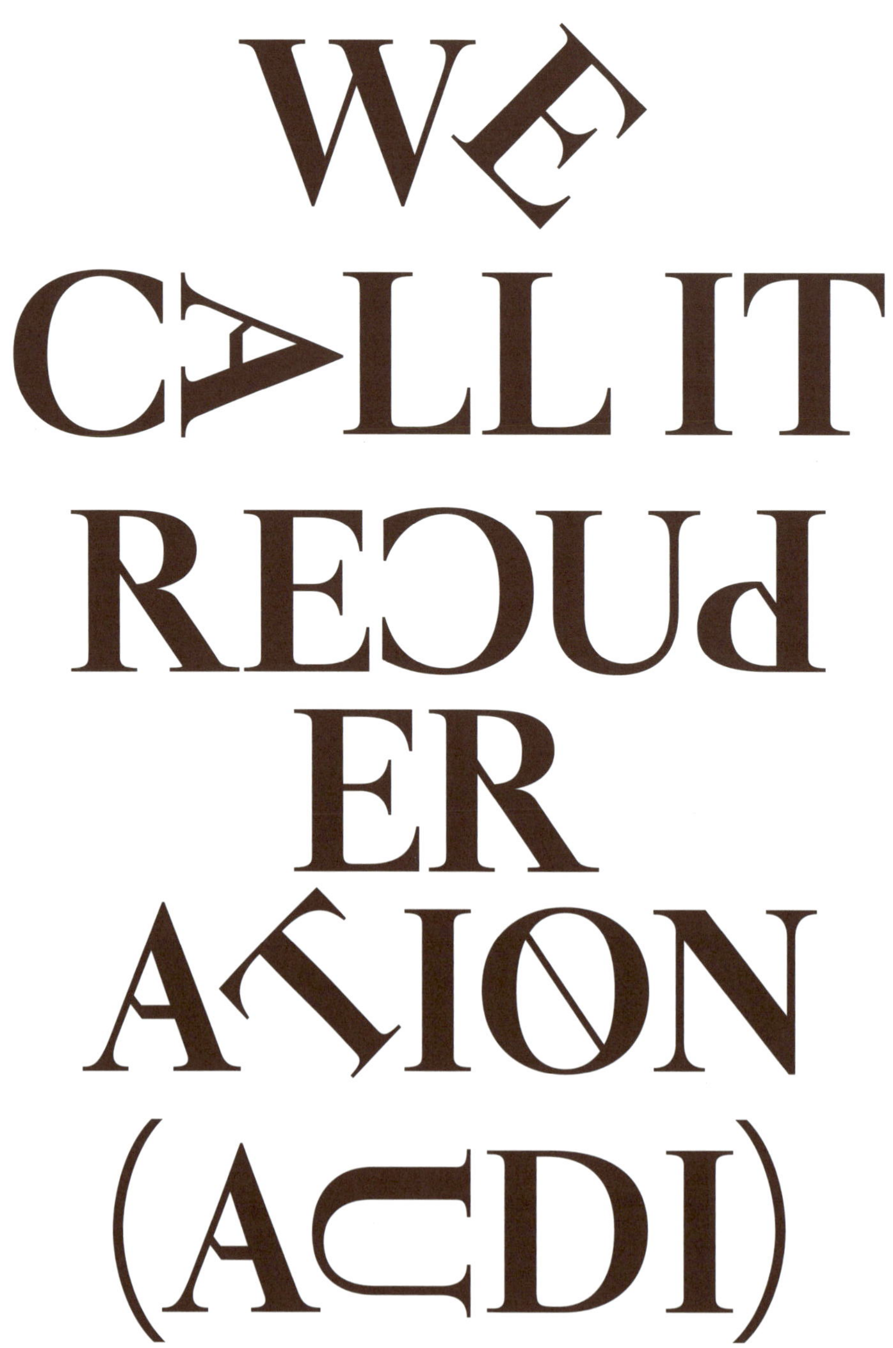

ESTHER LESLIE

INSPIRATION COMES STANDARD (Chrysler)
In the mid-1930s, at the close of the first thesis of his essay 'The Work of Art in the Age of its Technological Reproducibility', Walter Benjamin wrote of how various concepts used in the discussion of art had become outmoded, useless for both art criticism and artistic production. These categories included creativity and genius, eternal value and mystery, "concepts", he noted "whose uncontrolled [and at present almost uncontrollable] application leads to a processing of data in the fascist sense". Effectively Benjamin notes the recuperation of art into oppressive political and social systems through a language of criticism, or rather, more appropriately, and especially so in the Nazi context, where criticism as such was banned – recuperation through art appreciation.

I think about Benjamin's sneer at 'creativity' often these days, as the word 'creative' has returned forcefully. For a long time now there has been discussion of the co-option of the notion by the urban gentrifiers – at least since Richard Florida's well-distributed and implemented thesis on the Creative City, which stimulated countless 'creative city' branding exercises, hitching creativity to economic development as a motor, in the context of the New International Division of Labour. It might have been thought that such a political wielding of the term creativity would tarnish it, contaminate it, set it out of bounds for any contemporary *soi-disant* critical practice. But creativity persists, and as a politically loaded term wedded to the theory and practice of anti-globalists, artivists, art activists or hacktivists in its various forms. Creativity articulates how culture can re-animate democracy.

Recently there was an exhibition of ten years of anti-global art and culture called *Signs of Revolt: Creative Resistance and Social Movements Since Seattle.* Activist art comes in from the heat of the struggle or coldness of the outside-world and finds a refuge for a week, its energies, humour, anger and resistant creativity blu-tacked up for marvel. It is as uninterested in framing each piece, as it is uninterested in the gallery itself as a frame. The Artivism network of Germany website likewise mobilises the force of the creative: it "looks for creativity that threatens the conventional wisdom with progressive ideas". The group PLATFORM are engaged in "promoting creative processes of democratic engagement to advance social and ecological justice". And so on. Perhaps these initiatives have to proclaim their claim on the creative more loudly than the art that is 'political' but was always, all along, designed for the gallery, even as it fired off critiques of the institutions under whose spotlights it glowed. Incidentally, the high-end, high-tech 'political art', such as that curated at Laboral in Gijon, by Steve Dietz and Christiane Paul, *Feedforward: The Angel of History,* does not need to make reference to creativity nor the institution. It is comfortable enough with its own relation to both and to its funders global company Fundación Telefónica – no insecurity there, even as the show exhibits back to us the insecurities in which we exist, with "sections relating to five themes: the 'wreckage' of the 20th Century created by wars and conflict; the countermeasures of surveillance and repression that the state as well as global capital set up in an attempt to maintain control; the aesthetics and symbolic language of the media of our times; the forces of economic globalisation such as outsourcing and migration; and the possibilities of reconstruction and agency". The post-conceptual artists represented there are examples of what John Roberts has proposed as the collaborators in a 'general social technique', who gather up their new labour skills (post-creative ones in a traditional sense) from here, there and anywhere in the network that is the context of today's digital and media technologies of communicative action and build Guantanamo Bay in Second Life, a virtual Berlin Wall, a self-composed surveillance database the FBI can only dream of, fictitious off-shore finance companies, or technologies of obfuscation to parallel the media ones. And yet they remain artists. The ideology of the artist, the assertion of autonomy, are sustained – even as the world out there is mediated, sliced, recombined, broadcast and narrowcast in the gallery.

The artworld, that nebulous composite of galleries, funders, collectors, critics and theorists, have embraced all these different forms of being political and creative. Perhaps the thesis of the general social technique helps to explain it – political art, in all these contemporary guises, more or less draws on technology, media, mass forms and so appears to be a part of the general hubbub of the contemporary that is so sought after. But, in addition to being contemporaneous with what is, and therefore relevant, it remains art, which means it carries with it that irreducible meaningfulness, the gravity absent from all the forms that might approximate it, use the same technologies, the same points of reference. It is what it is with the creative added in as bonus.

PASSIONATE ABOUT CREATIVITY (Citibank)

Of course, it seems obvious. In the artworld how can there not be references to creativity. Creativity is the opposite of alienation. It is that which is expunged from the labour process as it becomes increasingly automated, rationalised, standardised, alienated, subdivided into tasks, unfree. Creativity is proper to art, but art is the problem. To re-spin that which has been spun so much, since Marx and Engels said it 161 years ago: art is – potentially – just another 'profession' now, another type of wage labour. Its quality, creativity, is recuperated into art, which is recuperated into the system of labour and consumption. As Adorno insisted, some 40 years ago, – without even having seen the TV show *School of Saatchi* – art is a branch of the culture industry. Though it is also, he maintains, imperceptibly, possibly, tendentially, hope against hopefully, also 'functionless', or rather its social function is to be, apparently, without function. It is for those reasons – that art is politically and socially and economically implicated and imbricated – that any mobilising of the notion of creativity need be probed to see what its attractions and detractions are. Benjamin's hostility to it might cast the term into suspicion for us and even allow us to understand that process whereby art and politics seem to collapse so desirably together in this way and now. Might the assertion of the value of the creative be the logical outcome of an aesthetics that refuses to remainder art, or, in other words, the spin-off a certain desire for recuperation – and one that now happily finds its recuperators in the galleries. As the Artivist network in Germany says "In a flashy culture of screens and Second Life, political artists are forced to the margins and must struggle to find exposure and support". Why? Or rather might not their continued insistence on their own existence as artists be a part of the problem of creativity? Is not thereby any 'political value' re-converted back into 'exhibition value' – and perhaps without remainder?

THINK DIFFERENT (Apple)

Benjamin's decision not to refunction the term 'creativity' (in a Brechtian sense) but to replace it with 'production' was a tactical move, made on the basis of the historical associations of the phrase, its relationship to genius, divine inspiration, otherworldliness, associations that stems from the Romantic period and characterise the artist as exception, visionary fool who is to be admired, then, later, perhaps rather tolerated, but not taken seriously in the workaday world. Creativity is outside society, outside the everyday and, for that reason, creativity is proposed as stimulus to a compassion that is unusual, or as an alibi for the world's usual coldness, or a catalyst of the new, when it is needed.

If creativity returns as sign that is as a sign of an alternative world, of course, something wonderful is being presented – a world organised in relation to the creative not the economically productive, a new economy or non-economy. But at the same time, the proposition of a creativity unleashed, motivating the anti-global movements, creativity showcased as proof of said mobilisations, in some sense, is to react, to reinstate a familiar situation. Artists are to assume for themselves all the creativity and the right to dispense it whenever and wherever they please – in the name of the better world. The rest get to watch the spectacle of themselves – or others – being marshalled in a more or less hopeless gesture towards a better world.

'The Author as Producer', from 1934, investigated the prospects for contemporary critical culture workers, examining strategies that would avoid the pressures on artists to be individualistic, competitive or promoters of art as a new religion or an evasion of the 'political'. Benjamin evaluated artists' efforts to work out cultural forms that could not be recuperated by fascism. He assessed what the new mass cultural forms that existed – radio, film, photography, photomontage, worker-correspondent newspapers – meant in the wider scheme of the social world, and how facts such as mass reproduction change humans' relationship to culture of the past and the present. The artist as producer abandons traditional skills and their associated creativity in favour of an alignment with new technical relations of production. That is to say he assessed and more importantly urged on the overhauling of relations between the creative and the non-creative, artists and audiences. The revised social and political relations of art proposed by Benjamin set out from a circuit of participants. When he wrote of "the author as producer" he meant thereby that everyone was an author of meanings or no-one was.

Rather more traditional relations of aesthetic production and consumption are proposed by something such as the Artivist network of Germany, whose starting point is that art has the power to inspire, imagine, dream. That may be true, but is it not a concern that it is the same starting point as that of business, as articulated quite succinctly in Carey Young's video piece, *Product Recall*, from 2007. Young is on the psychoanalyst's couch trying to remember what global brand used what slogan as its advertising tagline – all associate the product with inspiration and creativity: "Change the way you see the world", "Imagination at work", "Where imagination begins", 'It's not that hard to imagine'. In the advertising slogans, it is not the labour process that is to be associated with creativity, rather it is the product – or, more intangibly, the brand, the image of the product. The fetish object is sprinkled with the Disneydust of creativity. These brand tags stem from companies that have typically already recuperated the power of art – as quality of hipness, as humanising coating, through their sponsorship of art institutions, fairs and exhibitions. What does the endless roll-call of the creative mantras reveal: a simultaneous assumed power and actual blandness of the notion? Creativity makes for a limber politics – so unlike the old-style dull moralism of 'hardcore' politics. Creativity melds well with the out-of-nowhere, into anywhere, eventalism of Deleuzian *politique*. It's a flexible concept appropriatable by all who want to gesture towards their own virtuousness. And why shouldn't art galleries or funding bodies be the first amongst them?

YOUR POTENTIAL, OUR PASSION (Microsoft)
Recuperation is a powerful force – and it only works in one direction, in the Situationist schema, according to which there would be only one answer as to who is recuperating whom. In 'Basic Banalities' from 1963, Raoul Vaneigem notes that Situationist poetry, not that of the professional poet or culture worker, but that of everyday resistance to domination, "is irreducible and cannot be recuperated by power (as soon as an act is recuperated it becomes a stereotype, conditioning, language of power)". Once recuperated, any resistant object or technique crosses over to become part of the lifeblood of the system that gave rise to it as moment of negation in the first place. But the true poetry is that which cannot be recuperated, notes Vaneigem, though it is surrounded by power, which "encircles the irreducible and holds it by isolating it". Perhaps the culture industry is even more rapacious than it was in the 1960s – preferring to recuperate than isolate, where possible. Preferring to turn outwards – screening the world, interfacing with the world – as this gesture, which undoubtedly, under the same motivations that have propelled the success of reality TV, speaks to contemporary audiences who seek in culture some revelation about present-day iniquities, be that between self and celebrity, first world and third world, tourist and migrant, the self as worker and as consumer.

Indeed the culture industry, or in its new guise as creative industry, is so fearless, it is able not only to showcase something akin to constructed situations in galleries. It even re-releases the concepts into the city spaces for which they were originally destined. Thereby it recuperates even the base concept of Psychogeography, its fundamental unit, into its 'creative cities' visions: psychogeography, the 'plaque tournante', the turning plate or hub, those magical turbulent junctions in the city where an excess of energy, a clash of ambiences, a disruption of planning's logic generates resonant affectivities, proposes portals of transformation. We know the language of the hub. Indeed the Arnolfini's director has spoken of it: in relation to their location, in the interests of bringing in tourist revenue in a post-industrial context: "When we moved to our current venue, there was nothing here at all. Now the habourside is packed. This part of the city has become a real hub".[1]

The gallery is that agent that can make something out of nothing. That is the ultimate creative act – to pluck something from the air. That is the truly immaterial act.

None of this is to say that galleries, funding bodies, the artists who benefit from them are wrong or cynical. The question rather is what sort of space is the gallery, what sort of mechanism is funding? Do both do anything to the things they suck up? Or do they do nothing? Do they neutralise? Do they, in turn, put the brake on? Simply by turning the radical and creative gesture of negation into positivity and spectacle?

'We Call It Recuperation' comes from an Audi car advertisement from 2009. We call it recuperation. What Audi calls recuperation is the way energy produced by applying the brake is captured, stored and used later to recharge the battery. I wonder how much this notion of recuperation could be applied to the current affection between political art and galleries. The recuperated energy in the car is used to keep the system going, to top up the depleting energies of the engine. The energy produced by critical political art's efforts to apply the brake to the system – the global system, the neo-liberal device – is gathered up in the gallery, diverted even to the gallery, to keep at least it, if not the hub of which it is a component, dynamic.

1. Inflight Magazine of Brussels Airlines.

Esther Leslie a writer and editor, and is Professor of Political Aesthetics at Birkbeck, University of London.

RECUPERATOR/ RECUPERATED 5 FREEE

The Long Avant-Garde

Since Peter Bürger's *Theory of the Avant-Garde* did to political art what Adorno and Horkheimer had done to *Reason in The Dialectic of Enlightenment*, the accusation that art's critique of its own institutions has been recuperated by those very same institutions has been a perennial argument of art's discourse. In fact, the theory of the incorporation of the avant-garde into art's commercial and official mainstream has become almost too easy to assert. It is a cliché.

The problem with the theory of recuperation is the implication that prior to the process, or for those who steer clear of institutions etc, there remains the possibility of not being institutionalised. As a theory, recuperation is structured around a paired opposite of two terms, one signifying independence, critique, resistance etc, and the other signifying neutralisation, institutionalisation and corruption. This opposition, which is too black and white to navigate the complexities of art's relation to power, leads to simplistic tactics. Artists in the 1980s, for instance, attempted to dilute the effects of recuperation by announcing, up front, that they were corrupt through and through.

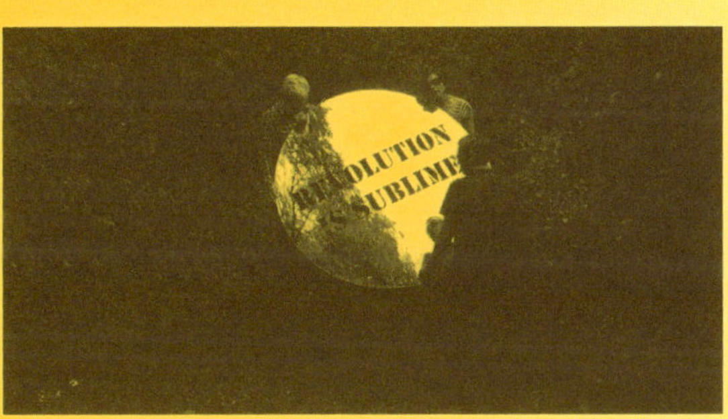

Revolution is Sublime, Freee, 2009, Billboard Poster

Why would anyone subscribe to this strict division? We should note that it is not only presupposed by those who cynically insist that since recuperation is unavoidable then there is no argument against business-as-usual. It is required, also, for the radical to pitch themselves against a corrupt and corrupting world. The division has another related purpose, too. Recuperation is used as an insult by one section of the left to another: it distinguishes between the true radicals who staunchly resist recuperation, and the liberal left who sacrifice the cause for a share of the spoils. Recuperation is an idea that lends itself to romanticised notions of resistance.

It is fair to say that critical art's recuperation is felt more keenly during periods of conservative backlash against previous avant-garde gains. As we can see with YBA, for instance, when the market leads developments in contemporary art the result is not a return to previously sellable works, but the commodification of the latest thinking. And one of the key elements of thinking on art at the time, evident in *Technique Anglaise, Blimey and High Art Lite*, was the recuperation of critical art.

How convenient! Imagine young artists in the company of fame and fortune being able to comfort themselves with the latest postmodern catchphrase from Baudrillard, telling them that there is no difference between complicity and critique in a world characterised by simulacra. Under such circumstances critical artists, political artists and engaged artists are regarded as naïve (or worse). John Roberts showed this fashionable position to be a "retreat from complexity" in his unflinching defence of 'critical postmodernism' in his agenda-setting book *Postmodernism, Politics and Art*.

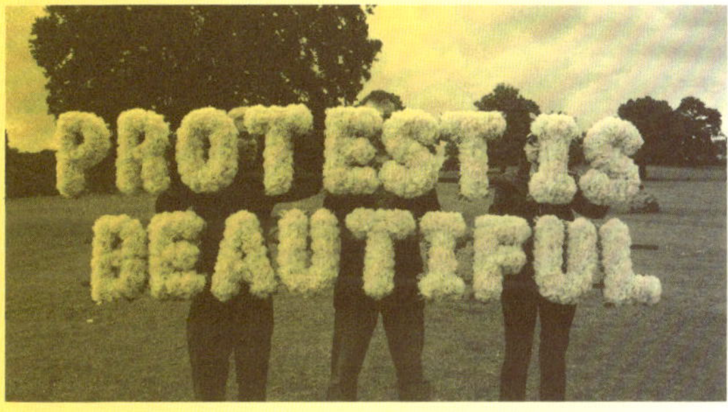

Protest is Beautiful, Freee, 2007, Billboard Poster

It wasn't just Roberts' arguments, impressive as they were, that convinced. Roberts' case was littered with examples of conceptually sophisticated politically engaged art, thus drawing together a formidable cast of critical artists, including Terry Atkinson, Art & Language, Jo Spence, Rasheed Araeen and Mark Wallinger. These artists were not ignorant or neglectful of the issue of recuperation, but their response was not to retreat from critique but to "problematise the political status of art *at the same time* as asserting this is where art is to find its conditions of relevance".

Peter Osborne is convinced that critical art (especially institution critique) can be judged in terms of its reception by the institutions it addresses. In 1971, he says, three major exhibitions were closed or cancelled, and this is a measure of their critical success. He argues that these rare moments of institutional rejection show that such projects "reveal where a limit was by surpassing it", but the epistemologisation of recuperation cannot hide the all-or-nothing opposition that it spells out for culture. When art's institutions came to understand the value of institution critique, or "smartened up", as Orborned puts it, such work "never seriously challenged" art's institutions again. Proof: no more shows were cancelled or closed.

In one sense Osborne introduces a Realpolitik of critical art, testing its success against whether the existing Ideological State Apparatus is pushed beyond its tolerance, but its binary is too stark to respond to specific historical circumstances. Crystal clear oppositions of this sort are always abstract even when their intention is to bring us firmly to the ground. Osborne adds urgency to the heroism of resistance (in one of the shortest windows of opportunity for avant-gardism available), but as a formula for recuperation it lacks nuance.

Compare Osborne's formula with what Rancière calls the politics of the *part des sans-part*. For Rancière something outside the system forces its way into the system but, by doing so, reconfigures the system itself. This is the work of politics. Following Rancière we would have to say that politics in its full sense does not take place until the act of recuperation backfires on the system. So long as the *part des sans-part* remains in its designated place outside the system then it has not fulfilled its political mission. Without such a shift, of course, the *part des sans-part* is depoliticised by occupying the very place that the system has allotted for it. We might think of recuperation as one aspect of the process by which this allotted place is challenged and changed, reconfiguring the whole system as a result. It is clearly too one-dimensional, therefore, to regard the process of recuperation as an event whereby the institution cancels critique by incorporating it.

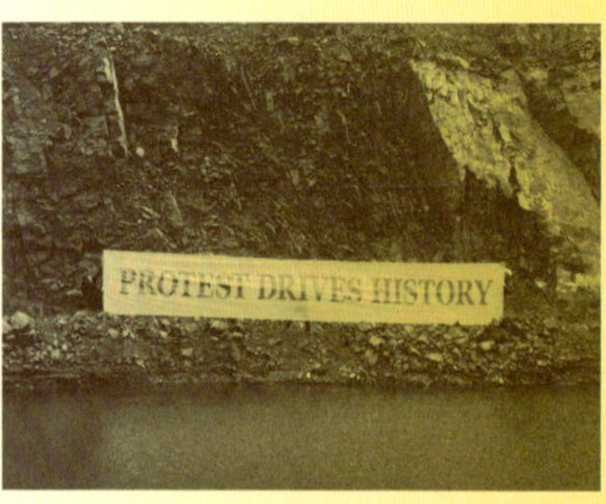

Protest Drives History, Freee, 2008, Billboard Poster

Recuperation is one of the names the Left in Europe has given to the various processes by which its critique of existing conditions is fatally compromised by being channelled through dominant structures. Debord points out that militants are transformed into passive consumers of their own militancy by the spectacle. This is recuperation. And the same effects are produced by the State, as well as market forces, when it legitimates and funds its own opposition. As such, the theory of recuperation is part of a shift in Left thinking that brought about an extension of the Left's agenda from politics and economics narrowly understood to questions of ideology and hegemony, that is to say, from production to reproduction. And the current state of play in political theory on the Left continues to develop these themes in the writing of Badiou, Rancière, Balibar, Habermas, Lecercle, Butler, Laclau, Mouffe, Žižek, and many others. Ideology remains at the heart of Left thinking today.

In order to understand the core issues raised by recuperation in terms of contemporary theories of ideology we need to grasp the essentials of Althusser's rearticulation of the material and social reality of the production of ideas within what he called the Ideological State Apparatuses. In addition to the State apparatus itself (comprised of the police, the courts, the prisons and the army) with its various mechanisms of coercive force, the Ideological State Apparatuses (including churches, schools, the family, the law, the political system, the media, and culture) reproduce the existing social relations (always relations of domination) not by repressing individuals but by transforming individuals into subjects.

He argues that the present society is structurally dominated by a combination of two ISA's, the school and the family. "What do children learn at school?" he asks. He answers that in the very process of learning techniques and knowledge: children learn to behave like good citizens. Althusser points out, therefore, that as well as being an Ideological State Apparatus, the school is protected from its ideological function by the ideology that it is a "neutral environment purged of ideology". The Ideological State Apparatuses are certainly the institutions where we encounter dominant ideas such as 'God' and 'beauty', but we do not understand ideology very well unless we see ISA's as the places where citizens are produced as subjects.

Althusser adds another new concept to the ISA's in order to explain the functioning of ideology. He uses the word 'interpellation' to name the process by which individuals are constituted as subjects. Althusser argues that subjectivity is not 'mental' but 'practical', existing not in consciousness but in rituals, practices and institutions. Interpellation is the process by which institutions produce the subjects they require. They do not just wish for subjects, they use rituals and simple physical acts (such as kneeling, praying, sitting, standing and singing) to produce these effects.

We can see then that Althusser's analysis does the opposite of vulgar ideological critique: instead of dismissing ideas as quickly as possible to reveal the reality behind appearances, Althusser sees the ideological content of simple physical acts and regards practices, rituals and institutions as the material existence of an ideological apparatus. This is why we have to think about recuperation through the Althusserian concept of Ideological State Apparatuses.

One can enter a church without being subject to it, without performing the subjectivity that it institutionally produces, but inevitably one will enter a church as one subject or another, as a tourist perhaps, or someone who appreciates architecture. And these other subjects will have been produced by their own institutions, rituals and practices. Here, ideology functions effectively without having to pass through the consciousness of the subject. It does this, not by persuading them, but simply by welcoming them into institutions, providing them with meaningful tasks, and identifying them as members of a community. So, if we know from J L Austin that speech acts "do things with words", we can say, after Althusser, that ideology interpellates individuals as subjects with speech acts and ritual acts.

Jean-Jacques Lecercle adds: "the function of ideology is to interpellate individuals as subjects – a task in which it never fails: all individuals are always interpellated". Hence, the individual will be interpellated as one kind of subject or another. No-one escapes, not even the agent of the Ideological State Apparatus who interpellates you. It is inevitable that, while teaching her class of toddlers to be good citizens, the teacher does not only interpellate her pupils, but interpellates herself as a 'good teacher'. Or, as Lecercle explains, the policeman does not only interpellate you as subject to his authority, he also interpellates himself as the holder of authority: "the policeman whistles not only at 'little Louis' but also at himself". As such, interpellation should not be thought of only in terms of something that happens to individuals, or even as things that one individual does to another, but as acts that we perform by ourselves and on ourselves.

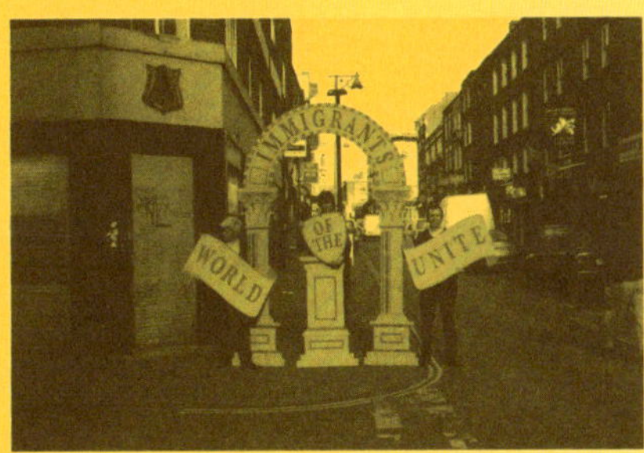

Workers of the World Unite, Freee, 2008, Billboard Poster

Since interpellation forms and reforms subjectivity, we can expect recuperation to have an emotional effect. If its interpellation is successful recuperation must feel great. Recuperation is an affirmation that feels like victory. If the interpellation of recuperation fails, however - which means that a previous interpellation still stands - then recuperation must feel awful, like betrayal or disgust. And, of course, one interpellates subject can feel disgusted on behalf of another who had been successfully recuperated.

At roughly the same time that Debord and the Situationists developed the idea of recuperation, Habermas articulated the twin processes by which the 'public sphere' - the social space designated for open critical opinion formation - had been 'colonised' and 'debased' by market forces and the state. Despite his reputation for a parliamentary and consensual politics, Habermas is one of the key theorists of the ways in which grass-roots activism and critique is colonised by the two 'steering media' of money and power. One of the key differences between Habermas' conception of the 'debased public sphere' and Debord's conception of the recuperation of critique is that when Habermas theorises the conditions of recuperation he also, simultaneously, provides a theory of the continual struggle, after recuperation, between power and emancipation.

During the same period Raymond Williams argued that the Left needed to supplement the theory of revolution as a *coup d'état* with an understanding of the 'long revolution' of culture. He, too, knew well that culture and the media had been cynically prevented from reaching its democratic potential for the sake of private gain. His conclusion was not to pronounce popular and critical culture as recuperated, but to argue that men like Rupert Murdoch "must be run out". Here, again, we see how a politics of critical culture need not be brought to a premature conclusion at the first recuperative blow. And, following Williams, we might develop a theory of the 'long avant-garde'.

Williams reminds us that recuperation is never final but calls for perseverance and resourcefulness if resistance and struggle are not going to be lost. The Left have been better at theorising the impossibility of social and cultural transformation, and they have excelled in theorising the ease with which the existing structures absorb all opposition. Williams is one of the few on the Left who have attended seriously to questions around the persistence of hope and critique in the most objectionable of circumstances. Recuperation is a complex, conflictual process. It is never one-way, automatic, inevitable, 100% complete and irreversible. It is the persistence of the avant-garde's struggle after recuperation that we would call the 'long avant-garde'.

Even when Althusser first devises his theory of ideology as always 'state ideology' through the Ideological State Apparatuses, primarily the family and the school, he refers to those teachers who resist the official dogma as 'heroes'. They are heroic because they act against the apparatus from within its own institutions. So, there is no call to be dismissive of art's institutions who "smarten up", as Osborne puts it. In fact, the very process of 'smartening up' shows that recuperation must be a two-way transformation if it is to occur at all. Institutions which do not change cannot recuperate practices that are critical of them. And what's more, those individuals within art's institutions who work against the existing "partition of the sensible", to use another of Rancière's phrases, should be given credit.

It is not better for critical art to stay in the wilderness for as long as possible. Critical art doesn't stay critical for longer because art's institutions lag behind developments. Art moves on anyway. We saw this during the period of what Bürger called the historical avant-garde, when artists moved on at an accelerated rate without needing institutional recuperation to egg them on. Any theory of critical art that prefers art's institutions not to 'smarten up' is irresponsible, trite and vulgar. The thesis of the short avant-garde had to be replaced with an understanding of the long avant-garde. The persistence of the avant-garde despite and through its recuperation is secured by the continuation of the struggle for emancipation in and against the current conditions.

Dave Beech is an artist and writer. Freee is a collective whose members are the artists, Dave Beech, Andy Hewitt and Mel Jordan.
www.freee.org.uk

DEMOCRACY 2.0

GEOFF COX

Today the enemy is not called Empire or Capital.
It's called Democracy. Alan Badiou [1]

Critique is an essential part of capitalist production. The ability to express one's opinions in public allows the system to verify itself as democratic. Through such means, it is able to generate its own critique and then quickly neutralise it. Within the neo-liberal spaces of contemporary art, thereby some opinions not readily acceptable in other public places can be displayed but the politics easily contained. The critical artist offers soft politics that is easily recuperated to legitimate the art institution's self-reflection. But it's not quite that simple – and far more dialectical. On the one hand, art appears to have lost its critical power as any form of critique is automatically recuperated; but on the other, the new situation opens up different strategies of opposition that respond to the ways in which power is organised.[2]

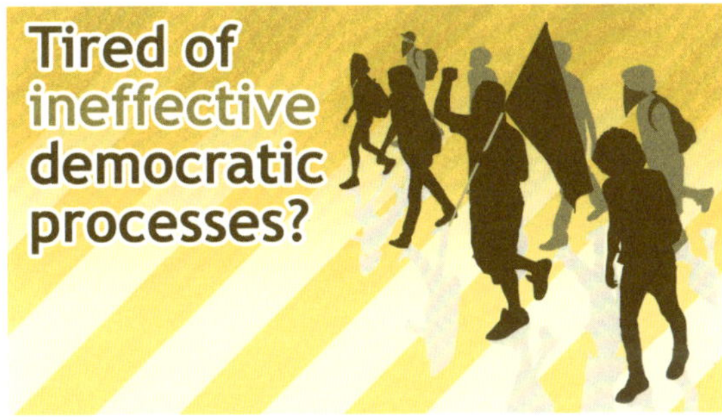

Repetitionr,
Les Liens Invisibles, 2010
Courtesy the artists

What is required is a more detailed examination of the power relations at work, and how they are configured as part and parcel of informational capitalism, and how social relations and control structures are managed. With no longer a centre of power to be found or established opposition as such, it is clear that the (class) enemy is increasingly hard to identify across its networks, and yet power continues to produce its own vulnerabilities. Correspondingly, the recommendation of those developing oppositional tactics is to take advantage of the vulnerabilities in networks (much like successful computer viruses do) by exploiting power differentials that exist in the operating system.[3] Such tactics draw on methods informed by network and information theory, as well as reverse engineering mass culture.[4] The approach offers direct responses to recuperative processes, and yet the effect of *tactical media* is paradoxical, as Lovink contends, leading equally tactically to "benign tolerance".[5] That may be sadly the case, but the reappraisal of recuperative processes and interventionist responses is necessarily ongoing, not least in the context of how social media have changed the face of the representational political process. This is evident in the apparent success of various campaigns that hope to influence the outcomes of elections and in the rise of services that offer effective participation in the political process.

The tactics of dissent have changed too. *Seppukoo*, a recent hack of Facebook by Les Liens Invisibles (2009),[6] provides an example where users were able to commit virtual suicide in a ritualistic removal of their virtual identity.[7] Critique here operates in the challenge to the living-death user-experience of Facebook and other similar programs that express the social relation in restrictive form. The action provoked a litigious response by Facebook not least.[8] Part of the friendly (inter)face of capitalism, restricted social relations are perpetuated through networks of friends (everyone is a potential friend rather than enemy), such that antagonistic social relations are masked and the politics nullified. Evoking Schmitt's notion of enmity (in *The Concept of the*

Political, 1927), the political differentiation of friend or enemy (aka Facebook or Seppukoo) lies at the heart of this, and offers a certain definition of politics. The reference to the Japanese ritual suicide of _Seppuku_ (literally _stomach-cutting_) evokes the stubborn refusal to fall into the hands of the enemy – and the preference for autonomy even at the cost of one's life.[9] Virtual suicide stands as the _refusal_ to operate under intolerable conditions of service and as an affirmation of creative autonomous practice. Refusal responds to the way in which those in power regenerate themselves through constant upgrades to break opposition; the position derives from Tronti's essay 'The Strategy of Refusal' of 1965, following the logic that capital uses workers' antagonistic opposition as a motor for its own development. But crucially, capital does not wish to destroy critique entirely, as it is fundamental to its operations, but obscure its origins and subdue its effectiveness. Moreover, this is its friendly face whether you like it or not. For instance, in the case of Facebook, they keep your account details for perpetuity and commercial exploitation. The _Seppukoo_ 'about' page explains: "Suicide is a free choice and a kind of self-assertiveness. Unfortunately, Facebook doesn't give to its users this faculty at all, and your account will be only deactivated."[11]

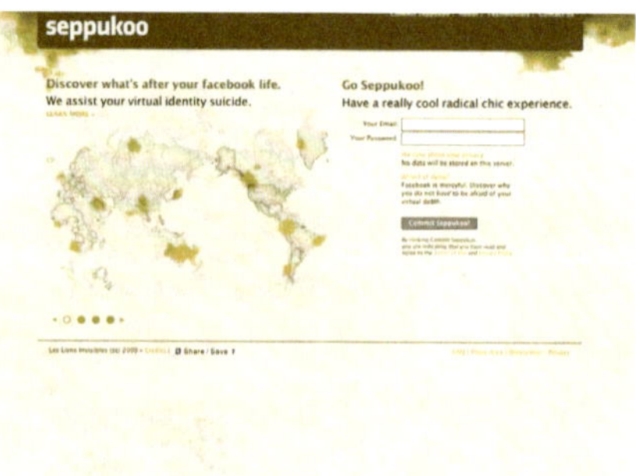

Seppukoo (screen grab),
Les Liens Invisibles, 2009
Courtesy the artists

Democracy and authoritarianism operate dialectically. This is in keeping with the liberal tradition, as Balibar explains, and the distinction between individual opinions and collective actions in the ways they "reciprocally 'underwrite' each other".[12] Individuals voice their diverse opinions, both for and against the ruling power, in order to legitimate its effects. Expressing the _violence of participation_, this is the basis of liberal democracy as well as the basis of its democratic renewal – what we together refer to as _participatory democracy_. Individuals actively imagine their participation in what ultimately is part of their subjugation. This comes close to Lazzarato's discussion of _participative management_ in the workplace as a technique of power in restructured form, and one that appears to grant special privileges to artistic labour. Indeed, Lazzarato thinks the technique is more totalitarian than the production line as it involves the willing subjectivity of the worker in the participatory process.[13] Again, popular social media platforms like Facebook come to mind, and more specifically applications such as _Causes_ through which users can imagine the effectiveness of their political engagement by creating petitions in support of a particular cause. The 'about' statement expresses the ambition of no less than changing the world:

> Facebook Platform presents an unprecedented opportunity to engage our generation, most of whom are on Facebook, in seizing the future and making a difference in the world around us. Our generation cares deeply, but the current system has alienated us. _Causes_ provides the tools so that any Facebook user can leverage their network of real friends to effect positive change. The goal of all this is what we call 'equal opportunity activism.' We're trying to level the playing field by empowering individuals to change the world.[14]

Another project by Les Liens Invisibles, commissioned by Arnolfini in 2010, uses the tactic of *over-identification* to respond to such tendencies.[15] In the age of over-mediated democracy, Repetitionr provides a platform for activism with minimal effort, an online petition service with a difference; offering advanced Web 2.0 technologies to make participatory democracy a truly user-centered experience.[16] The success of every campaign is guaranteed as just one click is all it takes to generate a whole campaign with up to a million automatic fake signatures. The project reflects the acknowledged need for new institutional forms that challenge existing systems of governance and representational structures, as a blatant expression of *non-representational democracy*.[17] The approach challenges the limits of representational democracy and the discourse of neo-liberalism in general, offering a means to rethink politics within network cultures. If this is an example of over-identification with real existing participatory democracy, then the provocation is that we need to develop far better strategies and techniques of organisation.

In opposition to informational capitalism lies commons-based peer production. Indeed, concerns over the commons are encapsulated by the title of Hardt and Negri's recent book *Commonwealth*, to indicate the 'common-wealth' of land, water and the atmosphere.[18] Current political, economic and ecological crises derive from aggressive and primitive forms of property (such as disputes over copyright and intellectual property) and energy production (geopolitical disputes over carbon fuels) – a lack of recognition of the common. Historical parallels between the ways in which the commons were turned in private property (through the enclosure movement), and the ways in which intellectual property is being privatised have been well established. In addition, the way that code is being privatised offers a useful focus to discuss wider issues of organisation and power struggles.

The cultural significance of this is captured by the term *recursive public* to account for the ways in which the public is "a collective independent of other forms of constituted power and is capable of speaking to existing forms of power through the production of actually existing alternatives".[19] Somewhat related to the concept of the public sphere, a recursive public is capable of modifying itself through participation, relatively unmediated by higher authority. For Kelty, the collective technical experiment of the Free Software movement is an example of a recursive public that draws attention to its democratic and political significance and the limitations of our understanding of the public in the light of the restructuring of power over networks, struggles over intellectual property rights and sharing of code. In this sense, the concept of the public sphere itself is taken as open to modification and reuse – made recursive in other words. As a consequence, a reconceptualisation of political action is required that combines traditional forms of expression such as free speech with coding practices and sharing associated with Free Software. Making reference to the work of Arendt, Kelty's intervention is to extend a definition of a public grounded in discourse – through speech, writing and assembly – to other legal and technical layers that underpin the internet in recognition of the ways in which contemporary power and control are structured – through both discourses and infrastructures.[20]

Such a reconsideration of public space or a politics of the common exposes the sad reality of liberal participatory democracy. To Rancière, the origin of the political lies in the properties of its subjects and in how they come together, how they 'part-take', or in other words how they participate in contradictory forms of action. "Politics is a paradoxical form of action" according to Rancière, and hence can be defined in the contradictions at the heart of action – between acting and being acted upon. It is the

very "axioms of democracy" (of ruling and being ruled) that require rupture to open up discussion of the constitution of the subject and its relations.[21] New publics are required – in coalitions of human and non-human agents involved in radical networks – to engage with and to modify the infrastructures they inhabit as an extension of the public sphere. Evidently publicness is constituted not simply by speaking, writing, arguing and protesting but also through modification of the domain or platform through which these practices are enacted. Democracy requires an upgrade but only if released fully into the public domain.

1. Badiou, A. "Prefazione all'edizione italiana." *Metropolitica.* Naples: Cronopio, 2002. There are far too many other references to mention here that take a critical view of Western representational democracy, but a particularly polemical view appears in the first section of Muammar Al Qathafi's 'The Solution of the Problem of Democracy' in his *The Green Book.*
2. I prefer the word 'antagonism' to 'opposition' in recognition of how important it is for neo-liberalism to dilute it in order to function effectively. Amongst others, this is in keeping with Chantal Mouffe's position in "Artistic and Agonistic Spaces." *Art & Research.* vol. 1. no. 2, 2007 <http://www.artandresearch.org.uk/v1n2/mouffe>.
3. Galloway, AR and Thacker, E. "The Exploit: A Theory of Networks." *Electronic Mediations.* vol. 21. Minneapolis: University of Minnesota Press, 2007.
4. The exhibition *Craftivism* at Arnolfini Nov 2009–Feb 2010, is an example of 'reverse engineering' aiming to question and disrupt the prevailing codes of mass consumerism <http://www.craftivism.net>.
5. Lovink says: "The ideal is to be little more than a temporary glitch, a brief instance of noise or interference. Tactical media set themselves up for exploitation in the same manner that 'modders' do in the game industry: both dispense with their knowledge of loop holes in the system for free. They point out the problem, and then run away. Capital is delighted, and thanks the tactical media outfit or nerd-modder for the home improvement." Geert Lovink quoted in Raley, R. "Tactical Media." *Electronic Mediations.* vol. 28. Minneapolis/London: University of Minnesota Press, 2009: 28. 'Tactical Media' broadly refers to contemporary forms of dissent somewhere between creative experimentation and a reflexive engagement with social change; particularly important are the collaborative writings of Lovink, as in 'The ABC of Tactical Media', 1997 (with David Garcia), and 'New Rules for the New Actonomy', 2001 (with Florian Schneider) and the *Next Five Minutes* conferences, held in Amsterdam from 1993.
6. Les Liens Invisibles are an imaginary art-group from Italy, comprised of media artists Clemente Pestelli and Gionatan Quintini <http://www.lesliensinvisibles.org>.
7. *Seppukoo* <http://www.seppukoo.com>. Also note similar projects, such as Cory Arcangel's *Friendster Suicide* <http://www.coryarcangel.com/2005/12/friendster-suicide-live-in-person-dec-2005> and moddr_lab's *Web2.0 Suicide Machine* <http://suicidemachine.org>.
8. See the 'cease and desist' letter from Facebook's lawyers, and the reply – both linked from the *Seppukoo* home page <http://www.seppukoo.com>.
9. Thanks to Tatiana Bazzichelli for pointing out that the inspiration for the project is *Seppuku,* the ritual suicide that some members of the Luther Blissett Project committed in 1999, to declare the end of their multiple identities project <http://www.lutherblissett.net/archive/452_en>.
10. Tronti, M. "The Strategy of Refusal." *Autonomia: Post-Political Politics, Semiotext(e).* vol. 3, no. 3. New York: Semiotext(e), 1980: 28–34.
11. Seppukoo <http://www.seppukoo.com>.
12. Balibar, E. *Spinoza and Politics.* London: Verso, 2008. 27.
13. Lazzarato, M. "Forms of Production and Circulation of Knowledge." *Readme! Filtered by Nettime: ASCII Culture and the Revenge of Knowledge.* Ed. Josephine Bosma et al. New York: Autonomedia, 1999.
14. <http://apps.facebook.com/causes/about>
15. The psychoanalytic term 'over-identification', often associated with Slavoj Žižek, has been taken up as a tactic by many activist-artists, including The Yes Men, to expose a position by exaggerating a position, wildly pushing the system to its extremes in order to conclude that it is unacceptable.
16. <http://www.repetitionr.com>
17. 'Non-representational democracy' describes democracy decoupled from sovereign power, as discussed in Ned Rossiter's *Organized Networks: Media Theory, Creative Labour, New Institutions.* Rotterdam: NAi, in association with the Institute of Network Cultures, Hogeschool van Amsterdam, 2006. 39. Rossiter also cites Paolo Virno's *The Grammar of the Multitude.* New York: Semiotext(e), 2004.
18. In addition, "love provides another path for investigating the power and productivity of the common. [... Such a] notion of love gives us a new definition of wealth that extends our notion of the common and points toward a process of liberation." Hardt, M and Negri, A. *Commonwealth.* Cambridge, Mass: Belknap Press/Harvard University Press, 2009. xi–xii.
19. Kelty, CM. *Two Bits: the Cultural Significance of Free Software.* Durham: Duke University Press, 2008. 3.
20. Ibid. 50.
21. Rancière, J. "Ten Theses on Politics." *Theory & Event 5.3,* 2001 <http://muse.jhu.edu/journals/theory_and_event/v005/5.3ranciere.html>.

Geoff Cox is a Researcher in Digital Aesthetics at the Digital Urban Living Research Center, Aarhus University, Denmark, and Associate Curator of Online Projects at Arnolfini.

Les Liens Invisibles is an imaginary art-group from Italy, comprised of media artists Clemente Pestelli and Gionatan Quintini.

"All the News We Hope to Print"

The New York Times

Special Edition
Today, clouds part, more sunshine, recent gloom passes. **Tonight,** strong leftward winds. **Tomorrow,** a new day. Weather map throughout.

/OL. CLVIV . . No. 54,631 | NEW YORK, SATURDAY, JULY 4, 2009 | FREE

IRAQ WAR ENDS

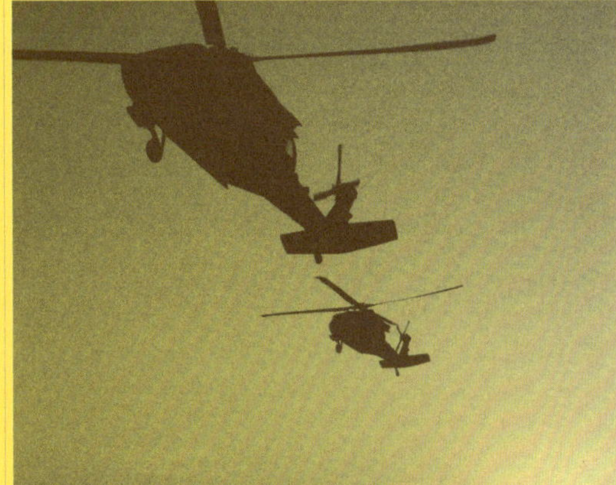

COURTESY ARMY.MIL
U.S. Army helicopters begin moving troops and equipment from Saddam Hussein's former Baghdad palace.

Troops to Return Immediately

By JUDE SHINBIN

WASHINGTON — Operation Iraqi Freedom and Operation Enduring Freedom were brought to an unceremonious close today with a quiet announcement by the Department of Defense that troops would be home within weeks.

"This is the best face we can put on the most unfortunate adventure in modern American history," Defense spokesman Kevin Sites said at a special joint session of Congress. "Today, we can finally enjoy peace — not the peace of the brave, perhaps, but at least peace."

As U.S. and coalition troops withdraw from Iraq and Afghanistan, the United Nations will move in to perform peacekeeping duties and aid in rebuilding. The U.N. will be responsible for keeping the two countries stable; coordinating the rebuilding of hospitals, schools, highways, and other infrastructure; and overseeing upcoming elections.

The Department of the Treasury confirmed that all U.N. dues owed by the U.S. were paid as of this morning, and that moneys previously earmarked for the war would be sent directly to the U.N.'s Iraq Oversight Body.

The president noted that the Iraq War had resulted in the burning of many bridges. "Yet our history with our allies runs deep," he said, "and we all know that friends forgive friends for anything. Or nearly." A spokesperson for the French Ministry of Defense confirmed that France would assist the U.S. withdrawal. "The U.S. helped the Soviet Union defeat Hitler. We do recognize that."

In conflict zones worldwide, leaders and rebels pledged peace. (See "In Conflict Zones Worldwide, Peace Moves," on Page A4.)

On Wall Street, reactions were mixed, with the Dow Jones Industrial Average up 84 points, to close at 4,212. While KBR stock was quickly downgraded to a "junk" rating of BBB-, defense contractors such as Lockheed Martin and Northrop Grummon started up.

Continued on Page A5

Nation Sets Its Sights on Building Sane Economy

True Cost Tax, Salary Caps, Trust-Busting Top List

By T. VEBLEN

The President has called for wift passage of the Safeguards or a New Economy (S.A.N.E.) bill. 'he omnibus economic package ncludes a federal maximum wage, nandatory "True Cost Accounting," a phased withdrawal from omplex financial instruments, nd other measures intended to nprove life for ordinary Americans. (See highlights box on Page 10.) He also repeated earlier calls or passage of the "Ban on Lobbying" bill currently making its way hrough Congress.

Treasury Secretary Paul Krugnan stressed the importance of he bill. "Markets make great serants, terrible leaders, and absurd eligions," said Krugman, quoting 'aul Hawken, an advocate of corporate responsibility and author f "Blessed Unrest, How the Largest Movement in the World Came nto Being and Why No One Saw It Coming."

"At this point, the market is our leader and our religion. No wonder the median standard of living has been declining so much for so long."

Krugman said that the new Treasury bill seeks to ensure the prosperity of all citizens, rather than simply supporting large corporations and the wealthy. "The market is supposed to serve us. Unfortunately, we have ended up serving the market. That's very bad."

Much as Roosevelt, after the Great Depression, put the brakes on C.E.O. wages and irresponsible banking practices, administration officials claim that today we need to rein in the industry that has caused such chaos and misery.

"The building blocks of post-World War II American middle-class prosperity have all been swept away," said House Speaker Nancy Pelosi, who initially op-

Continued on Page A10

Maximum Wage Law Succeeds

Salary Caps Will Help Stabilize Economy

By J.K. MALONE

WASHINGTON — After long and often bitter debate, Congress has passed legislation, fiercely fought for by labor and progressive groups, that will limit top salaries to fifteen times the minimum wage. Tying the bill to a plan of overall reform of the U.S. economy, the bill echoes a similar effort enacted by President Franklin Roosevelt in 1942, which was followed by the longest period of growth for the middle class in U.S. history.

"When C.E.O. salaries remain stable thanks to high taxation of high salaries, there's little incentive to take big risks with shareholders' money, and the economy remains in a steady growth mode," said Senator Barney Frank, one of the bill's co-sponsors. "But when C.E.O. salaries can fly through the roof, there's a very strong incentive for C.E.O.s

Continued on Page A10

TREASURY ANNOUNCES "TRUE COST" TAX PLAN

By MARCUS S. DRIGGS

The long-awaited "True Cost" plan, which requires product prices to reflect their cost to society, has been signed into law.

Beginning next month, throw-away items like plastic water bottles and other items which are wasteful or damaging to the environment will be heavily taxed, as in many developed countries. Steep taxes will also apply to large cars and gasoline.

The new plan calls for a 200 percent tax on gasoline, comparable to the one long in effect in most European countries. Companies and consumers are already switching in droves from inefficient gas vehicles to new electric cars. "We suddenly have a waiting list 200 names long for the EV1," said Jake Cluber, the owner of Cluber Chevrolet in

Continued on Page A10

Recruiters Train for New Life

As a ban is imposed on recruiting minors, ex-recruiters nationwide look for new work. The Times follows one on his job-hunt odyssey through Manhattan and surrounding areas.

BY BARRY GLOAD, PAGE A12

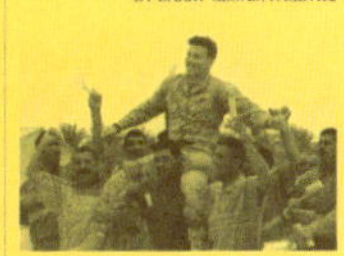

Last to Die

Two proportional monuments — one to the Iraqi dead, 300 feet high, and one to the American dead, 15 feet high — are unveiled in Baghdad, and a five-year-old boy whose lifespan coincided with that of the Iraq War is remembered.

BY J. FINISTERRA, PAGE A5

USA Patriot Act Repealed

Eight years later, a shamefaced Congress quietly repeals the much-maligned USA Patriot Act, unanimously… or almost.

BY SYBIL LUDINGTON, PAGE A8

Evangelicals Open Homes to Refugees

Up to a million Iraqi exiles — nearly half of the total — will find sanctuary in Christian homes across the U.S., vows the National Association of Evangelicals. Other denominations are expected to follow.

BY W. WILBERFORCE, PAGE A7

Public Relations Industry Starts to Shut Down

The public relations industry has been criticized for misleading the American people, corrupting politicians, and even helping to start wars. Now, it's beginning the process of shutting down for good.

BY LOUIS BECK, PAGE A10

Ex-Secretary Apologizes for W.M.D. Scare

300,000 Troops Never Faced Risk of Instant Obliteration

By FRANK LARIMORE

Ex-Secretary of State Condoleeza Rice reassured soldiers that the Bush Administration had known well before the invasion that Saddam Hussein lacked weapons of mass destruction.

"Now that all of you brave servicemen and women are returning, it's important to us to reassure you, and the American people, that we were certain Hussein had no W.M.D.s and that he would never launch a first strike against the U.S.," Ms. Rice told a group of wounded soldiers at a Veterans' Administration hospital yesterday.

"I want you to know that if we had had the slightest suspicion that Saddam could use W.M.D.s against you, we never would have sent hundreds of thousands of you to be sitting ducks on the Iraqi border for several months."

Mr. Rice was referring to the fact that by August 2002, eight months before the ground invasion, the US had over 100,000 troops stationed in countries throughout the Gulf, a number that grew to over 300,000 shortly before the 2003 attack on Baghdad. Most of these were within range of the Scud missiles used by Mr. Hussein in the 1991 Gulf War, that could easily have been fitted with chemical or biological weapons if they had existed.

Rice noted that in the 1991 Gulf War, Hussein had used missiles to launch attacks on Israel, which made him popular with Arab citizens throughout the Middle East.

"Do you really think we would have given Saddam a major public relations coup by allowing him to annihilate tens of thousands of you right there on holy territory?" asked Ms. Rice.

Former Secretary of State Henry A. Kissinger responded to Ms. Rice's revelation without surprise. "Of course this was the case. When Israel believed Iraq had nuclear weapons in 1981, they didn't attack on the ground — they bombed from the air. That's a pre-emptive attack. If you believe deterrence will not prevent an attack and that your enemy has W.M.D.s, then the last thing you do is station your troops right next door."

ABC's George Stephanopoulos

Continued on Page A5

Nationalized Oil To Fund Climate Change Efforts

By MARION K. HUBBERT

Congress has voted to place ExxonMobil, ChevronTexaco, and other major oil companies under public stewardship, with the bulk of the companies' profits put in a public trust administered by the United Nations, and used for alternative energy research and development in order to solve the global climate crisis.

While unusual, this is not the first time the government has chosen to take control of large corporations. From 1942 to 1944, U.S. car factories were retooled in order to produce tanks for the war effort. And Fannie Mae and Freddie Mac were both created as "government sponsored enterprises" with a significant amount of government oversight.

"We can do what needs to be done," said Senator Charles Schumer, Democrat of New York. "Our planet's survival is at stake. Plus, public pressure hasn't given us much of a choice."

Not everyone felt the move was a good idea. "The climate crisis may or may not be real," declared Senator Kay Bailey Hutchison, Republican of Texas. "I'm an agnostic and I'm staying that way. But sea

Continued on Page A5

Popular Pressure Ushers Recent Progressive Tilt

Study Cites Movements for Massive Shift in DC

By SAMUEL FIELDEN

The spate of reform initiatives undertaken by the Administration and both houses of Congress can be attributed directly to grass-roots advocacy, according to a comprehensive study due out this month.

"In education and health care, most notably, but also in housing, banking, and the environment, we have documented unprecedented responsiveness on the part of political leaders," said Dr. Joyce Wellmon, director of the Plains Institute for Policy Analysis, a New York-based think tank. "Our data show a direct correlation between the level of activity of particular coalitions, on the one hand, and specific legislative action, on the other. It's popular pressure that is responsible for the swiftness and scope of legislation emerging from the White House and Congress."

The institute's report shows a three-fold increase in the incidence of letters, phone calls, faxes, and email received by congressional offices, 88 percent of which were from people who identified themselves as new members of particular activist organizations.

See nytimes-se.com for more

The report includes extensive interviews with House and Senate staff, who speak of "unimaginable change," a "dramatic policy shift," and "a new era of accountability" since the elections.

"Not since the Great Depression has the interaction between popular movements and public leaders been so robust," said Jorge Lazaro, head of the U.S. Government Accountability Office. Lazaro cited, in particular, the Wagner Act, also known as the National Labor Relations Act of 1935, which recognized the right of workers to organize and bargain collectively with their employers.

"Roosevelt showed no interest in the Wagner Act until it became clear the unions were going to force it through regardless," Mr. Lazaro noted. "At that point he jumped on it and helped push it into law."

Mr. Lazaro also pointed to the Depression-era organizing of the Farmers' Holiday Association, when farmers refused to sell or bid on crops, blockaded roads, and even once used a torpedo to halt a train carrying livestock into Iowa. Such direct actions helped push courts and legislatures to adopt measures that granted relief from debt caused by low crop prices.

KC IVEY/THE NEW YORK TIMES
Protests organized by Witness Against Torture helped pave the way for the close of the Guantánamo facility.

"The similarities between the two periods are remarkable, and the lesson that emerges is simple: if you want change, keep our feet to the fire."

Dr. Wellmon agrees. "The only reason the current President and Congress have been able to implement all these changes, was because of pressure from popular movements that made them have to."

The Plains report, due out next month, cites the work of groups associated with United for Peace and Justice, an umbrella for anti-war groups, for galvanizing public support for ending the war, and for pushing the Administration to resist the oil lobby and other interest groups. It also cites the work

Continued on Page A6

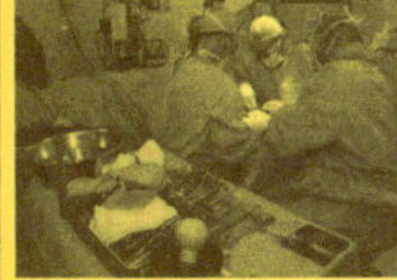

International

The New York Times

After Withdrawal Peace Spreads to Conflict Zones Worldwide

Leaders Worldwide Scramble to Follow American Lead

By F. NANSEN

In the wake of the U.S. withdrawal from Iraq and Afghanistan, government leaders and warlords in conflict zones worldwide seemed to be falling over themselves to pledge peace.

The President of Sudan declared an end to hostilities in Darfur. "We are modern, or at least we live in a modern world, near modern countries like the U.S. And like the U.S., we understand that blood cannot be the path to benefit, whereas peace can be."

In the Congo, where 45,000 people continue to die every month, dwarfing the toll in Darfur, reactions were more muted. "If the strongest country on earth can face not getting everything that it wants, I guess we can too," said Laurent Kabila, President of the Democratic Republic of Congo. "Now that the U.S. is facing its responsibilities in Iraq, what if Americans start doing that here in the Congo? We'd better clean up our act."

In Sri Lanka, Somalia, Columbia, the Kashmir, Chad, and elsewhere, fighters on all sides of the conflicts there pledged to take the U.S. withdrawal to heart. "We cannot continue this way," said one tribal leader in Somalia, who wished to remain anonymous. "The time has come to learn foreign policy just like the Americans."

In Belgium, Walloons and Flems promised to cooperate. "We've been idiots, like pinheads from outer space," said Filip Dewinter, leader of the secessionist Vlaams Belang. "If America is a real country, so is Belgium. They've shown us how to behave."

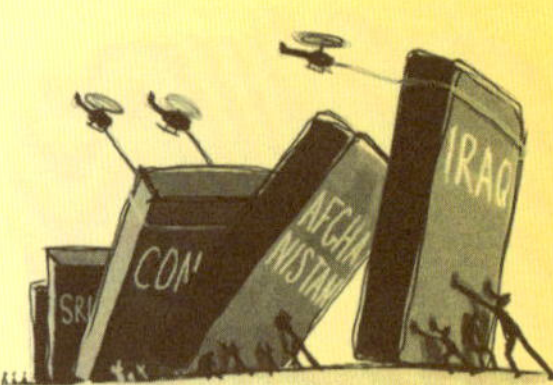

FRED WOLFF

United Nations Unanimously Passes Weapons Ban

By HELEN PREJEAN

NEW YORK – A spontaneous celebration erupted in the U.N. General Assembly after representatives of 192 member states unanimously ratified the Comprehensive Arms Ban Treaty. The treaty outlaws possession, production and trade of military equipment ranging from small arms to nuclear warheads.

"This is watershed moment in the security of people and the security of the planet itself," said U.S. President Barack Obama. "With weapons off the table, we can finally focus on the world's real threats: global poverty, pollution, and climate change."

The Comprehensive Arms Ban Treaty is an initiative of the U.N.'s new Global Security Protocol, which identifies environmental sustainability as its prime directive.

"We cannot have any kind of security unless our planet remains livable," said Secretary-General Ban Ki-moon. "The tens of trillions of dollars freed by disarmament makes it easier to focus on the big-picture issues."

The weapons ban includes extensive subsidiies for the retooling of arms manufacturers. Hours after the agreement was reached, German weapons giant Heckler & Koch announced its first contract to take advantage of the incentive packages by refitting its P11 assault pistol factory to produce an improved "life straw," an individual water filtration system that greatly reduces waterborne disease. The company's plan will use former weapons brokers to deliver the straws, and they will train former child soldiers to handle the labor-intensive task of local distribution.

TELSTAR LOGISTICS

The U.S.'s stockpile of W.M.D.s, which includes arms like the one above, will soon be a relic of the past.

Impetus for the C.A.B.T. developed after the 1998 European Union Code of Conduct, which prohibits selling weapons to countries that may use them for external aggression or internal oppression, went largely unheeded. In one contravention of the code, Europe did not cease trade with the United States and Britain despite their unprovoked invasion of Iraq in 2003.

In Britain, massive public protests, including a sit-in that blocked exit from the British Parliament for two weeks, convinced the government to reverse course and uphold the E.U. Code of Conduct, as well as to support passage of the C.A.B.T.

One of the primary focuses of the C.A.B.T. is small arms, which kill one person every minute, 75 percent of them women and children. A survey conducted last May showed fewer than one-tenth of one percent in favor of continuing these deaths. In addition to mandating the immediate cessation of production, the C.A.B.T. includes a buyback program to repossess most of the 640 million small arms already in circulation, and melt them down in small mobile smelters which will recycle the steel into agricultural tools and equipment to be distributed locally.

As for the 20,350 nuclear warheads known to exist, they will be destroyed using monitoring procedures developed under the Strategic Arms Reduction Treaty. The last country to sign off on the new plan was North Korea, who agreed to dismantle their last warhead simultaneously with that of the U.S. The disarmament will take place in a ceremony organized and televised by members of the now defunct Olympic Games Committee. The Olympic Games were canceled in December after most member nations realized that contests to see who could do useless things in the name of archaic national boundaries are not helping anyone.

Ailing leader Kim Jong Il made a rare appearance to comment: "Finally, we have rid ourselves of the Olympics. Our best athletes will do useful and strenuous things. And we are very pleased to no longer need bombs to protect ourselves from Americans with more bombs. We can now focus on avoiding the collapse of our planet's ecosystem, and on other pursuits the Great Leader would have applauded. The people of North Korea will enjoy this challenging bright future immensely."

Iraqis Around the World Celebrate U.S. Withdrawal, Rebuilding Plan

By F. WUNDERLICH

JORDAN — With the news that U.S. forces were withdrawing from Iraq, nearly five million Iraqi refugees learned that the nightmare that started in 2003 was over. However, most are convinced that going back to a pre-sanctions or even pre-war Iraq is a mere pipe-dream.

"All Iraqis wanted the war to be over, but the Iraq that existed before has disappeared from the face of the earth, and no one has any idea how living in the new one will feel," said Malik Abdul-Razzaq, a 37-year-old Iraqi refugee now living in Amman, Jordan. Abdul-Razzaq left Baghdad, where he had lived all his life, in early 2006, after being threatened by an "unknown armed group" due to his relationship with a human rights organization.

> For two million exiles, tempered hope of return to a shattered land.

"Politically what will happen? The country is destroyed, the militias are everywhere," said Abdul-Razzaq, whose feelings of bewilderment were a common theme among refugees.

Of the 4.7 million people that are estimated to have been uprooted since 2003, half of them remain in the country, but far from their towns and cities and separated from family and friends. Approximately two million have spilled into Syria and Jordan, where they have been living in what human rights organization Amnesty International calls "ramshackle camps and struggling to meet basic needs, like food and medicine."

About 200,000 have made it beyond the Middle East, mainly to Europe. In most cases, Iraqi refugees are not allowed to work and must depend on the black market.

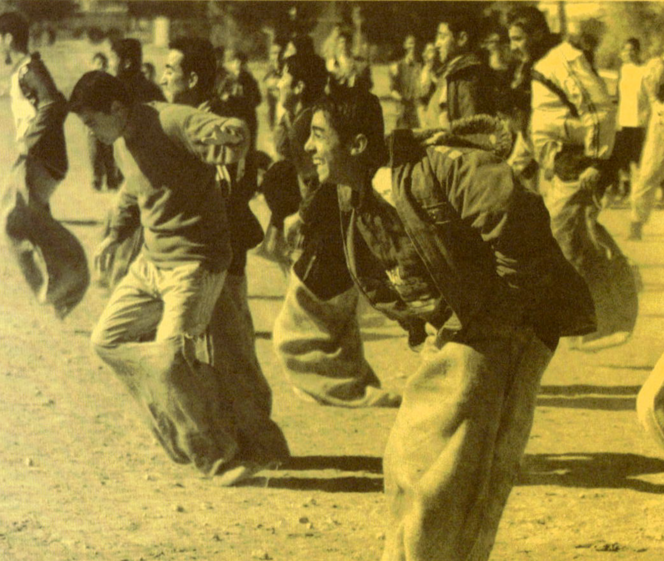

RASHID HAMASHANI/REUTERS

Iraqi teens participate in team-building exercises organized by aid workers in a Jordan area refugee camp.

Amira al-Fadl, 31, now living in Stockholm, says that "since the Samarra bombing in February 2006 [when a dome of the Al-Askari Mosque was destroyed by bombs], my parents have been locked in their neighborhood, away from my sisters." Al-Fadl is doubtful that she will return. "To leave, I had to peddle my house, my furniture and the family jewelry, and I still needed to borrow $10,000. I'm sleeping on a relative's couch, but I'm not sure what I have to go back to."

Leyla Jarrah, 33, also in Stockholm, can't keep tears of joy from coming down her cheeks. But she is not planning to go back either. "I've lost most of my family and I don't think I'd be able to find my friends. As promising as people say it now is, I can't see myself starting all over again."

Harun Saeed, 45, is planning to return to Baghdad. He is one of only 2000 or so Iraqis to have made it to the U.S. "Two of my Air Force colleagues were assassinated. I spent 14 months and all my savings in Syria. Now, I am barely surviving." Despite extensive experience as a technician for the Iraqi Air Force, Saeed has been unable to find a job paying more than minimum wage. He is now dreaming of going back and seeing his wife and two children. "I have no idea what will happen now, but for the first time in many years, I am hopeful."

When Timur Barzani, 47, heard the news, he thought of his children. "Life in Damascus is hard and my wife and I have had to send our sons to work. My sons now say they will be too embarrassed to go to school, they think they are too old to learn the ABCs. But I think in Najaf we will find many children in the same situation, and they will not be embarrassed," Barzani explained.

Until the U.S. withdrawal, Iraqi refugees usually had only two options. Either they could face the humiliation of living as refugees without rights or hope for a better future, or they could face likely death if they returned to their shattered country. The common feeling among Iraqi refugees today is of hope for their country, for their friends and relatives, and for their lives.

They know that the social fabric of the county has been destroyed by the war and the occupation, and that the challenges are huge. But as Abdul-Razzaq says, "The withdrawal is only the first step. At least now, we Iraqis will be free to choose our own future."

Iraqi journalists for The New York Times contributed reporting from Damacas, Amman, and Stockholm.

Times Reporter to Embed with Peace Groups

By DARLA ZIMBALIST

Recent studies have shown that embedded reporters lose perspective and objectivity. Thrust into high-tension situations of dangerous conflict, and surrounded by a corps of strong personalities devoted to a single objective, journalists almost inevitably write subjectively and sympathetically of situations that are best addressed analytically.

Yet there are other subjects that might be better served by a more sympathetic approach—like the cause of those who work to correct injustices done by our country abroad. Yet The Times' coverage of protesters has often been anything but sympathetic. This paper has belittled the movement, marked its participants as wingnuts, and all in all written as if it were beholden to those against whom the protests were aimed.

Veteran Times reporter John Hess noted that during his 24 years of service at the paper he "never saw a foreign intervention that the Times did not support, never saw a fare increase or a rent increase or a utility rate increase that it did not endorse, never saw it take the side of labor in a strike or lockout, or advocate a raise for underpaid workers." When anti-war protesters are covered, the Times has regularly undercounted the numbers and glossed over violent acts by riot police. It has never given the demonstrators editorial support.

After returning stateside from 16 weeks embedded with the 101st Airborne division in Iraq, this reporter decided to right this imbalance herself, beginning with some of the most interesting anti-war protest groups: Iraq Veterans Against the War, who stage simulated military operations in American cities in order to "make the truth of this war visible"; United for Peace and Justice, a coalition of 1400 peace groups nationwide; and CODEPINK, a group singled out by former President Bush as setting a "dangerous, radical agenda" for American politics.

> To right a longstanding bias, a focus on those fighting for change

Beginning next week, embedded reports from this movement will be featured every week in this space. You, like The Times, will come to see these organizations in an entirely different light.

What the Future Holds for Afghanistan

By EMIL LEDERER

A 400-page plan, written by Afghani leaders under U.N. supervision, outlines the final stages of U.S. and NATO withdrawal, and details a rebuilding effort on a scale not seen since World War Two.

Core to the plan is the presence of the U.N. peacekeeping and humanitarian forces in order to guarantee the quality of life of all citizens through assurances of peace, a means to earn a living, and basic food and health care. "Afghani warlords and the Taliban use access to resources as a source of power. When these resources are readily available, their authority will be neutralized or minimized," the report states.

The plan focuses heavily on rebuilding schools and retraining teachers who have not taught since the Soviet-backed regime was toppled by U.S.-backed Mujahedeen in 1992. "An abundance of research has shown that individuals worldwide who are literate are less likely to address problems with non-diplomatic means" the report states, adding that this is also true for U.S. political leaders.

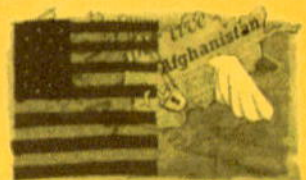

NICK TUCKER

One Taliban official, who was in a minority opposing the plans, explained that his group was being supported by Baptist groups in the U.S. which "understand the need for men to rule women and the legitimacy of martyrdom as a political strategy."

Afghani leaders are hopeful that future powerful states will finally attend to the lessons learned by previous imperial powers, including Britain, Russia, and now the U.S. Mikhail Gorbachev, in a recently-published book on the collapse of the Soviet Union, has revealed that he warned President George W. Bush against attempting to occupy Afghanistan. Mr. Bush's response: "Hey, Gorby, lighten up. The Taliban and the Mujahedeen may have brought you down, but it was we who provided the funding. They're in our pocket and they know it."

"I wonder what he thinks now that U.S. missiles are bringing down U.S. drones, and the U.S. had to nationalize banks because Americans wanted control of the means of production and not just blank checks for the financiers," Mr. Gorbachev said.

Global Problem Turned Into Global Solution

From Page A1

level rise has been overblown. And one thing I'm sure of, is that nationalizing private industry is just another name for theft."

"The private oil interests have been involved in theft for decades," responded Deputy Under Secretary of the E.P.A. Gavin Newsom. "They've stolen our air, our oceans, our health, and our land. They've proven they can't run their business without massive theft."

"If we're going to give corporations the same rights as people,"

'They've stolen our air, our oceans, our health, and our land. They've proven they can't run their business without massive theft.'

said House Speaker Nancy Pelosi, "then we need to hold them accountable like people. When parents abuse their children, the government takes over. When oil companies abuse the planet, the government needs to take over too."

Arco C.E.O. Rex W. Tillerson was philosophical. "We fought this long and hard. We did everything we could do. But do we want more blood in the streets? Or do we want to move on?"

"You can't fight the street," said Mr. Newsom. "The people are going to do what the people are going to do. And the oil companies are just going to have live with it."

Last to Die in Battle Remembered, American and Iraqi

By J. FINISTERRA

BAGHDAD — Secretary of Defense Scott Ritter was joined by Iraqi Prime Minister Nuri Al-Maliki and representatives of the former "Coalition of the Willing" in Baghdad this afternoon for the groundbreaking of a monument to the last to die during the allies' occupation of Iraq.

An enormous granite obelisk to the Iraqi dead, 300 feet high, will stand in Firdos Square, where coalition troops famously attempted to topple a 40-foot-tall statue of Iraqi tyrant Saddam Hussein in April 2003. A 15-foot-high obelisk will stand nearby, honoring the coalition casualties.

The difference in size between the two obelisks will represent the different numbers of casualties. For the Iraqi dead, the most conservative estimate of 93,067 was chosen to avoid the coalition monument being absurdly small or the Iraqi monument prohibitively large.

On the side of the allies, the last to die was Corporal William Whitman, age 28, of Quinnesec, Michigan. Just as fighting began to wane, he took up an exposed position while on a foot patrol and was struck by a sniper's bullet. He died instantly, the 4,314th American casualty of the war. In retaliation, a U.S. attack helicopter fired rockets into a nearby apartment building, killing the sniper and six Iraqi civilians. Moments later, U.S. soldiers received word that they were to cease fire immediately and prepare to return home.

Mr. Al-Maliki commemorated Ahmed Yahya, a 5-year-old boy who was inside the building the sniper had fired from. Rescue workers dug him out of the rubble from the rocket blast. The boy survived overnight but succumbed early the next morning to internal injuries, and was either the 93,067th, the 755,265th or the 1,233,657th Iraqi civilian casualty of the war. (No accurate records were kept, and estimates from different sources conflict wildly.)

"Ahmed's life coincided with the absolute worst episode in the his-

An American representative tells the Iraqis that some Americans tried, to polite applause.

tory of the Middle East," Mr. Maliki said of the boy, who was born just after the Iraq War started. "May his life and death represent the importance of never again seeing such catastrophe rain on our heads, whether for false pretences or even real ones."

"I stand before you as a representative of the American people to tell you that some of us tried," Mr. Ritter told an audience of mainly Iraqi veterans and their families. "We may have failed to stop this in time, but at least we did try. It only remains for us, the heirs of our victims' legacy, to have the courage and the character to make sure it never happens again."

Ritter's statements were met with polite applause.

ONLINE **EXCLUSIVE TIMES 3D INTERACTIVE MODEL**

To explore the interactive, full-color, virtual monument in a digital 3D architectural rendering, featuring zooming and panning capabilities, see:

nytimes-se.com/world/virtual/~3D.html

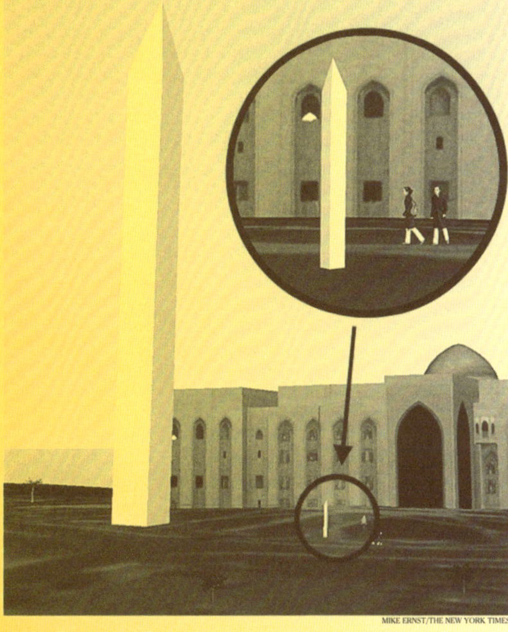

MIKE ERNST/THE NEW YORK TIMES

The last American and Iraqi to die during the war will be commemorated by obelisks in downtown Baghdad.

Court Indicts Bush on High Treason Charge

By BART GARZON

WASHINGTON (AP) — George W. Bush, the 43rd President of the United States, was indicted Monday on charges of high treason. The charges, filed by Attorney General Russ Feingold late in the evening, allege that Mr. Bush, knowing full well that Iraq possessed no weapons of mass destruction, falsified information in order to pursue the disastrous Iraq War. (See "U.S. Knew No W.M.D.s in Iraq," on Page A1.)

Federal District Judge Michael Ratner denied Mr. Bush's request to represent himself. Ratner is the former president of the Center for Constitutional Rights.

High treason is usually defined as participation in a war against

A move to avoid the death penalty brings its own risks.

one's own country; attempting to overthrow its government; spying on its military, its diplomats, or its secret services for a hostile and foreign power; or attempting to kill its head of state.

"In this case, high treason has been interpreted to include pursuing an illegal and devastating war that has cost hundreds of billions of dollars and the lives of over 4,000 Americans and perhaps a

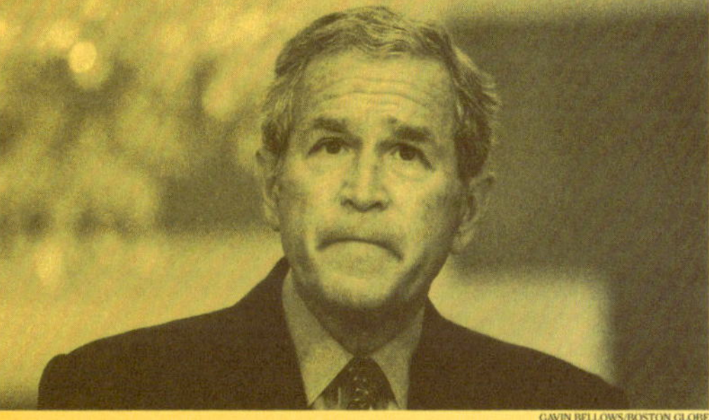

GAVIN BELLOWS/BOSTON GLOBE

The former President appeared perturbed by his own charges against him.

million Iraqis, for essentially insane ends," said Vincent Bugliosi, a former federal prosecutor whom Feingold named lead special prosecutor in the case. "In effect, the Iraq War amounted to a war against America," added Bugliosi, who is also the author of the book, The Prosecution of George Bush for Murder.

Although the treason indictment came as no surprise to most observers, what was completely unexpected was the party who brought it.

"The case is highly unusual in a number of ways," said Bugliosi, "not the least of which is that the defendant is actually accusing himself."

In a press conference held close to midnight yesterday at his Crawford, Texas ranch, former President Bush cited his renewed Christian faith as the catalyst for this unprecedented action. "Last month, I had a conversation with Jesus Christ. A new conversation. And I've been very blessed to have been born again, again. This time, for real," Mr. Bush read in a prepared statement to half a dozen stunned reporters.

"It's taken a lot of soul searching, or more like deep-soul diving, I think is the term. But now I see that it was wrong to lead our nation to war under false pretenses. Millions have suffered for my sins, and I see now that it is only fitting that I should suffer as well."

Mr. Bush's self-accusation seems largely to have been plagiarized from years of accusations made against him in the press. It refers to his "political propaganda campaign to sell the war to the American people," and describes how he and his team attempted to make the "W.M.D. threat and the Iraqi connection to terrorism appear certain, whereas in fact we knew there wasn't one at all."

"The death and economic collapse that resulted has been completely devastating to our nation and, most of all, to me," read Mr. Bush's indictment. "I want to make amends, and it is for this reason that I am requesting that I be indicted for high treason. I thank the court for allowing me to right my grave wrongs. Bring it on!"

Some analysts suggest that Mr. Bush's self-indictment is part of a strategy to avoid the death penalty. Although treason carries a potential death sentence, Mr. Bush and his team of attorneys are seeking a triple life sentence without possibility of parole.

"We don't want to be too cynical about Mr. Bush's motives," said a spokesperson for AfterDowningStreet.org, one of the main groups that had been pursuing Mr. Bush's indictment. "But even if it doesn't get moved to the I.C.C., requesting his own conviction is so unusual it could move some jurors, or even help with an insanity plea."

A friend of Mr. Bush, speaking on condition of anonymity, revealed that Mr. Bush would attempt to move the case to the International Criminal Court, which does not have a death penalty, and was quietly pressing Secretary of State Naomi Klein to bring the U.S. under the court's jurisdiction. In 2002, then-Secretary of Defense Donald Rumsfeld rejected the I.C.C.'s jurisdiction, saying it was "unaccountable to the American people."

Mr. Bush maintained his characteristically jovial manner throughout the proceedings. "I could be executed, but what good would that do anybody? Especially me. I think the nation would rather I spend a good long while considering what happened — not only the tragic end of hundreds of thousands of lives, but the end of American capitalism, that I liked, I sincerely liked," Mr. Bush said. (See also "An Exclusive Interview With George W. Bush," on Page A9.)

The treason charge does not address compensation for the hundreds of thousands of Iraqis killed in the war. It is expected that surviving family members of fallen American soldiers will file thousands of civil lawsuits alleging wrongful death.

What's Fair?

Americans favor life in prison over death penalty.

64%	Life in Prison
31%	Death Penalty
3%	Charges Dropped
2%	Community Service

Source: New York Times/CBS News poll

Ari Fleischer contributed reporting.

With War Over, Troops Return

From Page A1

"Now that the war's over, we're going to get to go back to developing exciting new weapon systems, instead of just trotting out the ones that are proven to work," said a visibly excited Robert Stevens, Lockheed C.E.O., before a reporter informed him of the Senate moratorium on new weapons systems development.

"Oh," said Stevens, looking

A general learns his difficult history lessons late.

flushed, and quickly excused himself.

General David Petraeus had a distinctly ashen look as he attempted to put a good face on the situation. "I've been trying to make sense of all this, and I have to say that in perspective, we did pretty well," Petraeus told reporters.

"It turns out that in 1917, the British made exactly the same mistakes we did," Petraeus noted. "They told the Iraqis they had come 'not as conquerors but as liberators, to free you from generations of tyranny.' Like us, they were surprised the Iraqis didn't feel quite the same. The insurgency against the British started in Fallujah too, and like us, the British Prime Minister warned against leaving Iraq on the grounds that there would be civil war."

Petraeus smiled wearily. "I guess it's never too late to learn."

A number of mothers contributed reporting.

Rice: Troops Never Faced Annihilation Risk

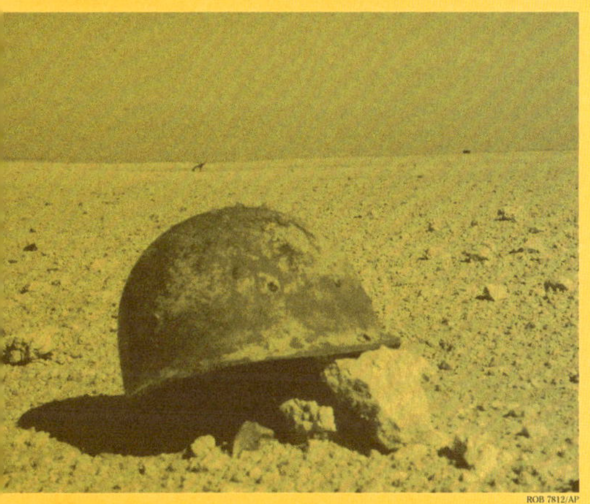

ROB 7812/AP

A lone helmet lies in the desert near Atrush, Iraq, a monument to absence.

From Page A1

believes that it was former President Bush's trial for high treason that spurred the revelations.

"There's nothing to hide anymore," said Ms. Rice. "We are relieved to finally be able tell you, the troops who fought for us, that we love our soldiers and we always have. We would never have put you in such obvious harm's way."

A sheepish former secretary expresses respect and concern for the troops.

Ms. Rice also confirmed Secretary of Defense Scott Ritter's revelation that he had provided the C.I.A. with documentation in the 1990s, when he was a U.N. weapons inspector, that Iraq lacked biological or nuclear weapons programs. "We were then already far more than 99 percent certain that Hussein had zero W.M.D.s and that if he did, he would not be able to use them against us."

War Brides (and Husbands) Find Their Place in a New Iraq

By LEN G. WILKINS

BASRA — Following service in Iraq and an honorable discharge last April, Lieutenant Samantha Blaine returned to Iraq to start a small construction company.

She is far from alone. The growth of the postwar economy in Iraq has proven so tempting that dozens of members of the U.S. military chose to remain in Iraq. Thus a region long associated with its citizens fleeing abroad has seen unprecedented volumes of immigration.

Seven years ago, Ms. Blaine had no experience with safety engineering or building codes but was sent to Basra to assist in the rebuilding of the Iraqi infrastructure. Today, her private contracting company is benefiting from a local building boom.

"For the first year of our business, most of the work was government contracts," said Blaine, "but after the major infrastructure work was done and the Iraqi economy began to rebound, there was a surge in demand for new housing."

Ms. Blaine met her husband, Ibrahim Khan, when he was hired to work as her translator during the war. It is a role he continues to serve as Ms. Blaine's Arabic improves.

Ms. Blaine claims that it hasn't been hard to adjust to life in Iraq. "I expected to have to deal with a lot of sexism. But until the invasion, this was a modern, secular society."

Sergeant Rahim Rafiqi has also benefited from the new construction, opening an insurance agency that caters to the construction industry. Prior to joining the military, Mr. Rafiqi had worked at his father's small insurance company. "I was able to get backing for what some would have seen as a risky investment, but we were in the black pretty quickly," says Mr. Rafiqi.

According to the recent émigrés, the cultural adjustments that are necessary to move from the United States to Iraq are more than worth enduring to be a part of the new Iraq. "Getting sent to Iraq was the best thing to happen to me," said Ms. Blaine. "I'm finally living the American Dream."

Biofuels Ban Act Signed Into Law, Seeks to Ease Food Shortage

By WILLIAM PETTY

WASHINGTON — In a dizzying about-face, the White House announced that the president will be signing the Ban Biofuels Act tomorrow.

The controversial legislation was pushed through Congress by newly elected Democrats uncharacteristically willing to stand up to big agribusiness, bolstered by intense public pressure in part due to the efforts of international organizations like Friends of the Earth, Greenpeace and the Rainforest Action Network.

The shift was cheered by environmental activists as well as average Americans worn down by the steep rise in food prices. "Vegetable oil and corn are for feeding people, not cars," said Elizabeth Johnson, a hospital worker and mother of three, at yesterday's demonstration outside Capitol Hill. "There was only so much more we could keep paying."

Six nationwide protests over the last four months had prepared the terrain for the bill's success, according to Andrew Kohut of the Pew Research Center, who said that national polls indicate a sharp decrease in public approval of biofuels and increased concern about global warming. "The public sees the use of biofuels as profoundly irresponsible both environmentally and socially," Kohut said.

He added that recent investigative reporting on the effects of biofuels, including one piece in the New York Times and several on C.N.N., had been key in sparking public outrage. "Television and print journalism haven't done this type of reporting for years," Kohut said. "We found that when people weren't barraged with disinformation, they developed a much sharper analysis of the situation."

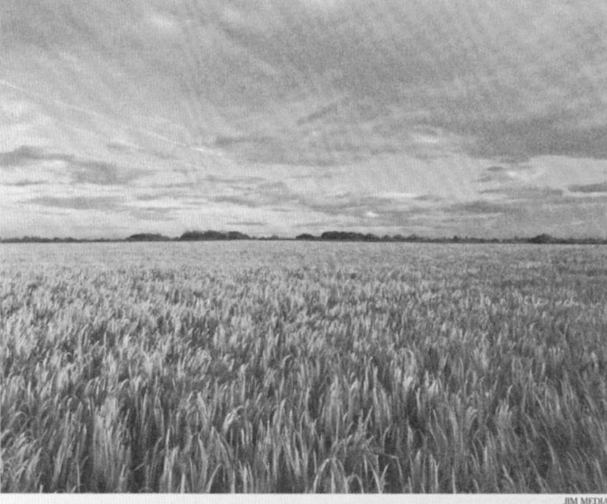

JIM MEDIA

Acres of corn now to be used for feeding people, rather than being converted to car and truck fuel.

In addition to turning off the tap on plant-based petrol, the Ban Biofuels Act sets out an ambitious plan of shifting over $10 billion in annual direct and indirect subsidies from oil companies to the construction of wind farms in rural areas of Texas, Kansas and Wyoming.

"One of the great things about the act is that it mandates the building of transmission lines, which has been a big infrastructural hurdle to getting renewable energy on track in the United States," said House Speaker Nancy Pelosi at a press conference yesterday. In acknowledging her failure in the past to support alternative fuels in a meaningful way, Pelosi credited activists for her increased understanding of the need for renewable energy.

Delivering yet another jolt to Republicans, House Democrats tacked onto the act a mandatory transition of cropland from chemical-intensive "conventional" farming to chemical-free organic cultivation on all acreage that receives subsidy payments from the federal government. "We've been getting a lot of heat from our constituents on this issue," explained Rep. Daniel Seals, Democrat of Illinois. "We had to do something and now was the time."

Top executives from Cargill and Archer Daniels Midland rushed to the Capitol late last night for an emergency closed-door session with the vice president. According to an aide who attended the meeting, negotiations quickly unraveled when congressional leaders sent a memo announcing they would refuse all future campaign contributions from the powerful firms.

Today the stock of both corporations registered their sharpest single-day drop on record at the Dow. Neither company would return calls for comment.

International response has been mixed. "I must admit, no one saw this coming," said a World Bank official who spoke on condition of anonymity. "We've all known there were big problems with our subsidies for biofuel crops in developing countries, especially as they encroached on other crops, and on native ecosystems. We were examining that. We just never expected to be pushed on it by U.S. officials."

Analysts at the World Bank predict that the legislation will have a ripple effect, eventually easing pressure on the remaining rainforests.

Food riots highlight a need for real solutions

"If the demand for biofuels drops, then there's far less incentive to clear-cut native forests," explained a spokesperson from Friends of the Earth Indonesia, also known as Walhí. "This is what the people in the rainforest have been fighting for for years."

The spokesperson added that the struggle would not be over until similar controls are implemented by governments around the globe. "Ecological destruction is a systemic problem, it's not just one company or one place. The only way we'll have real justice is if those who prosper from exploitation have nowhere else to go, and have to go somewhere else."

TORTURE, RENDITION "NOT SUCH GOOD IDEAS AFTER ALL"

By DIEGO TAVERA

WASHINGTON — In response to 36 million handwritten letters, the president made a formal apology today to Canadian citizen and extraordinary rendition victim Maher Arar and presented him with the Presidential Medal of Freedom.

Mr. Arar was a software engineer changing planes at J.F.K. Airport on his way home to Canada from a family vacation when he was detained, kept from counsel, and sent to Syria for a year of torture and interrogation.

The letters in support of Mr. Arar were part of a campaign organized by a coalition of human rights groups including Witness Against Torture, Amnesty International, the Center for Constitutional Rights, and MoveOn.org. His case has come to represent some of the worst excesses of the previous administration's national security policies.

The context for the apology is the White House's new Truth and Prosecution Program, which has exposed and reversed policy on secret C.I.A. interrogation and torture centers worldwide, warrantless wiretapping, illegal infiltration of activist meetings (and Quaker quilting bees), and extraordinary rendition, the extrajudicial transfer of suspected terrorists to countries known to torture prisoners.

The program works to assist the Attorney General's criminal prosecutions of former Bush administration officials for their role in torture policy and taking the country to war under false pretenses.

In a prepared statement, White House Press Secretary Samantha Bee said, "We will not condone torture, nor outsource torture. Maher Arar can never regain that year of his life, when our country sent him to be tortured in Syria, but the Medal of Freedom at least recognizes his heroic fight to assure that what happened to him will never again happen to anyone else." Bee also noted that the U.S. is matching Canada's $10 million compensation to Mr. Arar for his ordeal, "but in real money."

In a tearful interview on ABC's daytime talk show "The View" earlier this week, former Secretary of Defense Donald Rumsfeld, currently awaiting trial, told Elisabeth Hasselbeck that he hoped the world would not remember him as the man who brought torture out of the dungeon and into the Executive branch. "Maybe the whole torture thing wasn't such a good idea after all," he said. "I just hope people also remember my way with words, and peer through that to the essence, where I am also a, at least some kind of, father."

What do you think?

Send your feedback, or leave comments online at our website: nytimes-se.com

Congress Returns Civics to High School Curriculum

Part of Broader Agenda to Restore United States Constitution

By JOSEPH BRISTELLO

WASHINGTON — Wild applause broke out at the Parent Teacher Association national offices early this morning when several congressional spokespeople announced a funding appropriation to return the subject of civics to high school curricula nationwide.

The initiative is emblematic of the new bipartisan agenda to restore the United States Constitution to its pre-Bush-era status. In a joint statement, Senators Harry Reid, Democrat of Nevada, and Mitch McConnell, Republican of Kentucky, proclaimed that the initiative proves the two parties can work together on an issue of tremendous national importance.

The announcement came following a coordinated series of school strikes organized by parents outraged over a recent study by the National Opinion Research Center. The findings revealed a profound ignorance of government structure and citizens' rights by graduating high school seniors.

Some of the false, but widely held, opinions and beliefs highlighted in this cross-country study included: the legislative and judicial branches of government are subordinate to the executive branch; the president has the power to interpret treaties; the president is not bound by law; the vice president is independent of all three branches of government; torture is not a punishment and therefore cannot be considered "cruel and unusual"; in matters of national security, no warrants need be acquired by law enforcement.

The study noted that many students' political consciousness dated back only three years — in other words, their awareness of constitutional rights had been entirely formed during the Bush administration.

The study also found that students were growing incapable of differentiating between living figures, historical figures, and corporate-licensed figures such as cartoon characters and Internet avatars.

The revived civics courses will teach students about the structure and function of each branch of government; the theory of checks and balances; theories of the role of government; and of the role of the public in government; and constitutional law.

"We have so much work in front of us," said Los Angeles area high school teacher Roberta Morales. "Trying to instill in students a sense of citizenry and the public good and undo so many self-centered individualistic messages will take tremendous effort."

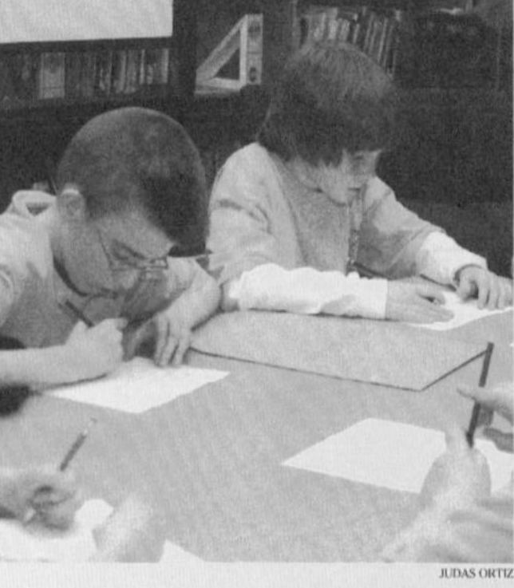

JUDAS ORTIZ

In an American History classroom in San Antonio, Texas, students learn about the Bill of Rights.

Labor Dept. Launches Job Creation Program

By ROBERT OWEN

WASHINGTON — The Department of Labor is scrambling to propose new standards that will affect every American worker. "This job report is a blueprint for job creation and economic stability," said Secretary of Labor David Bonior, who worked closely with unions like the S.E.I.U. and UNITE in crafting the standards.

By reducing the work week by five hours, to 35 hours per week, Bonior anticipates a 12 percent increase in new hires, particularly in the burgeoning sustainable energy sector. But new jobs aren't the only benefit. Coupled with the mandatory six-week paid vacations each year, worker health and satisfaction among U.S. workers will be on a par with those in Western Europe, according to Bonior.

Other new employment laws currently being developed will guarantee workers rights to equal protection when in dispute with employers. This includes giving workers full freedom to unionize unimpeded by employers.

USA Patriot Act Repealed

By SYBIL LUDINGTON

Eight years after being enacted, and three years after being reauthorized, the controversial USA Patriot Act was repealed by Congress by a vote of 99 to 1 in the Senate and 520 to 18 in the House.

No fanfare greeted the repeal in either house. Absent were the 40-minute speeches and foam-core charts predicting Armageddon. The act was repealed with a simple vote cast late in the day by a Congress ashamed of what it had done and what the Act had meant for Americans.

In related news, Congress yesterday repealed the Animal Enterprise Terrorism Act and agreed to permanently shelve the Violent Radicalization and Homegrown Terrorism Prevention Act. "These acts were worded in such a way that they could be interpreted to equate political dissent with terrorism. In any case none of these bills did a thing to protect Americans," said Speaker of the House Nancy Pelosi.

An obvious error, quietly buried.

Most past supporters of the act refused comment, but Senator Jon Kyl (R-AR) explained his lone vote to retain the Act: "I wish I could say I was as principled as Russ Feingold [the only Senator who opposed the Patriot Act in 2001], but the truth is that I had too much wine at lunch, hit the wrong button, and then was too inebriated to notice. I hope my constituents, who overwhelmingly wanted me to vote for the bill's repeal, will forgive me."

Popular "America's Army" Video Game, Recruiting Tool Cancelled

New Game Will Recruit Young Diplomats

By WILFRED SASSOON

WASHINGTON — The Department of Defense announced yesterday the cancellation of its highly successful and popular "America's Army" online game and recruitment tool. The program has already been converted into a new game, operated by the State Department, entitled "America's Diplomat." State Department spokesperson Donald Demsfold called this "a pretty good step towards nurturing a generation committed to the principles of diplomacy and peaceful negotiation."

America's Army was an online game designed by the Army to attract young recruits via simulated combat missions, many of which were modeled on actual battlefields in the Middle East.

During its use as a recruitment tool, America's Army consistently ranked among the top 20 Internet-based games. First launched in July of 2002 at a cost of $10 million dollars, America's Army's annual support budget was estimated at $1.5 million.

The cancellation of the game comes as part of the elimination of the Army's entire $583 million recruiting budget.

Early versions of the game were only moderately successful with young people, but the more subtle game is expected to inspire longer-term dedication. "I've never experienced such an exciting simulation of international negotiations," Greg Hauser, 14, told the press. Hauser is president of the Eastern High School debate club.

The State Department has high hopes for America's Diplomat, given its predecessor's highly successful history. In 2005, 40 percent of all recruits surveyed had played America's Army game prior to enlisting. As the game's popularity grew, and after dozens of new releases, the America's Army brand expanded to include console and cell-phone games, T-shirts, and the Real Heroes program, a section of the America's Army website that highlighted actual soldiers in Iraq and Afghanistan, and even recreated them as action figures.

The avowed purpose of America's Diplomat is to encourage young people to consider careers in the diplomatic corps, and to present non-military alternatives in a positive light. Where the ability to aggressively attack and kill opponents spelled success in America's Army, America's Diplomat stresses situations that demand negotiation, dialogue and peaceful outcomes.

Reactions from gamers have been intense as those attempting to access the America's Army website have been redirected to the new America's Diplomat site.

Lenny Purvill, a 16-year-old player, noted an initial disappointment in finding his favorite online game replaced. "I liked to pretend I was in the army going on missions in Iraq. And blowing stuff up was fun," he told the press. Purvill, who has been playing the game since he was 13, had been considering signing up when he turned 18.

His initial disappointment, however, was replaced by fascination as he facilitated a peaceful negotiations between Sunni and Shiite militiamen. "It was like, are they gonna shoot each other? No! They're not! 'Cause I'm helping them settle their differences with diplomacy. It's so awesome," he said.

Purvill also said he excitedly anticipates the expansion of the game in the coming months. This is expected to include new mission updates such as "United Nations," "Peace Corps," "Swords to Plowshares" and "Gandhi's HungerStrike!"

Demsfold acknowledged that the game represents a major shift in focus. "The next generation of government game-playing kids may not be able to kill very well, but they'll be able to practice diplomacy. That's what our national security calls for."

Defense Secretary Scott Ritter acknowledged that national security could benefit from the new game. "One of the most important lessons of the wars in Iraq and Afghanistan is that military success is not sufficient to win," he noted.

Unlike its predecessor, America's Diplomat has been pronounced suitable for children of any age by the Entertainment Software Rating Board.

America's Diplomat is available online: americasdiplomat.com

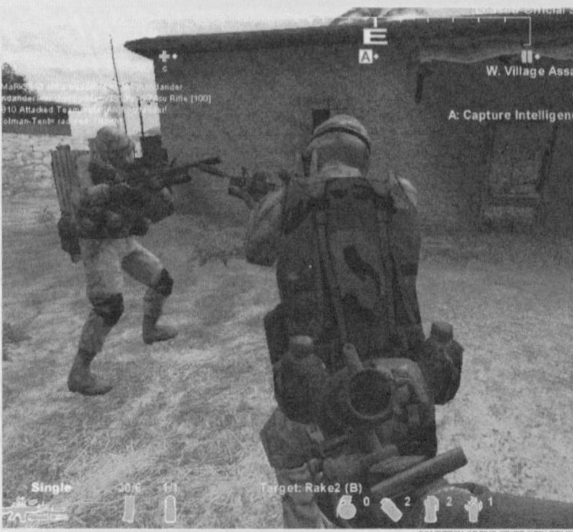

COURTESY OF THE STATE DEPARTMENT

In the discontinued "America's Army" video game/recruiting tool, players stormed villages.

High-Speed Internet Hits Fast Track to Appalachia

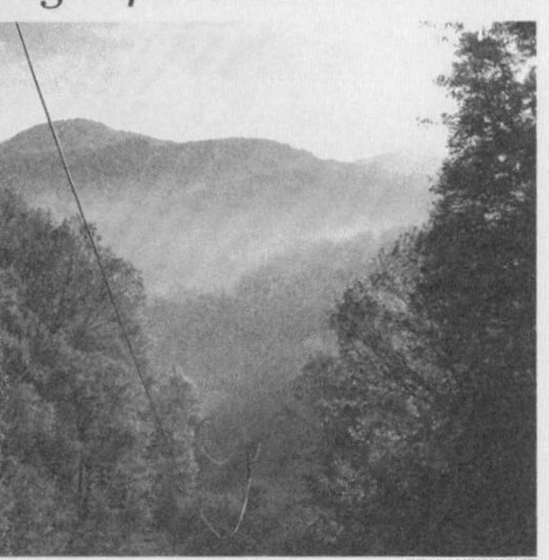

WILLIAM KNOXCRUFT

High-speed lines connect rural counties across the U.S. with the rest of the world at no cost to the user.

By B. VANNEVAR

WASHINGTON — The Internet Freedom Preservation Act has passed both houses of Congress, thanks in part to overwhelming and well-organized support of millions of Internet users. The act will ensure "net neutrality" — i.e., that all users have equal access to the Internet and that large corporations like Time Warner, AT&T, Comcast, and Verizon can no longer act as gatekeepers, determining which sites go fast and which slow.

The act also includes provisions to eliminate billions of dollars in subsidies and tax breaks for telecommunication corporations, and to use the proceeds to build a fiber-optic network providing free high-speed Internet service to even the most remote towns throughout the United States. This new network is expected to bring the U.S. up to speed with countries like Japan, France, and Korea, which have had extensive fiber-optic networks for years. The improved access for all communities is expected to help narrow education and socioeconomic gaps.

In the late 1970s, the Supreme Court ruled that companies providing communication services shouldn't interfere with smaller users. Two years ago, that decision was reversed and the largest telecommunications companies effectively became the gatekeepers of the Internet. The Internet Freedom Preservation Act guarantees that these companies can no longer decide which Web sites on their networks go fast or slow and which won't load at all.

"This law is a huge step forward for not only technology, but for the sharing of ideas," said free speech advocate Lawrence Lessig, who is head of the new Network Communications Bureau, which will be charged with protecting the network against all surveillance including that of other government agencies.

Education Department Plans National Tax Base for Schools

Takes Cue from Ohio and 23 Other States

By M.M. BETHUNE

Twenty-three states have announced plans to fund primary and secondary education on a statewide tax basis instead of per county, following the lead of a landmark decision in Ohio.

Ohio's S.B. 320 follows the Ohio Supreme Court ruling that funding schools from local property taxes and private initiatives does not comply with the Ohio Constitution's guarantee of a "thorough and efficient" public education system. The new statewide system means that resources are more equitably distributed, with inner-city schools receiving the same amount as suburban ones.

The Ohio decision began with Governor Ted Strickland's 2006 campaign promise to assure that "where you grow up in Ohio should not determine where you end up in life." Hundreds of grassroots campaigns throughout the state, including The Ohio Coalition For Equity and Adequacy of School Funding, took the cue from Mr. Strickland's statement and spent the last two years working hard to hold him to it.

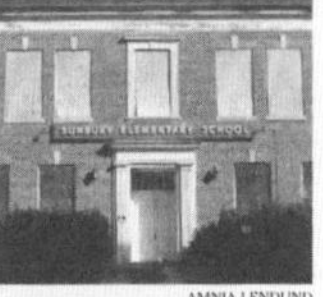

AMNIA LENDUND

"Finally, this is a real step towards the equality our Constitution recommends," says Amanda Fullerton, of Columbus. Ms. Fullerton, a mother of two, voted for Mr. Strickland because of his long history of support for educational reform, but was soon disappointed by the governor's inaction in office. When she first heard about the proposed bill in the Ohio Senate, Ms. Fullerton decided to occupy the Governor's office to demonstrate how important she felt the bill was. Over two hundred mothers soon joined her, camping out for six days. Many observers feel that actions like the mothers' played a key role in convincing Governor Strickland to push hard for the bill.

Following the announcements of twenty-three states that they would be voting on similar bills, the U.S. Department of Education said it would be developing a plan for a national tax base for schools, to finally assure that as in most other developed countries, a child's opportunities to learn will not depend on his or her birthplace.

Pharmaceutical Law Revised to End Corruption

By JASON BREMARSA

Revisions in the Physician Payments Sunshine Act (S.2029) will now make it a Class D federal felony for physicians to accept more than $25 annually in gifts or other rewards from pharmaceutical companies or biological product and medical device manufacturers.

The revised bill, introduced last fall by Senators Chuck Grassley, Republican of Iowa, and Herb Kohl, Democrat of Wisconsin, requires full disclosure of gifts, through a Department of Health and Human Services online system, by both companies and individual physicians, and it revokes caps on non-disclosure penalties for companies.

The legislation targets offending individual physicians, hospitals, schools, and other medical institutions that deal directly with patients. It also makes it a federal offense for medical industries to circumvent customary gift-giving practices through third parties, such as lawyers and insurance companies, or via "educational" events.

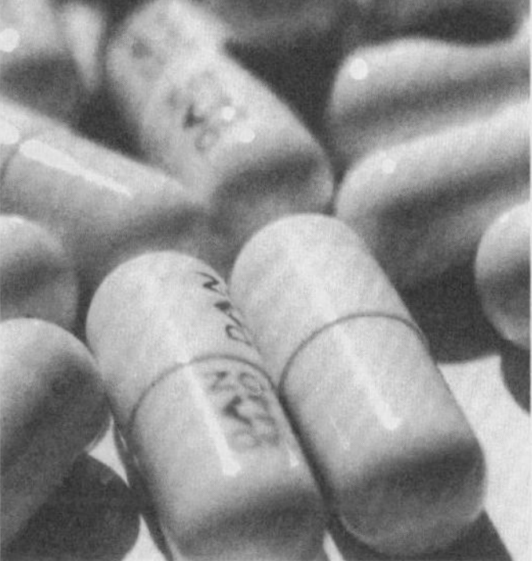

CAVUTTO/THE NEW YORK TIMES

It reverses earlier legislation that would have preempted more stringent physician sunshine laws passed by the states. The previous version of the law limited penalties to $10,000 for non-disclosure, and $100,000 for companies that "knowingly" fail to disclose gifts to physicians. The new bill establishes a lower limit for fines, but not an upper limit, and requires that that penalties take into account histories of gift-giving, product specifics and histories, overall corporate revenue, and other variables, before appropriate fines can be assessed.

Patients' rights and medical ethics groups, like the New England Medical Ethics Commission in Boston, are exultant. "It's not like the A.M.A. or [pharmaceutical trade association] PhRMA were ever going to comply with their own stated standards," says Patty Williams, Director of Communications for the commission. Williams is referring to the American Medical Association's 1991 guidelines on gifts to physicians from industry, which stemmed a tide of blatant gift-giving in the 1980s, but have been criticized for allowing new byways for abuse: free lunches and dinners, travel and honoraria, and the hemorrhaging of complimentary pens, coffee mugs, and other product-related paraphernalia into doctors' offices.

"What we really need is a sea change in the medical profession wherein physicians realize that it isn't O.K. to get gifts or fill our offices with advertisements for products. It demeans patient care," says Mount Sinai School of Medicine professor Dr. Joseph Ross. While programs like the Prescription Project, which scrutinize pharmaceutical company information and sales practices, have been in place for several years in states like Massachusetts and Pennsylvania, their effect is limited by the willingness of doctors to abide by ethical standards.

A series of tiny bribes corrupts a profession.

"This will definitely make it a lot harder for us to get our products to customers," says Sampson Browning, spokesperson for Eli Lilly, which anticipates large losses of revenue due to the new legislation.

"I haven't paid for lunch since last February, and I think I ate at home that day," says Dr. Bruce Arbogast, Director of Pine Grove Medical Center in Chicago. "Do the math. Do you think I can afford to say no when the drug reps knock on my door?" From now on, doctors will have to, or risk up to ten years imprisonment.

Prison Industry Looks Within

By ELIZABETH FRY

An experimental new program spearheaded by the Department of Justice and the Department of Corrections will place federal and state lawmakers, criminal court prosecutors and judges, wardens, and guards in five randomly-chosen prisons for a period of three days per year.

The National Prison Rehabilitation Program aims to give those in the prison-industrial complex the experience of those they condemn, and the time and space to discuss ideas for reform. It leverages empathy to reduce the incarceration rate in the U.S., the highest in the world by far.

Giving those with power a chance to reflect.

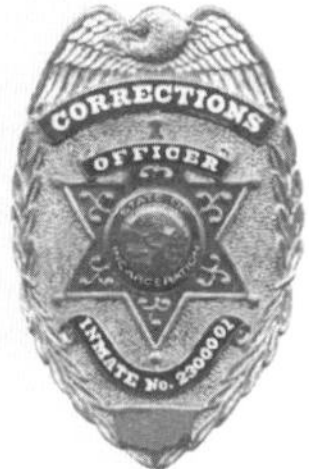

JOHN HOWARD

"It's part sentence, part all-expenses-paid meditation retreat," said Department of Corrections head Tom Hayden. The conference-like structure will feature keynote speakers and breakout discussions. "Once we get some of these players together in these facilities, I think it's pretty certain that great things will happen."

Bush Resumes Golf Game

By JAMES BRAID

WASHINGTON (AFP) — Former U.S. President George W. Bush returned to the fairway this week, after previously giving up the game out of respect for the families of U.S. soldiers killed in the conflict in Iraq in 2003.

"I saw him polishing his clubs last week," stated a White House security agent, who wished to remain anonymous. "Of course, we all assumed he was just sneaking out to play like he usually does."

In an interview with Yahoo! News and Politico in 2003, Bush resolved to refrain from his leisure pursuit out of solidarity with the families of soldiers in Iraq. "I think playing golf during a war just sends the wrong signal," he said.

"I don't want some mom whose son may have recently died to see the Commander-in-Chief playing golf."

The U.S. President claims to have renounced the game during the August 19, 2003 bombing of the United Nations headquarters in Baghdad, in which Sergio Vieira de Mello, the world body's top official in Iraq, was killed.

"I remember when de Mello got killed in Baghdad as a result of these murderers who were taking this good man's life." The tragedy forced Bush off the fairway at the 12th hole, and home to his ranch in Crawford, Texas.

Meticulous records kept by CBS News, however, trace the President's last official round of golf to October 13, 2003.

One source close to the President's caddy claimed that Bush's dismal score at that last game did, in fact, come out of solidarity with

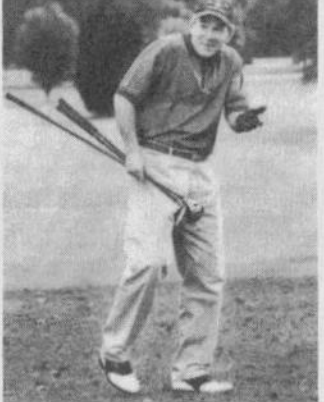

REUTERS

troops stationed in Iraq. "It's like, they're having a hard time, he was having a hard time.... At some point, I think he was just like, 'I've been out here for, like, six hours. I was sure I was gonna win at the 2nd hole. When is this gonna end?'"

Bush assured The Times that the game will not interfere with his continued search for Osama bin Laden.

An Exclusive Interview with Former President Bush

Former **President George W. Bush** gave his first post-indictment interview yesterday to **Scott Pelley** of 60 Minutes. The interview, conducted at Bush's Crawford, Texas ranch is scheduled to air Sunday evening. 60 Minutes has provided the Times with excerpts of their discussion.

PELLEY: It's been several months since you left the White House, and although you've condemned the war in Iraq, and your own role in leading us to it, you've also made clear you have some business you'd like to finish. What do you have planned for the next year?

BUSH: First, Scott, let me tell you where I'm at. I've had more time to look at the big picture since I left office. Abu Ghraib was a mistake. Using posturing language like "mission accomplished" and "bring it on" was a mistake. Troop levels may have been a mistake. Getting us in there in the first place was obviously a big mistake. I think history is going to look back and see a lot of ways we could have done things better, no question about it, all the way from day one to day now.

But the reason I bring all this up is mainly that I don't want people out there blaming the folks in the military for what's happened in Iraq. If regular American people need a scapegoat, well they can look no further. I'm your scapegoat, right here, made to order. Me.

Of course that doesn't stop me from picking up firewood! (Laughter.)

PELLEY: Mr. President, what are your plans now, besides being a scapegoat?

BUSH: Well, just because I'm not in that Oval Office, doesn't mean I can just sit down. I started out with a plan, and my obligation to this country is to fill out that plan, fulfill it.

PELLEY: So you will be...

BUSH: I'm going to pursue Osama Bin Laden.

PELLEY: I'm sorry?

BUSH: I'm going on my own search for Osama bin Laden to bring a killer to justice. I have set up a $500,000 reward, of my own money, for tips. Laura helped me set up a toll-free hot line to field those tips.

Near the beginning of my terms, my nation was attacked by Saudi Arabian terrorists. So I started a hunt for Osama bin Laden and the Taliban in Afghanistan. We got the Taliban, we didn't get the main man. Then, Iraq.

I'm going to finish the job. It's not just the good thing to do, it's the need to do it thing. And that's what I'm going to do.

PELLEY: Why didn't you do this during your terms as President?

BUSH: Scott, Osama bin Laden, he's our enemy. Make no mistake, he's our enemy, and he's not down. And we have not really pursued him. I wouldn't say that I didn't do anything. But sometimes what you want to do, or think you might do, is not really all there is, and you eventually see that.

We did remove Osama bin Laden's enemy, Saddam Hussein. I'm proud of our servicemen and women who did that. Maybe I wouldn't do that today, but that's what I did back then. And now here I am.

But what's important is that we made mistakes, and one thing when you make mistakes is you can't undo them. And now I'm not undoing them, I'm doing the only right thing for right now.

PELLEY: Sir, forgive me, but many people will say that you're not equipped for this. Your health — this isn't a one-man job.

BUSH: A lot of people thought I wasn't equipped to be President either. (Laughs.) But really, once I make up my mind, I need to follow through and give it my best shot.

See this, Scott? This is the same rifle we issue to our Marine marksmen. I've been training with this for the past 6 months here on the ranch. I'm ready for this. We can shoot some cans later, if you need any proof. (Laughs.)

PELLEY: Pardon me, sir, but I just find it incredible that you are personally going to hunt Osama bin Laden. I mean, jail...

BUSH: Well, "personally" is an awfully big word here, Scott. A business organization has a lot of members, we have a lot of resources. Over the last eight years, private-sector fighting organizations have developed in a way I am amazed to see.

So obviously I'm not going to do it alone. But I'm going to have the time and also the resources, and the freedom, to do what I want to do, which is finish the search for Osama bin Laden. We will have resources that I never had as president. When you're commander in chief there are laws,there's limitations and diplomacy you have to work within. Now I'll have more freedom, frankly, even in jail.

The presidency isn't a popularity contest. I had to make tough decisions. But I was the president when this war happened. I want to be the one to bring closure for the American people.

Maybe you can think of it as a second career, or a retirement, but I'm going to have more time on my hands. And what I will do is shoulder this burden, and do this work that has not been done, myself. I will spend whatever time needs to be spent to hunt that killer, I will find him, and I will bring him to justice.

SATURDAY, JULY 4, 2009

Business

The New York Times

Public Relations Industry Forecasts a Series of Massive Layoffs

By LOUIS BECK

SACRAMENTO (AP) — Public relations firms across the country predict massive layoffs in the coming months due to recent legislation outlawing the firms' most lucrative practices.

The new regulations carefully scrutinize government contracts with for-profit public relations companies, and apply much higher standards to public relations work overall. The new rules would have forbidden the creation of the National Smokers Alliance, a front group formed by Philip Morris with the help of P.R. giant Burson Marsteller, which presents itself as a grassroots group opposed to smoke-free laws.

The regulations would also have rendered impossible the notorious "Kuwaiti incubators" episode of 1992, in which P.R. giant Hill & Knowlton worked with the U.S. and Kuwaiti governments to galvanize public opinion in favor of the Persian Gulf War. Among other things, the firm helped stage a press conference in which a 15-year-old girl named Nayirah claimed to have witnessed Iraqi soldiers flinging Kuwaiti babies to the ground from their incubators. Nayirah was later revealed to have been performing on behalf of her father, the Kuwaiti Ambassador to the U.S. The "Kuwaiti incubator" hoax was considered decisive in turning popular opinion toward war against Iraq.

An industry that helped launch wars begins to shut down.

"It's unfortunate that our hard work is being discussed under these circumstances," said Cynthia Knowlton, granddaughter of Hill & Knowlton founder David J. Knowlton III and a spokesperson for the company.

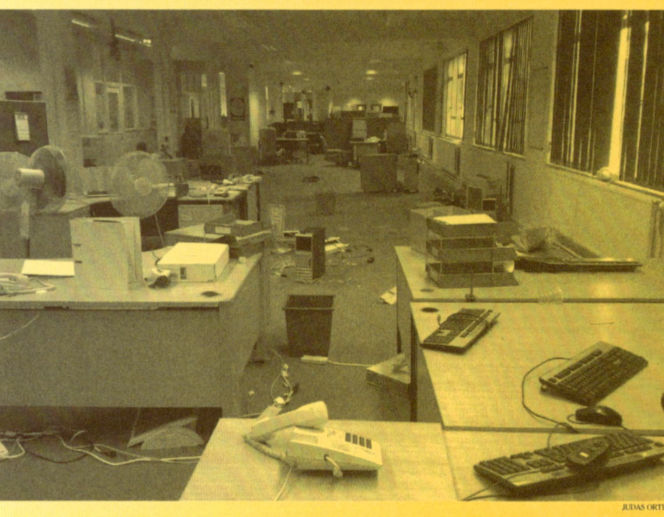

JUDAS ORTIZ

Hill & Knowlton's New York office after layoffs were announced yesterday. Cutbacks have rippled through giants across the industry.

While most industries suffered during the Iraq War, the P.R. industry remained buoyant. As overall consumer spending decreased, government spending increased, and the coffers of some private firms expanded. Of the 40 percent of Iraq War spending that went to private military contractors since the 2003 invasion, a full 10 percent is rumored to have gone to P.R. firms. Campaigns like "Army Strong" and "Be All You Can Be" were created by private firms, and companies are even alleged to have been paid hefty sums to guarantee returning veterans prominent placement on television programs such as "Wife Swap," "Trading Spaces," and "Punk'd."

One P.R. firm, MediaLink Worldwide, plans to cut its media commentator funding, a substantial portion of its budget. "We are forced to cut back, and that does mean letting excellent and qualified candidates in all fields go," company spokesperson Fred Donahue said in an official statement. Saatchi & Saatchi, one of the largest ad firms in the world, fired over 300 employees in its Word-of-Mouth Division. Leo Burnett in Chicago is expected to release all part-time staff later this week.

It's a vast network of influence, all crumbling down around the feet of culture producers.

"P.R. companies have been doing whatever it takes to maximize their profit," contended media activist Ben Jefferson at a hearing which shortly preceded the passage of the new regulations. "The mystical power of the consumer isn't going to change that — whereas the actual power of the citizen is. That's where legislation comes in."

Harvard Will Shut Business School Doors

By JOHN LEVERETT

Harvard University Business School will be closing its doors following an unprecedented drop-off in applications this fall. The school will be renamed the Harvard University School of Integrity, and students will receive Masters in Integrity and Compassion, or M.I.C.s.

"We believe that the recent increase in visibility of progressive movements and ideals, coupled with the demotion of free-market capitalism as a viable belief system, has led students away from training in accumulation for its own sake and into fields where they can advance peace and justice," said Harvard spokesperson Susan Morrison.

It became apparent in early 2009 that enrollment in fields like marketing, advertising, corporate communications, and management dropped 44 percent, while enrollments in fields like social work, journalism, and community organizing were up 53 percent in the same period.

"We're not sure if it's an anomaly or an indicator of a long term trend, but there's definitely a change," said Morrison.

Morrison said the new Integrity School is contacting campuses around the world to encourage graduating seniors to apply. "We see as our job to help students tap into their desire for integrity and compassion, rather than their greed. That's what they need, and that's what our society needs."

Plan Encourages Steady Growth, Will Boost Bottom 95%

From Page A1

posed the proposals before overwhelming public support helped change her mind. "This bill brings a level of sanity and restraint back to the system that allowed companies like Enron, Bear Stearns, Fannie Mae, and Freddie Mac to fleece Americans for all they were worth."

Merrill Lynch C.E.O. John Thain disputed Ms. Pelosi's account. "High C.E.O. salaries, sophisticated financial instruments, and the freedom to speculate freely have for the past thirty years been instrumental in driving us to achieve the highest shareholder returns in the world outside of Russia. Shareholders have been very grateful for those returns. We mustn't look at one rash of foreclosures, or one system collapse, and forget the decade of high returns that enabled a new wave of prosperity for a certain number of people."

Treasury Secretary Krugman cited the pressure applied by progressive activist groups as instrumental in the S.A.N.E. Act's success despite overwhelming counterpressure from financial industry lobbyists, who have been working overtime in anticipation of the likely passage of the "Ban on Lobbying" bill, which prohibits lobbying on behalf of private individuals or corporations earning more than $1 million annually.

"We've got popular pressure to thank for letting us make the market serve humans once again," Mr. Krugman said. He also stressed that even passage of the S.A.N.E. bill would be meaningless without passage of the "Ban on Lobbying" bill. Only by banning lobbying, Mr. Krugman added, would it be possible to assure that the changes mandated by the S.A.N.E. Act are not rolled back through the influence of big corporations.

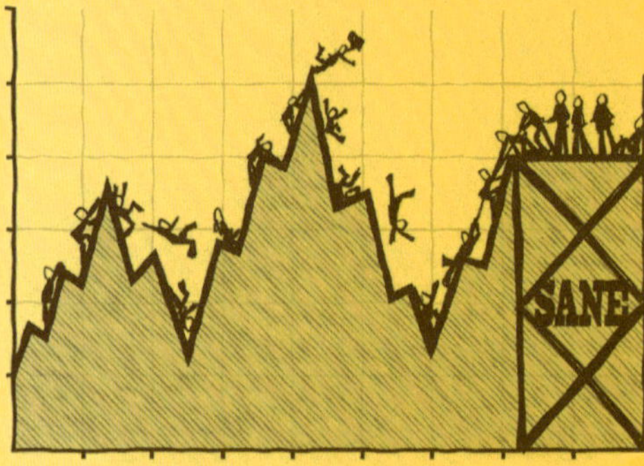

DETAILS OF S.A.N.E. ACT

CAPS WAGES. Caps salaries, in part to reduce the incentive of C.E.O.s to speculate wildly with investors' funds.

BUSTS TRUSTS. Breaks up financial conglomerates and reinstate the 1933 Glass-Steagall Act keeping investment banks and commercial banks separate, in order to reduce speculation.

TAXES SPECULATION. Spearheads an international 1 percent tax on financial transactions, to slow speculation and reduce market volatility.

STABILIZES MORTGAGES. Keeps Fannie Mae and Freddie Mac, which were formed to boost home ownership, under government management, and imposes a moratorium on foreclosures.

INVESTS IN HOUSING. Reinvests in public housing and renews rent control, until the "ownership society" becomes real.

PRICES FOR TRUE COST. Establishes a "true cost" pricing system to ensure that prices reflect the true cost to society of products, services, and practices.

TAXES INHERITANCE. Establishes a 100 percent tax on inheritance for fortunes over $500,000. These revenues will enable a quicker implementation of universal health care, affordable housing, guaranteed college education, and other measures considered standard in almost every other developed country.

SETS EMERGENCY TAX. Provides for an emergency surtax on the wealthy in case of future financial meltdowns, to further discourage the sort of reckless speculation that fueled the latest banking crisis.

LIMITS DERIVATIVES. Regulates and streamlines the market in abstract financial instruments, especially those derivatives and derivatives of derivatives which serve no social purpose whatsoever.

"TRUE COST" PRICING SET

From Page A1

Pelham Bay, New York, referring to General Motors' EV1, an electric car it developed in 1996, before scrapping it shortly after. GM was required to reintroduce the EV1 last month by the Clean Car Act.

"Ever since it came back, the EV1 is five times more popular than the next car down," Cluber said. "I hope we never have to sell a combustion engine again."

Three months after a 90 percent "True Cost" tax on bottled water went into effect, the high premium has already prevented many tons of plastic waste, according to Environmental Protection Agency Deputy Under Secretary Gavin Newsom. "When we banned plastic shopping bags in San Francisco in 2006, it reduced waste enormously. The recent tax on plastic water bottles has prevented even more needless environmental damage, including many tons of CO_2 emissions from the transportation of water," said Mr. Newsom in a press conference. "Imagine transporting water across oceans. What were we thinking?"

"It's great to see this extended to the whole spectrum of products with which we're destroying our world," Mr. Newsom added.

Treasury Secretary Paul Krugman believes the "True Cost" system will serve not only as an incentive to manufacture certain products instead of others, but will help to make people aware of the effects of their behavior.

"We complain about high gas prices," said Melissa Schwarzwald, spokeswoman for the Sierra Club, pressure from whose members was instrumental in getting the tax implemented. "But how much does it really cost, to our health, to the planet's health, and to the health of the country we destroyed in the interest of a steady supply? We're cut off from what we're really doing, and that's the whole problem."

New Wage Cap Will Stabilize Economy

From Page A1

to rake in massive dividends, often at the cost of the company's, and the country's, stability."

The first time the U.S. implemented a maximum wage was in 1942, when President Roosevelt said that "no American citizen ought to have an income, after he has paid his taxes, of more than $25,000 a year," the equivalent of $315,000 today.

Some version of a maximum wage law was in effect until 1980. Before 1964, income over $400,000 in today's dollars faced a 91 percent federal tax rate, and the top-bracket tax rate never dipped below 70%. Under Reagan, the top tax rate slid down to 28 percent — a shift that is now understood to have been one of the prime contributors to the mortgage meltdown and other market failures.

The current minimum wage is $5.85 ($12,168 annually) making the new maximum wage $182,520/year. Any amount over that will be taxed at a rate of 100 percent.

The Center on Executive Compensation is an industry-backed group based in Washington whose goal is to tell corporate America's side of the executive pay story. Richard Floersch, the center's chairman and the chief human resources officer at McDonald's, defended high salaries. Most companies, he said, are "dedicated to a very strong executive compensation program with very strong principles around pay for performance."

In the two days since Mr. Floersch made these comments to a reporter, the Center on Executive Compensation has dissolved. A statement on their website now reads: "We have decided that in light of recent changes in economic policy, and the failure of hedge fund managers and banks to prevent massive losses despite their astronomical pay, our Center has lost its relevance." The statement also acknowledges the problems caused by Fannie Mae and Freddie Mac executives falsifying profits of $9 billion so their firms would appear attractive to investors and then, instead of being fired, receiving retirement packages upwards of $10 million.

House Speaker Nancy Pelosi celebrated the bill's passage with an impassioned speech. "The struggle on behalf of human dignity continues. We need investment in productive enterprises and public services. The era is over of C.E.O.s who receive millions in bonuses as their employees go without health care and the company fails."

In her speech, Ms. Pelosi extensively quoted Treasury Undersecretary E. Merrick Dodds, who stated, shortly after passage of the first maximum wage under Roosevelt: "The modern period has been one in which a new impulse towards regulation has gathered strength as a result of our experience of the evils to which unlimited freedom of contract gives rise in a postindustrial society characterized by extreme inequalities of wealth and bargaining power and by sudden oscillations between booms and depressions."

Don Cortland contributed reporting.

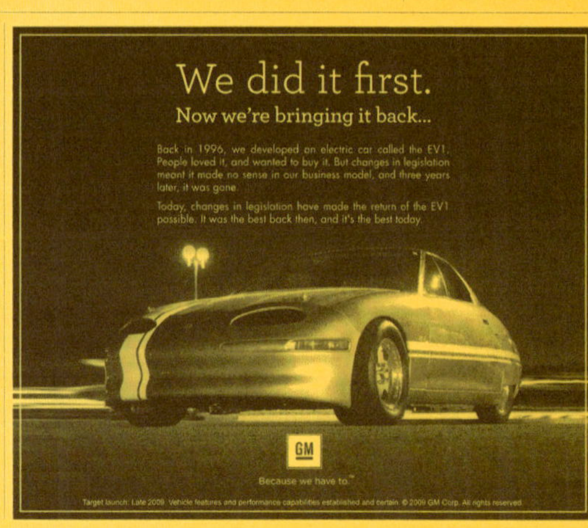

Senate Gets Tough On "Limited Liability" to Rein in, Humanize Corporations

By CARLTON DONALLY

Senator John McCain, Republican of Arizona, has launched a bold new "tough on crime" initiative that would imprison or fine shareholders for corporate crimes committed in their name. Punishment would depend on the severity of the crime and the number of shares owned.

Mr. McCain outlined his unique two-tiered punishment program, which would punish corporations for legal infractions according to their severity. Mr. McCain explained that there would be two "suites" of punishment, for levels of crime roughly corresponding to misdemeanors and felonies.

In one "suite" — for "misdemeanors" like bilking taxpayers of seven-figure dollar amounts, overcharging consumers, attempting monopolies, and contributing to simple human troubles like asthma and brief bouts of homelessness — punishment would take the form of short- or long-term share confiscation. Dividends of confiscated shares would pay for remedial action, where possible, as well as public-good programs like health care.

"I know a number of people whose companies were players in the Savings and Loan scandal," Mr. McCain said, "and they're prepared to face the consequences. Remedies for serious problems are never easy, especially when they hit at the root."

The second punishment "suite," for "felonies" — spreading diseases, committing homicide or manslaughter, contributing to national disasters in the U.S. or abroad, large-scale bilking of taxpayers, etc. — would involve direct punishment of the shareholders in question.

Mr. McCain used Union Carbide's 1984 Bhopal massacre, in which thousands of Indian villagers were killed by lethal gas, as an example of a crime that would be classified as a felony. While retroactive prosecutions based on new laws are usually not permissible, in such extreme cases they would be, as they were in the Nuremberg prosecutions of 1945.

In the Union Carbide example, Mr. McCain noted that each death would cost the company a "negligent homicide" charge, for approximately twenty years of incarceration each. Twenty years multiplied by 2000 equals 40,000 years in prison, with aggravating factors such as a demonstrated lack of remorse or compassion tripling the total.

This penalty would be divided among Union Carbide shareholders, each of whom could expect to spend from a few weeks to several years in prison, depending on the size of investment. A minimum penalty could be set by a judge — so that an investor with even a fraction of a share would be liable for, say, two weeks in jail. This would apply even to those who had invested via mutual funds, without knowing the precise direction of their investments.

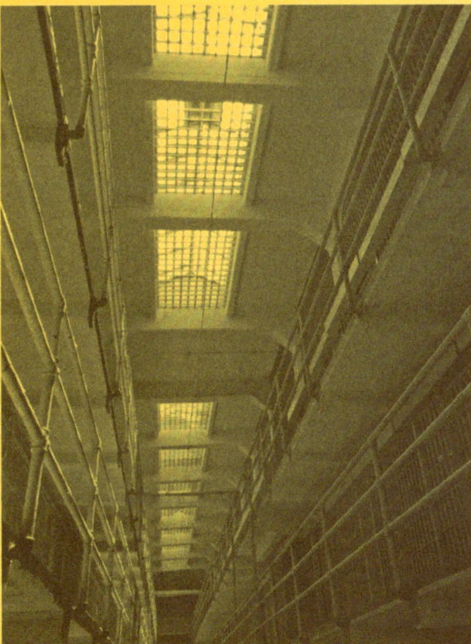

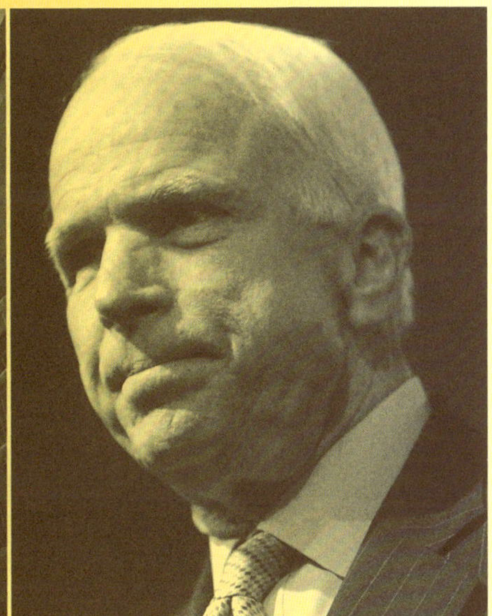

CFINKE AND OBORLOO HOCHMANKS

Left: An old prison being remodeled for white-collar criminals. Right: John McCain reclaims "maverick" status with strict new sentencing to put corporate criminals behind bars.

Mr. McCain said that while "tough on crime" policy has been shown to be useless with humans, it would work with corporations. "Corporations are just machines, not like teenage kids. They can be forced to act as if they knew right from wrong."

"Corporate behavior has become a very loud cry for 'tough love,'" the governor said. "We've got to adapt to a changing world, and sometimes that means changing laws."

"Fines are not punishment, they do not build character," Mr. McCain said. "What's a ten-million-dollar fine to a giant corporation? Fines seldom if ever affect the pocketbooks of shareholders or managers, those who make the decisions or power the machine. Hitting pockets and people directly is a different thing."

Mr. McCain admitted that several major problems remain to be solved. The death penalty, for example, while often merited in corporate crime cases, had no obvious application — "We can't talk about 'little deaths' here," said Mr. McCain, making an obscure bilingual pun better left unexplained.

Also, the issue of global markets poses some problems, Mr. McCain said. "These penalties will eventually have to be agreed on by a global governing body like the W.T.O., not only here at home in Arizona or the U.S. Otherwise we may create a better market here, but the changes will be irrelevant in the bigger picture. And influencing such a powerful and state-independent body as the W.T.O. is a very involved process."

The ultimate aim of the program, Mr. McCain said, is to help corporations achieve their long-term goals. "Corporations have spent the last century and a half trying to obtain all the legal rights of people," Mr. McCain said. "They're now technically persons, but they're not really human. We owe it to them — and to our species — to help them finish their quest."

Mr. McCain went on to explain that corporations still, even today, lack one distinguishing human characteristic: a conscience. "Corporations were invented to keep investors innocent of crimes committed with the help of their money, accidentally or not. But now that corporations have become legally almost human, they have to be taught that their actions have consequences."

Mr. McCain called corporate efforts to obtain the legal rights of humans "compassionate greed," and said that it was "not entirely about getting richer."

"You'd have to be very cynical to think that corporations, when they won protection as 'persons' under the 'Freed Slave' Amendment, were thinking only of their own wealth," Mr. McCain said. He was referring to the 14th Amendment, which had been designed to protect the rights of freed slaves, and which was used in 1886 to establish corporations as "natural persons" under the law.

"It's clear that corporations just admire humans and what we have. We should be good hosts and help them however we can. Right now, that means making them responsible and responsive."

While most experts scoff at the idea that corporations could actually become human beings, most agree that punishing corporations for the crimes they commit will at the very least have a positive effect on the world. "If each shareholder is personally responsible for corporate crimes, then you've got real controls — and without regulation!" said Mr. McCain.

Mr. McCain dismissed concerns that personal liability for corporate crimes might discourage individual investors from taking a risk. "People love to gamble," he said, "and this will make it all very real."

For those who do not thrive on such risks, Mr. McCain suggested that the mutual fund industry would easily adopt new decision-making processes, just as it has in the past. "The prime mechanism of regulation will be shareholder judgement. If investment in one company is likely to land you in jail, you'll invest in another instead. Mutual fund companies will find it an exciting challenge to obtain and keep investor confidence. It will reinvigorate the industry, and in fact the whole concept of investment."

Chad Woolin contributed reporting.

New York

The New York Times

Army Recruiter Goes from Marketing the Military to Marketing Himself

By BARRY GLOAD

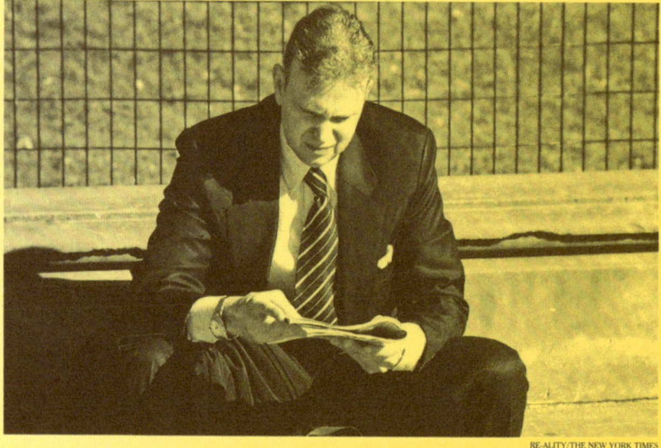

RE-ALITY/THE NEW YORK TIMES

Former recruiter, Staff Sgt. Joe Pascanic, pages through job listings before an interview at a used car lot in Elizabeth, New Jersey.

MANHATTAN — "I have plans, and I have backup plans," explained retired Staff Sgt. Joe Pascanic, a former recruiter for the U.S. Army. "That's one thing I learned in the military. Always have your Plan B, and your Plan C."

"Plan D is called Unconditional Surrender, a.k.a. filing for Unemployment Insurance. We're not gonna need to go there."

Pascanic, 36, of Rahway, New Jersey, was looking for a new job in the civilian sector. The Times spent a day with him as he took the train from this blue-collar town into New York City to pound the fresh post-war pavement.

Pascanic is a medium-tall man, with blonde short hair and brown eyes, trim and nattily dressed in a professional, well-pressed, blue pinstriped suit. He thanked me for my compliments on his "civvies," and said, "I'm very happy to be wearing them."

He appeared lost in thought for a moment, and then shook off the reverie with a gruff statement.

"I have to say, however I felt about the war, I'm glad I don't have that job anymore," Pascanic admitted as we waited on the New Jersey Transit platform. "That was serious pressure."

Indeed, while many antiwar activists denounced military recruiters as liars during the war, this time Pascanic was telling the truth. The Army's strict and harsh quota system for recruiters made it one of the highest-stress jobs in America. As the war grew more bloody and news of "stop-loss" and other involuntary extensions of soldiers' combat tours made it harder to get new recruits, rates of suicide, drug and alcohol abuse, divorce, and stress-related illnesses such as ulcers skyrocketed amongst Army recruiters.

"I used to say, the only more stressful positions are the ones they put you in at Abu Ghraib, those and the only more stressful occupation was the U.S. in Iraq." Pascanic laughs a little, gives me a self-conscious glance, and says, "That was an after-work, at-the-bar kind of line, of course.

"I did get a lot of skills from it, though. Besides the working under pressure, I learned so much about marketing. It's hard to fill your quota when that means getting kids to sign up to go fight in a shooting war. Trust me.

"I mean right after September 11th, it was no problem, the product sold itself, so to speak. To go fight in Afghanistan, where the bad guys were, the ones who attacked us. I didn't have to do any pitching, the kids came right to me in droves to sign up. The product made its own sauce. Just add water."

As we got off the train and made our way on foot into the city, Pascanic warmed to the subject of his skills. He repeated some of his key advantages a few times, apparently rehearsing out loud the lines for his first job interview, at a medium-sized advertising firm in midtown Manhattan not far from Penn Station.

"Now obviously I had to develop massive marketing skills in my old job. Sometimes it was just in terms of what to focus on. So I want them to sign up to fight in Afghanistan? Now I happen to know from Military History class that the British and the Russians both lost in Afghanistan. Empires get bled to death in that place. Now that's very interesting information, but is it helpful on the job? No, actually it's counterproductive. So that doesn't go in the patter. See? It's not just what you say. It's what you don't say."

'I've sold people trips to Iraq!'

And how did he feel about his chances at this job interview? As we entered the sleek lobby, he adjusted his cuffs and said "Hey, maybe my military service got me here to the target. But now I have to deliver the payload." He spun on his heels and marched to the elevator.

Coming out forty-five minutes later, Pascanic seemed shaken. "They heard my pitch, but they're really looking for guys with M.B.A.s from Ivy League colleges. They said they'd keep my resume on file. I think they were impressed with my recruitment rate, but I don't know. I don't think I should wait around for that phone call."

We took a taxi down to Chelsea for our next stop, a real-estate firm where Pascanic was hoping to use his work experience to sell co-op apartments. He recovered his confidence and talked himself up as we rode. "I've sold people trips to Iraq! We're talking about desert and urban guerrilla warfare. And they signed! Of course you have to promise them competitive job training, money for education, maybe insinuate they probably won't ever go to a combat zone, or that they'll all get assigned to be military journalists or photographers or whatever they're interested in that sounds safer. But you're also selling an adventure, a chance to be all you can be, be an army of one, be army strong. It's a complicated mix of practical bread-and-butter promises and an appeal to the beautiful spirit in all of these kids, their desire to help, to protect, to be a real part of America. It's tough, but you know what? You're selling the American Dream. And that's what I'd like to do as a real estate agent. Sell the American Dream of home ownership."

And how did he feel about the fates of the people he'd convinced to sign up with misleading promises? Pascanic did not argue the facts — that veterans' training yields them a lower rate of employment than their civilian peers, not higher; that only a small percentage of veterans ever qualify for the education funding due to hidden restrictions and costs; that military contracts include a catch-all disclaimer to nullify obligations the recruiter has promised.

"Let's talk about this when I get out from this next interview. I'm not debating! I'm not denying! But I gotta make sure I'm at that front desk on time." He grinned and jumped out of the taxi, jogging into the company's front office.

Twenty-five minutes later, Pascanic came back out on the street, frowning. "They gave me a good listen, but they seemed a little offended. I wasn't trying to compare selling open-ended trips to a war to selling studios to wealthy N.Y.U. students. But I might have come across that way. They didn't think we'd be a good match."

Pascanic slowed his pace, then stopped, and asked if I'd mind if we went into the church we were passing. As we sat in the pews of the huge, solemn hall, he said, "About your question . . . yeah, sometimes I do think about my job and what I promised the kids, and what ended up happening to them." He pointed at the ceiling and said, "And I wonder what He would think."

"But I don't know, you know, this is America, we're all selling something, right? The President sold the country a war, wholesale; I just did the same thing at the retail level. But what am I gonna do now?" He looked around him at the relative sanctuary of the church. "Maybe I'll get a job here. Maybe I'm not meant for the private sector. Maybe I can sell salvation. You know, I'd much rather sell Heaven and Hell than Iraq and Afghanistan. Because these products have stood the test of time. People still believe in them. And you know what? They're for after you die, you don't actually die in them. I can feel better selling that. How do you apply to be a priest?"

At that moment, Pascanic's cell phone rang, piercing the silence. His ringtone, Bon Jovi's In and Out of Love, played for several maximum-volume bars before he patted down his pockets, found, and answered the phone. At that moment, he snapped to attention and darted out of the church.

It was Chris Sorrentino calling. Sorrentino, 24, was one of Pascanic's first recruits to go to Iraq, instead of Afghanistan as he'd expected, in 2003. He lost his right arm in an I.E.D. explosion five months into his deployment. Pascanic and Sorrentino had kept in touch.

Sorrentino was calling to offer Pascanic a sales job at his family's used-car lot in Elizabeth, New Jersey.

This reporter, who felt solidarity with Pascanic because The Times, too, had helped to sell the war to the nation, paid for a car service to drive him to the lot. After a few minutes of friendly Jersey-boy small talk, vulgar ribbing and tasteless jokes, Pascanic had nailed the job. Since he was already wearing a dapper suit, Sorrentino's father, Bill, put the former recruiter out on the lot immediately. Pascanic thanked me for the ride and said goodbye, studying the specs of the car inventory and rehearsing a new pitch under his breath as he marched off to the sales floor.

I asked Sorrentino if he bore any grudges against Pascanic for misrepresenting the reality of the war that had cost him his arm. Sorrentino hesitated, he frowned, shook his head, and answered "Well, I mean... yeah, I wish... but — hey, hey, hey ... the war's over."

New York Bike Path System Expanded Dramatically

Miles of Segregated Bicycle Lanes Will Be Paved by 2010

By MEDE SIVRAC

NEW YORK — Officials from the Department of Transportation today opened the 9th Avenue bike lane, which now extends the entire length of Manhattan. The festivities were then moved to 2nd Avenue, where ground was broken on a similar path to extend the full length of the island.

Over the next two years, every other avenue will also receive a full bike lane, blocked off from traffic, while every fifth crosstown street will be opened exclusively to bicyclists and pedestrians beginning next month.

Mark Blair, a transit worker from Queens, was busy re-timing traffic lights for bicycle speed. "Riding your bike up or down the avenue, the traffic lights are going to change in sync," explained Blair. "You ride 10-15 miles per hour, and you'll be hitting all greens."

"Now that our country is taking its rightful place among the world's developed nations," said Mayor Bloomberg, "it is time for our greatest city to take its place among the world's great cities."

Bloomberg recently visited Paris to examine its popular public bicycle rental program. Although he initially expressed doubts as to whether it could work, public pressure has helped convince him it can, and national legislation sealed the deal. (For more on the new transportation initiatives, also see "Crumbling Infrastructure Brings Opportunities," Page A6.)

Blair, watching the dedication from a cherry picker above 9th Avenue commented, "From cesspool to world city, it's just fantastic. I love this place."

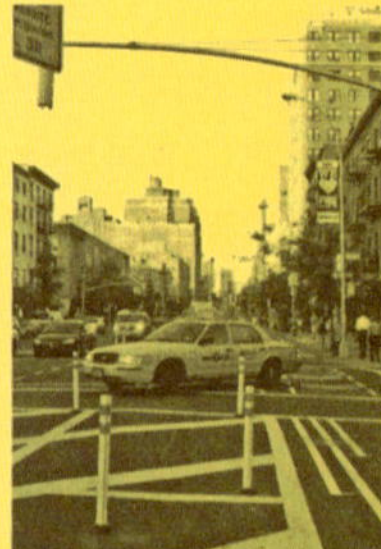

PAYTON CHUNG

University to Rescue Iraqi Scholars

By AMAL MAAMLAJI

The New School University in New York announced yesterday the launch of the New University In Exile, a program to provide small grants and visas to scholars from Iraq. The program is inspired by the University In Exile, a New School program that rescued over one hundred Jewish scholars from Nazi Germany beginning in 1933.

"As in World War II, scholarship today faces one particular crisis that dwarfs all others," said New School President Bob Kerrey. "In Iraq today, almost four hundred scholars have been assassinated, and most others have been sent into permanent exile. Iraq's universities, libraries, museums, and archeological sites have for the most part been completely destroyed. The scale of devastation places it among the worst tragedies in all history."

The New School will make available small grants to scholars, facilitate visas, and provide shared office space with New School faculty members.

Mr. Kerrey acknowledged that the program faced significant challenges. "The situation for Iraqi scholars today is even worse than for Jewish scholars in 1933, but it's our doing this time, and so the available funding is a whole lot less. It's psychologically easier to help people when one's tax dollars aren't instrumental in killing them, which is probably also why there's more concern for the victims of Darfur than of the much larger crises in Iraq or the Congo." But we've got to do what we can.

"While the academic riches of Iraq will never be restored, and its archaeological sites, museums, and libraries will remain a mere memory, the academic community must attempt to in some small measure make amends for what our country has done, and do what it can to save the scholarly heritage of a nation," Mr. Kerrey said.

The New School hopes to be joined in the effort by other universities anxious to live up to their stated ethical aims.

See also "Hope for Iraqi Refugees?" Page A13.

City Council Votes to Beat Swords Into Plowshares

R.O.T.C. Funding Reallocated to Organic Gardens for Youth

By ED SHARSNEK

NEW YORK — The New York City Council is scheduled to vote later this week on a measure that may finally close the doors on the City's Junior Reserve Officer Training Corps, following complaints by parents and teachers, and a recent spate of student walkouts.

Critics contend that the training corps, whose official mandate is educational, is a recruiting arm of the U.S. Army. They note that the J.R.O.T.C. provides no non-military training, and that the firearm training offered by 90 percent of the J.R.O.T.C. programs undermines the no-weapons policies widely promoted on high school campuses.

At Jesuit-run Xavier High School in Manhattan, 33 percent of students belong to the J.R.O.T.C. "It's the only gang the Fathers let us join," bubbled Senior Cadet Leader Bernard Goetz Jr. "But it's plenty good for me."

Not all the Jesuits support the program. Father Jon Sobrino, who supervises the school's ethics curriculum, said that the J.R.O.T.C. obedience training seemed to stunt some students' reasoning skills. "'Lock-and-load' is not a recognized ethical philosophy," Sobrino said.

With the end of the war in Iraq, concerns voiced for months at Parent Teacher Association meetings around the five boroughs received renewed urgency. "We are asking Secretary of Defense Scott Ritter to shift these funds into training programs in nonviolence and communication," Queens Borough P.T.A. head Estelle Chavez said. "If our leaders of the past eight years had had that sort of training, we wouldn't be in the huge mess we're in."

Retired General David Petraeus defended the program. The only way a volunteer army can recruit is if we can get them early. The fact is, it works. Plus, J.R.O.T.C. students who don't join the army tell us the leadership training they receive helps them find work in security and related fields."

Critics argue that those students who do go on to join the Army fare especially poorly. According to the Veterans Administration, veterans earn less than non-veterans; one-third of homeless men are veterans; and at least 10 percent of federal and state prisoners are veterans.

The City Council vote follows outrage by area principals over Mayor Bloomberg's proposal to cut $180 million from the Department of Education's budget in the current fiscal year, and $324 million in the following year, cuts which will most likely effect after school programs, arts programming, and programs for children with special needs.

One group of critics has been working with Schools Chancellor Joel I. Klein to redirect the $2 million J.R.O.T.C. budget to Urban Green, an after-school program that promotes environmental leadership for youth by creating organic gardens in vacant lots. Klein's office issued a memo yesterday acknowledging the effort. "Our office feels that the J.R.O.T.C. budget might best be redirected to what we might call Victory Gardens, in celebration of a new direction for our country and for our nation's youth."

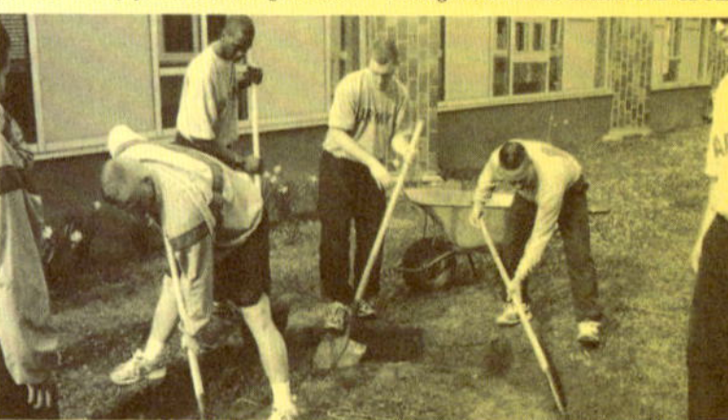

HERALDPOST

J.R.O.T.C. members-turned-gardeners, planting eggplant for the fall semester.

Streets Come Alive as Relief and Exuberance Greet End of Conflicts

By SCHUYLER FRANK

Thousands are already taking to the streets of Manhattan, mainly around Times Square, to celebrate the announced end to the wars in Iraq and Afghanistan. Police are responding by organizing water distribution centers and places to rest.

"We're all guaranteed the right to peaceably assemble," said New York City Police Commissioner Raymond W. Kelly. "Today, we're going to try responding the way police do in many other developed nations." In the past, New York City police have usually responded to demonstrations with forces in riot gear.

After pausing a moment Kelly added, "You know, everyone on the force, we're all just glad we're here to help celebrate peace this time."

The spontaneous street celebrations were the manner in which many first heard about the withdrawal. In Manhattan, as thousands thronged the city streets with Commissioner Kelly, only a few tuned in radios or checked news sites on the Internet. "I've just gotten overwhelmed by all the bad news, and I'm tired of learning that so much of what were told was lies," Linda Negrobi, 42, told The New York Times in Washington Square Park, which was full of revelers. "At some point or other, I just stopped watching the news."

Juan Villarosa, 18, agreed. "My brother was killed in combat last year in a war that never should have happened. You don't turn to Wolf Blitzer for answers in that situation," he said. The crowd at the uptown sandwich shop bubbled with conversation about America's new direction.

"People are saying hello to each other in the street. I just had lunch with a group of total strangers where we just talked about what's going on right now," said Carrie Moore, a photographer's assistant living in midtown. "It's like this huge stress has been lifted."

Makeshift signs were visible in office windows, among them: "Sleep with me"; "The end of our lives" with the V crossed out; and, simply, "YES."

The street celebrations were unusual in the preponderance of business suits and professional attire. One celebrant, Farsala LaRue, 72, speculated on the somber hues.

"This is an issue that affected us all, on a daily basis, for seven years," she said, pausing from a hopscotch game she was playing with her 7-year-old neighbor. "Not just the anti-war people, not just young people, not even just Democrats," she said. "All of America is here today. I think it's wonderful."

The New York Times

THOMAS J. FRIEDMAN

The End of the Experts?

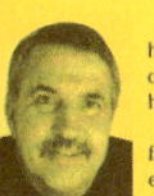

The sudden outbreak of peace in Iraq has made me realize, among other things, one incontestable fact: I have no business holding a pen, at least with intent to write.

I know, you're thinking I'm going too far. I haven't always been wrong about everything. I recently made some sense on global warming and what we needed to do about it, for instance.

But to have been so completely and fundamentally wrong about so huge a disaster as what we have done to Iraq — and ourselves — is outrageous enough to prove that people like me have no business posing as wise men, and, more importantly, that The New York Times has no business continuing to provide me with a national platform.

In any case, I have made a decision: as of today, I will no longer write in this or any other newspaper. I will immediately desist from writing any more books about how it's time for everyone to climb on board the globalization high-speed monorail to the future. I will keep my opinions to myself. (My wife suggested that I try not to even form opinions, but I think she might have another agenda.)

Baffled? I don't blame you. So I'll cite some facts to support my decision — a practice, I must admit, I have too seldom followed.

Let's start with the invasion itself. I was pretty much all for it. Mind you, I was not one of the pundits, reporters, or public figures who said that Saddam Hussein was a threat to the United States. I knew better — but I said it didn't matter!

Back in February of 2003, I wrote in this space: "Saddam does not threaten us today. He can be deterred. Taking him out is a war of choice — but it's a legitimate choice." In other words, we should invade a sovereign state and replace its government in order to remake the world more to our liking.

Now the simple fact is, an unprovoked attack on a sovereign state is a war crime, even when linked to grand ideas of the future of mankind. In fact, that's exactly what Hitler did, for exactly the same reasons. The Nuremburg War Crimes Tribunal called it the "the supreme international crime, differing only from other war crimes in that it contains within itself the accumulated evil of the whole."

What was I thinking? And more importantly, why didn't anyone stop me?

But wait, it gets worse. Having expressed how acceptable it was to commit Hitler's signature crime, I then applauded the invasion of Iraq as an "audacious roll of the dice." It should have occurred to me that this gamble would be unspeakably painful for an untold number of Iraqis who had done nothing to us — in other words, any of them.

Soon, when it became obvious that my pipe dreams for a peaceful and democratic subject nation were just that, I decided to say it was too soon to tell how things would turn out in Iraq, but that we would definitely know in six months to a year. I said this pretty much every six months for five years. And The Times just kept giving me more and more column-inches.

I'm not trying to beat myself up here. I've done that plenty already, believe me — and my wife has done the rest! But I have one question: why are newspapers like The New York Times letting people like me make fools of themselves, mislead the American people, and, worst of all, give their wives a lifetime of ammunition?

To err is human, but to print, reprint, and re-reprint error-mad humans like me is a criminally moronic editorial policy.

Nor, of course, is it only me. Just consider who populates the opinion pages of America's top newspapers. Bill Kristol, who was actually hired by The Times long after being proven wrong on Iraq. Charles Krauthammer. Robert Novak. Mona Charen. Fred Barnes. The list goes on and on of officially-approved wise men (and a woman or two) who never once doubted that Iraq had vast stockpiles of W.M.D.s. And that's just in newspapers.

We were all wrong again and again — and the consequences were devastating. Can anyone tell me why any of us should ever be asked, let alone paid, for our opinions ever again? Or, for that matter, why Richard Perle or Paul Wolfowitz should be allowed behind any sort of desk whatsoever as long as they live?

Peace in Iraq will undoubtedly have many far-reaching consequences. As promised, I'm not going to speculate publicly about what they might be.

Except one. As of today, I'm putting down my pen, to take up a screwdriver. I am going to retrain as an engineer and spend the rest of my life working to build non-carbon-based energy technologies. And I'm going to spend a lot of time washing my hands.

We Apologize

The momentous occasion of the end of the war in Iraq also marks a time for reflection at The Times. As many of our readers have pointed out for years, this newspaper played no small part in making the case for the war in the first place, and in supporting the costly and deadly U.S. occupation of Iraq for five years — long after public opinion had turned against it.

We have in the past acknowledged botched reporting. In May 2006, we published an editors' note acknowledging no fewer than nine articles that uncritically repeated erroneous claims about W.M.D.s by anonymous officials.

Those admissions, we realize, didn't go nearly far enough. Notably, we failed to single out the instrumental role that Times reporter Judith Miller played in bringing unfounded W.M.D. allegations to a national audience.

Miller's prominent stories hyping purported Iraqi weapons go back to 1998, and were full of dramatic but unverified claims and unreliable sources. "All of Iraq is one large storage facility" for W.M.D.s, she credulously quoted one source (September 8, 2002). Miller systematically played down skepticism and conflicting evidence, both of which were readily available to any reporter. In so doing Miller lent crucial support to the Bush administration's agenda. It took Miller's involvement in the vengeful leak of a C.I.A. officer's name before we finally let her go — with a hefty severance package.

Even after this episode, we continued publishing articles based on claims by anonymous officials advancing unverified claims — this time, against Iran.

As for our opinion pages, what we passed off as "debates" on the Iraq war have consistently excluded the views of people with a track record of being right. Conversely, in January 2008, we boosted Bill Kristol's already considerable national platform by offering him a regular column. It is hard to say why.

As early as 1997, Kristol had penned a Weekly Standard cover story, "Saddam Must Go," in which he and contributing editor Robert Kagan called for war against Iraq: "We know it seems unthinkable to propose another ground attack to take Baghdad. But it's time to start thinking the unthinkable." They argued that Saddam Hussein had humiliated the United States by expelling U.S. officials from U.N. weapons inspection teams. The editorial cited unspecified sources about Iraq's chemical and biological weapons capabilities, and concluded with this dark warning: "If you don't like this option, we've got another one for you: continue along the present course and get ready for the day when Saddam has biological and chemical weapons at the tips of missiles aimed at Israel and at American forces in the Gulf. That day may not be far off."

Why did we decide to reward Kristol for having been utterly — and lethally — wrong on Iraq? We can't say for sure, but as of yesterday Mr. Kristol has been terminated as a columnist at The Times. In the same spirit, we also welcome Thomas Friedman's resignation.

Beginning today, you will see a giant overhaul of our paper, from the front page to this page, as, belatedly shouldering our responsibilities as the newspaper of record, we make a practice of hiring writers who get it right.

Hope for Iraqi Refugees?

One of the many terrible consequences of the Iraq war has been the displacement of millions of Iraqis since the Iraq War began in March 2003. According to the most recent statistics from the United Nations High Commissioner for Refugees, more than two million Iraqis have fled to neighboring Syria, Jordan, Turkey and Lebanon, as well as Australia and Europe, and another 2.5 million or more have been displaced within the country, most of them between 2006 and 2008.

These numbers are staggering. If a similar proportion of the U.S. population were displaced, that would mean 30 million refugee Americans.

The Iraqi refugee crisis is the worst in the history of the Middle East. The number of refugees surpasses the number of Palestinians displaced in 1948 by a factor of at least four. And while in 1948 the international community and the United Nations established entities to provide refugees with the bare minimum of education and aid, the response to the Iraqi refugee problem has been seriously inadequate on all levels. Many women have been forced into prostitution, and many children have no educational opportunities.

Among the displaced are most of the doctors, teachers, nurses, and educated professionals who formed the basic fabric of Iraqi society and are an integral building block of any reconstruction effort. Iraq's recovery, which will take a few decades at best, will be impossible without the return of these citizens.

The Bush administration ignored this disaster, as to acknowledge it would have been an admission of its role in creating it. The number of Iraqis so far granted asylum in the U.S. is still less than that accepted by Sodertalje, a village in Sweden, as reported recently in the Washington Post.

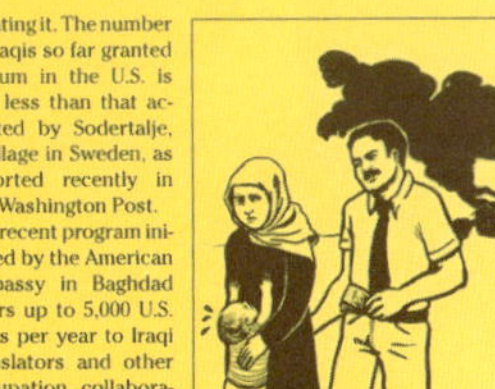

RICHARD SORGE

A recent program initiated by the American Embassy in Baghdad offers up to 5,000 U.S. visas per year to Iraqi translators and other occupation collaborators. But high-ranking U.S. officials do not believe that this allowance can cover even direct employees of the American Embassy itself, let alone of other occupation entities such as Halliburton, Bechtel, and the U.S. Armed Forces.

Now that the war is over, no one can afford to neglect Iraqi refugees, and a serious and comprehensive plan to resettle them must be a priority for the new administration. The Evangelicals' generosity is terrific (see "Evangelical Churches Announce Policy of Sanctuary for Iraqi Refugees," Page A7), but what is really needed is a major policy change.

From the Editors

Two years ago, who would have dared to image we'd elect, as President of the United States, an African-American community organizer?

Six months ago, who would have predicted we'd enact universal health care, reform our education system, establish a maximum wage and "true cost" tax, and start taking steps to make our cities more livable — or that we'd so swiftly end the war in Iraq, and try for treason the leaders who took us there?

Yet we've done all that. Although we demanded change of Barack Obama, we understood that only we could bring about that change. And that's why it happened.

Of course even with all these victories, we can't let up for a second, and we can't get tired. But if there's one thing we've learned in the past two years, it's that the most restful, energizing thing we can do is fight for a better world.

See the fine print on page A2 for a few ways to do that.

Lobbyists Are Citizens Too

You won't read many stories critical of the recently-passed "Ban on Lobbying" bill, H.R. 27865, whether in this newspaper or any other media outlet. Lobbyists have been treated as pariahs by the press, by both candidates in the latest elections, and in popular culture. They have been called "the root of the problem" in Washington, and much worse. The newly proposed ban on capital punishment even has a temporary exemption clause — for lobbyists!

As a lobbyist I vehemently object to this treatment.

Let me remind you of something. We are people. We are citizens. All U.S. citizens are guaranteed the right to petition the government for redress of grievances; nowhere in our founding documents does it say those citizens can't be well paid to do so.

We have worked closely with most politicians — including both Barack Obama and John McCain. What lobbyists do is figure out how to sway politicians to vote on legislation in a way that favors the interest they represent. They educate and inform members of Congress on issues that will come before them for a vote. Much of the information provided to elected officials by lobbyists cannot be found in any library or newspaper, nor in any way whatsoever... except from the lobbyists themselves. This is what makes us indispensable.

It is indeed true that our services are only available to those who can afford them, and it's true that on any issue, both sides can't always afford the same things. But that's exactly where the problem lies. The problem isn't lobbyists, it's a lack of sufficient money in Washington.

For example, the top five spenders among mortgage bankers and brokers invested more than $31 million on lobbying and campaign contributions during the past election cycle. With the help of us lobbyists, the financial services industry successfully stopped the government from regulating the frenzy of borrowing and buying during the housing boom, a frenzy that enriched hundreds.

Lobbyists were also successful in preventing Congress from taking steps to help families keep their homes despite an inability to repay their mortgages — which would have hurt bankers and brokers.

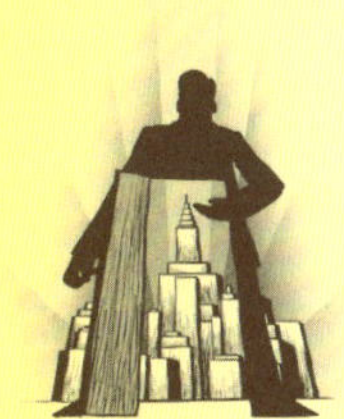

But we lobbyists would be more than willing to work for whomsoever could afford us. That is why Congress needs to grant first-time homeowners, indigenous peoples, the urban poor, recent immigrants, working-class families, and other embattled groups enough funding to compete for our services against those with opposite interests.

We lobbyists have been willing to comply with the rules and laws that Congress adopts. For example, the Fair Elections Now Act (S.1285), which mandated that candidates for Senate run on public funding only, made our role nearly irrelevant in those races. We fought against that legislation with all the influence we had, but we lost, and we accepted our loss. We did not attempt a coup.

If Congress passes the "Ban on Lobbying" bill, we will likewise comply with it, though not without a fight. Because the "Ban on Lobbying" bill is not only unfair, it is wrongheaded.

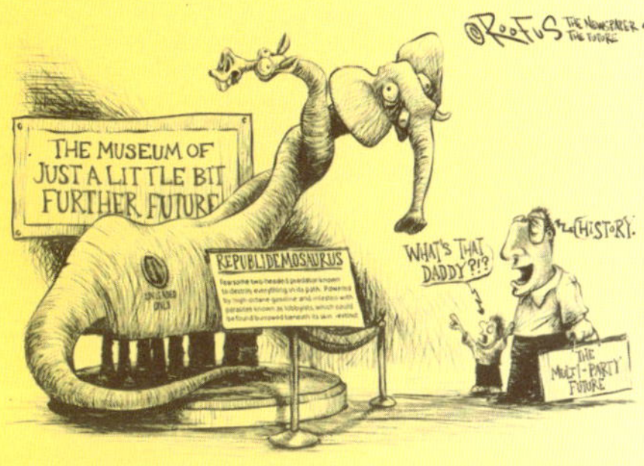

©RooFuS THE NEWSPAPER OF THE FUTURE

A Baboon Study Remembered

While thinking about the recent changes in this country, I recalled an article by Robert M. Sapolsky (in Foreign Affairs, January 2006), who lived for a while among a troop of baboons in the wild, and witnessed a remarkable transformation.

Forest Troop was initially composed of a regular mixture of baboons: gentle ones, mean ones, and a few in-between. One day, a nearby hotel expanded its garbage dump, and another troop of baboons claimed the dump as territory and primary food source. Forest Troop's meaner males (let's call them Clique W) decided they would raid this exciting new resource, even if that meant beating up a number of the newly obese males from the garbage dump troop.

After feasting on the other troop's half-rotten hamburgers for a while, Clique W got what was coming to them and died of food-borne tuberculosis. All that remained in Forest Troop were females and nice males. And even today, at fifteen years after all the original docile males died of old age, Forest Troop remains a gentle culture, much more welcoming to new members, with a lot less fighting and a lot more cooperation, and a lot more playing with each other's hair, even among adult males. And new members quickly learn that things are different in Forest Troop.

Until very recently, we in this country couldn't imagine life without the aggressive baboons who, by hook and by crook (mostly by crook), were dominating our politics. But then one day, those baboons ate out of the garbage dump of a deeply mad foreign policy, and quickly killed themselves off.

We are not baboons, of course. For one thing, no microbes killed off our jerks; rather, we nicer folks did it. For another, the resource-hunting adventures of our own hostile males didn't result in just a few dinged-up fat guys, but rather one million dead and four and a half million refugees.

Another key difference between us and Forest Troop may be that in our case, it wasn't enough to rid ourselves of some of the creep baboons at the top. A lot of the supposedly gentler ones voted for war as well. Rather, right after the elections, and for many months after, we had to keep pushing with all our might to make sure that everyone, at all levels of power, understood that America would now be a culture of peace and generosity.

Fortunately, that's just what we did. And though human nature hasn't changed, nor the nature of politics, we've made our desires so clear that there is now no more room in Forest Troop U.S.A. for the garbage adventuring that dominated our last thirty years.

Letters to the Editor

To the Editor:

Re "Viva Free Trade with Cuba!" Page A6, July 2, 2009.

In addition to the benefits from ending the embargo on Cuba listed by your reporter (family visits for some of us, fabulous cigars for all of us, and affordable vacations that include the rental of vintage red Thunderbird convertibles), there is one more that went unmentioned: world-class public health medical schools.

In contrast to the United States, where students have been learning what the biotech, medical engineering, and pharmaceutical companies want them to learn, Cuba's medical schools will be a natural destination for the new crop of medical students who will be the foot soldiers of our country's shift to universal health care.

Your readers may remember that in 1998, following the public health emergencies occasioned by severe hurricanes, Fidel Castro offered free medical education for low-income students from anywhere in the Americas, including the United States. Since then, the Latin American School of Medicine has become the world's largest medical school and has graduated tens of thousands of students.

At a time when the mortality rate in the U.S. has been rising, and the average U.S. lifespan declining, the lifting of the Cuba embargo provides an invaluable opportunity to partner with the world expert on training doctors in inexpensive, preventative treatments for common illnesses. Cuba will be the perfect partner for training the doctors who will revolutionize health care in this country.

MEREDITH KOHR
Miami, Fla., July 3, 2009

▪

To the Editor:

Here at the nursing home we've all been glued to the TV set watching the withdrawal from Iraq. For as long as I remember, in all my 93 years, war has been all around me. My grandfather fell as a Rough Rider during the Spanish-American War, my mother and father served in World War I (my mother as a nurse). And I grew up a military brat, moving from base to base. When I met him, my second husband was the most active American Legion Post director you'd ever hope to meet!

So I feel slightly lost in this new world of peace. But I'm glad to leave behind the military lingo, uniforms, and sacrafices. Can I get used to it? Can I really attend my great-grandson's graduation without worrying if I'll see him live to 24? Should I go ahead and tell my niece that even though I'm not sure I fully approve, that if I ask, she can tell?

I suppose I'll adjust to this strange new environment.

RUTH PRINCIPE
Summit, N.J., July 2, 2009

New York Times Special Edition, Yes Men, 2008

The Yes Men are an activist-duo consisting of Andy Bichlbaum and Mike Bonanno.

IF YOU CAN'T HACK 'EM, ABSORB 'EM, OR THE ENDLESS DANCE OF THE CORPORATE REVOLUTION

TATIANA BAZZICHELLI

What were once the values and philosophy of the hacker ethic has become the domain of business companies contributing to the development of Web 2.0 and the notion of social media. According to Steven Levy, the first to use the term, the hacker ethic was a "new way of life, with a philosophy, an ethic and a dream".[1] With its own language and rules, and its own representative community, its roots go back to the 1950s and 1960s, crossing the activity of the hackers at the Massachusetts Institute of Technology (MIT), and in the 1970s, the rise of the sharing computer culture in California (well represented by the Community Memory Project in Berkeley and the Homebrew Computer Club in Silicon Valley). Embracing the ideas of sharing, openness, decentralisation, free access to computers, world improvement and the hands-on imperative (Levy 1984), the hacker ethic has been a fertile imaginary for many European hackers as well, who started to connect through BBSes in the 1980s.

At first glance it may seem evident that business enterprises in social networking and Web 2.0 built their corporate image by re-appropriating the language and the values of the first phase of hacker culture – a language once very representative of certain networking art practices as well, from mail art to net.art. Tim O'Reilly, one of the main promoters of the Web 2.0 philosophy, and organiser of the first Web 2.0 conference in 2004 (San Francisco), wrote in the autumn of 2006: "Web 2.0 is much more than just pasting a new user interface onto an old application. It's a way of thinking, a new perspective on the entire business of software."[2] However, both what has been called Web 2.0 since 2004 (when Dale Dougherty came up with the term during a brainstorming session) as well as the whole idea of 'folksonomy' which lies behind social networking, blogging, and tagging, are nothing new.

According to the software developer and venture communist Dmytri Kleiner, these forms of business are just a mirror of the economic co-optation of values of sharing, participation and networking which inspired the early formation of hacker culture and peer2peer technology. As he pointed out during a panel at the Chaos Communication Congress in Berlin in 2007, "the whole point of Web 2.0 is to achieve some of the promises of peer2peer technology but in a centralised way; using web servers and centralised technologies to create user content and folksonomy, but without actually letting the users control the technology itself."[3] But even if the Web 2.0 business enterprises do not hide their function as data aggregators, they make openness, user generated content and networking collaboration their main core strategies. The user contribution becomes a key to market dominance. Google was one of the first companies to base its business in involving users to give productive feedback, releasing beta versions of its applications, such as Gmail for example, to be tested by users without being formally part of the production process.

This idea of 'perpetual beta' (O'Reilly 2006) was well anticipated by the 'bazaar method' of Eric S. Raymond (1999), as the capability to create software and other products of intelligence and creativity through the collaboration of a community of individuals acting to make communication channels open. Raymond's well-known essay 'The Cathedral and the Bazaar' is obvious support of the open source 'cause' (Raymond is co-founder of the Open Source Initiative) but also an apology for greater involvement in the free market.[4] His metaphor juxtaposes the methodology of open source and its deterritorialisation of development (the bazaar method) to the one of free software, often developed in laboratories or closed groups of programmers (the cathedral). This text, considered controversial by many hackers for being heavily negative towards the work of the Free Software Foundation, created a shift from the idea of open source (as user rights of free infrastructures, well explained by the Free Software Definition and the Open Source Definition), to the model of networked collaboration, "not only referring to computer programs, but evoking broader cultural connotations" (Cramer 2006). By shifting the target from users to producers, this vision focuses more on business opportunities than on an ethical idea of software distribution. It makes open source more a branding exercise than a philosophy, moving away from the emphasis on freedom and rights for users stressed by the free software movement – the same conceptual trick used by the Creative Commons initiative, as Anna Nimus (aka Joanne Richardson and Dmytri Kleiner)[5] and Florian Cramer pointed out in 2006.[6]

A predictable consequence of Raymond's networking vision emerges when O'Reilly, involved since the early days of the Open Source Initiative, openly refers to what he calls the "open source paradigm shift", showing the business advantages in building applications on top of open source software. This shift implies the idea of building modular architecture to allow cooperating programmes, encouraging Internet-enabled collaborative development, having users as co-contributors, and creating viral distribution and marketing (O'Reilly 2007). The idea of applying collaborative software development in Web 2.0 companies therefore, becomes a strategic business advantage without stressing the accent on the rights of users and making life easier for producers, with subsequent decreases in costs. Many companies have adopted the bazaar method and the open source built-in communities model, from IBM, Google, Apple and Facebook, to Creative Commons and Wikipedia.

Writing about the problem of intellectual property and the producer-consumer dichotomy that the CC licenses fail to resolve, Nimus pointed out:

> What began as a movement for the abolition of intellectual property has become a movement of customizing [sic] owners' licenses. Almost without notice, what was once a very threatening movement of radicals, hackers and pirates is now the domain of reformists, revisionists, and apologists for capitalism. When capital is threatened, it co-opts its opposition.[7]

This shift of the hacker principles of openness and collaboration into commercial purposes is the mirror of a broader phenomenon. We are facing a progressive commercialisation of contexts of software development and sharing, which want to appear open and progressive (highly emblematic is Google's claim "Don't be evil"), but which are indeed transforming the meaning of communities and networking, and the battle for information rights, placing it within the boundaries of the marketplace. The artistic works of Aaron Koblin, based on crowdsourcing and the Amazon Mechanical Turk, are good examples of this phenomenon of the aestheticisation of networking practices, which become part of the business field.[8]

Like Google, many social networking platforms try to leave an image of themselves as 'a force for good'.[9] At the same time, the free software community is not alien to this progressive corporate takeover of the hacker counterculture. Google organises the Summer of Code festival every year to get the best hackers and developers to work for the company.[10] It encourages open source development, supports the development of Firefox and funds hackerspaces – i.e. the Hacker Dojo in Mountain View. Ubuntu One, an online backup and synchronisation utility, uses Amazon S3 as its

storage and transfer facility – while the Free Software Foundation bases its GNewSense, a free software GNU/Linux distribution, on Ubuntu.[11] This ambiguity of values, which is contributing to the end of the time of digital utopias, is described well by Matteo Pasquinelli: "a parasite is haunting the hacker haunting the world" (2008), analysing the contemporary exploitation of the rhetoric of free culture, and the collapse of the 'digitalism' ideology, corroded by the 'parasite' of cognitive capitalism.[12]

However, there are other possibilities for analysing the matter, which once again could probably open a field of action for artists and activists. The question is whether the co-optation theory of the counterculture might be the right explanation to understand the present development, or better, implosion, of the hacker and networking culture. Thomas Frank's *The Conquest of Cool* (1997) and Fred Turner's *From Counterculture to Cyberculture* (2007) may point the way; both books analyse how the endless cycles of rebellion and transgression are very well mixed with the development of business culture in Western society – specifically in the US. As Thomas Frank suggests;

In the late 1950s and early 1960s, leaders of the advertising and menswear businesses developed a critique of their own industries, of over-organisation [sic] and creative dullness, that had much in common with the critique of mass society which gave rise to the counterculture. The 1960s was the era of Vietnam, but it was also the high watermark of American prosperity and a time of fantastic ferment in managerial thought and corporate practice. But business history has been largely ignored in accounts of the cultural upheaval of the 1960s. This is unfortunate, because at the heart of every interpretation of the counterculture is a very particular – and very questionable – understanding of corporate ideology and of business practice.[13]

The American counterculture of the 1960s was very much based in mass culture, promoting "a glorious cultural flowering, though it quickly became mainstream itself" (Frank 1997) and becoming attractive for corporations from Coca Cola to Nike, but also for IBM and Apple.

Fred Turner explains how the rise of cyberculture utopias is strongly connected with the development of the computer business in Silicon Valley, as the background of the Whole Earth network by Stewart Brand and the magazine *Wired* demonstrate.[14] It should not surprise anyone today that Google is adopting the same strategy of getting close to counterculture – hackers, burners at Burning Man, etc. – because many hackers in California were already close to the development of the business we face today. The cyber-utopias of the 1980s and 1990s were pushed by the market as well, and they were very well connected with its development. Turner demonstrates how the image of the authentic counterculture of the 1960s, antithetical to the technologies, and later co-opted by the forces it opposed, is actually the shadow of another version of history. A history which instead has its roots in a "new cybernetic rhetoric of systems and information" born already in the research laboratories of World War II in which scientists and engineers "began to imagine institutions as living organisms, social networks as webs of information" (Turner 2007). Once again, with Web 2.0 enterprises, we are facing the same phenomenon.

Accepting that the digital utopias of the 1980s and 1990s have never been completely extraneous to business practices, might be an invitation for artists and hackers to subvert the false idea of 'real' counterculture, and to start analysing how the cyclic business trends work, and what they culturally represent. Analysing how the hacker culture became functional to accelerate capitalism, as it happened for the youth movement of the 1960s, might

change the point of view and the area of criticism. The statement "if you can't beat 'em, absorb 'em" could be reversed by the artists and hackers themselves. If hackers and activists can't avoid indirectly serving corporate revolutions, they should work on absorbing the business ideology for their own advantage, and consequently, transforming it and hacking it. A possible tendency might not just be refusing business, but re-appropriating its philosophy, making it functional for our purposes. Some artists are already working in this way, creating art projects that deal with business and which subvert its strategies, such as The People Speak (*Planetary Pledge Pyramid* 2009), or Alexei Shulgin (*Electroboutique* 2007), UBERMORGEN.COM (*Google Will Eat Itself* 2005, and *Amazon Noir* 2006), both created with Paolo Cirio and Alessandro Ludovico (*The Sound of Ebay* 2008), and the community of Seripica Naro (2005), just to mention a few.[15]

Even if it is easy to recognise co-optation as a cyclic business strategy among hackers and activists, it takes more effort to accept that business has often been part of counterculture and cultural development. In this phase of ambiguity, it is fundamental to look back to analyse the reasons for the shift in networking paradigms and hacker values, but it is also necessary to break some cultural taboos and avoid dualistic oppositions. Artists should try to work like viruses to stretch the limits of business enterprises, and hack the meaning of business itself. Instead of refusing to compromise with commercial platforms, they should try to put their hands on them, to reveal hidden mechanisms of social inclusion and exclusion, and to develop a critique of the medium itself. Once again adopting the hands-on strategy of the hacker, hacktivists should directly face the economy that has made these strategies its core business.

1. Levy, S. *Hackers: Heroes of the Computer Revolution*. New York: Penguin, 1984.
2. Musser, J, O'Reilly, T and O'Reilly Radar Team. "Web 2.0: Principles and Best Practices." *O'Reilly Radar* Autumn 2006 <http://oreilly.com/catalog/web2report/chapter/web20_report_excerpt.pdf>.
3. Panel with Kleiner, D, Mars, M, Prug, T and Medak, T. "Hacking Ideologies, part 2: Open Source, a capitalist movement." *24th Chaos Communication Congress*. bcc Berliner Congress Center, Berlin. 23 Nov 2007 <http://chaosradio.ccc.de/24c3_m4v_2311.html>.
4. Raymond, E. "The Cathedral & the Bazaar." *O'Reilly* 2000 [1999] <http://www.catb.org/~esr/writings/cathedral-bazaar/cathedral-bazaar>.
5. Nimus, A. "Copyright, Copyleft and the Creative Anti-Commons." *Subsol* 2006 <http://subsol.c3.hu/subsol_2/contributors0/nimustext.html>.
6. Cramer, F. "The Creative Common Misunderstanding." *nettime* 2006 <http://www.nettime.org/Lists-Archives/nettime-l-0610/msg00025.html>.
7. Nimus, A. "Copyright, Copyleft and the Creative Anti-Commons." *Subsol* 2006 <http://subsol.c3.hu/subsol_2/contributors0/nimustext.html>.
8. Aaron Koblin <http://www.aaronkoblin.com>.
9. Panel with Fry, S. Stone, B and Hoffman, R. "Social Media – A Force for Good." *Silicon Valley Comes to the UK*, Cambridge University. 19 Nov 2009 <http://www.stephenfry.com/2009/11/19/social-media-force-for-good>.
10. Google Summer of Code <http://code.google.com/soc>.
11. As Florian Cramer made me notice, discussing Ubuntu in private e-mail correspondence.
12. Pasquinelli, M. *Animal Spirits. A Bestiary of the Commons*. Amsterdam: Institute of Network Cultures, 2008.
13. Frank, T. *The Conquest of Cool. Business Culture, Counterculture, and the Rise of Hip Consumerism*. Chicago: Chicago University Press, 1997.
14. Turner, F. *From Counterculture to Cyberculture. Stewart Brand, The Whole Earth Network, and the Rise of Digital Utopianism*. Chicago: Chicago University Press, 2007.
15. Respectively: <http://www.pledgepyramid.org>; <http://electroboutique.com>; <http://gwei.org>; <http://www.amazon-noir.com>; <http://www.sound-of-ebay.com>; <http://www.serpicanaro.com>.

Tatiana Bazzichelli is a communication sociologist, currently undertaking PhD research at Aarhus University, Denmark, on the evolution of social networking.

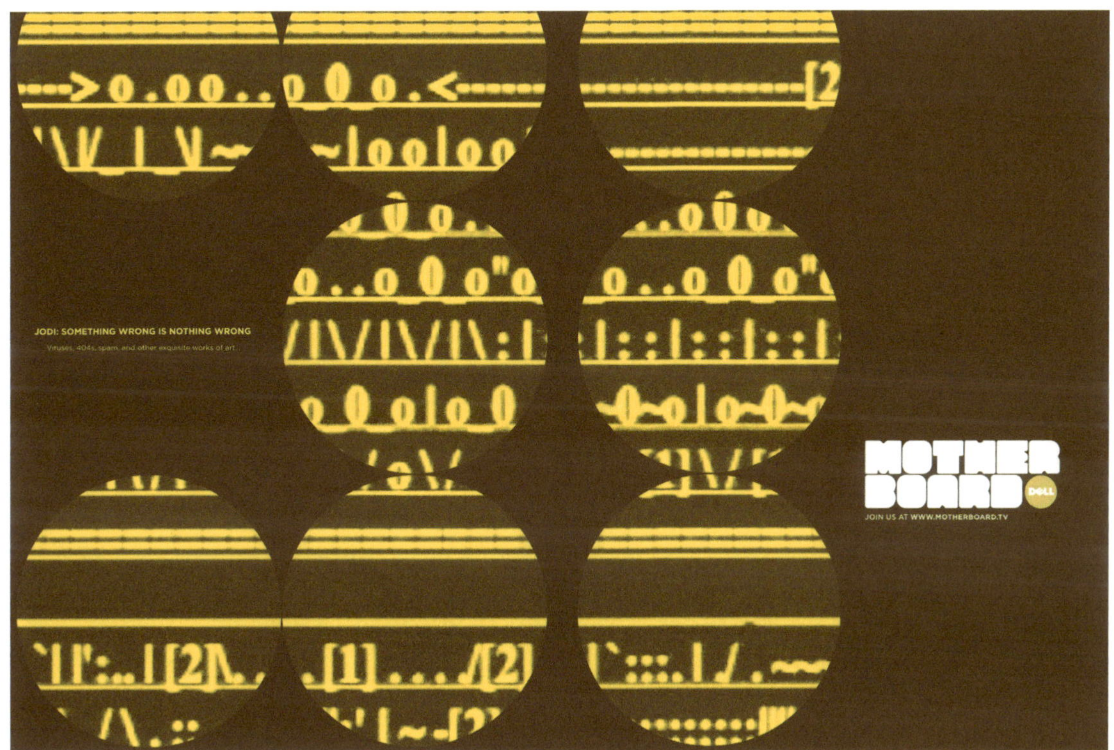

Something Wrong is Nothing Wrong,
JODI and Adam Mignanelli, 2010
Courtesy VICE

JODI: Something Wrong is Nothing Wrong, Ad by Motherboard TV (DELL). The image, published in VICE magazine Vol 7 Nr 2 (2010), is an advertisement for the social networking platform Motherboard TV, sponsored by DELL. Those familiar with digital culture will immediately recognize something else. The advertisement shows a reconstruction of the homepage http://wwwwww.jodi.org, a work by the Dutch artists JODI, a very well known symbol of early net.art. The advertisement, branded by DELL, might also be a symbol of something more as my article explores.

Что дѣлать?

Наболѣвшіе вопросы нашего движенія

Н. ЛЕНИНА.

…„Партійная борьба придаетъ партіи силу и жизненность, величайшимъ доказательствомъ слабости партіи является ея расплывчатость и притупленіе рѣзко обозначенныхъ границъ, партія укрѣпляется тѣмъ, что очищаетъ себя“… (Изъ письма Лассаля къ Марксу отъ 24 іюня 1852 г.).

Цѣна 1 руб.
Preis 2 Mark = 2.50 Francs.

STUTTGART
Verlag von J. H. W. Dietz Nachf. (G. m. b. H.)
1902

Chto dielat'? Nabolievshie voprosy nashego dvizheniia.
Stuttgart, 1902
Courtesy of British Library

RECUPERATOR/ RECUPERATED 6 PIRATBYRÅN

We have always followed the way of Kopimi, the will to be copied, which flips the question of recuperation around.[1] It is 'we' that recuperate 'them'. If you think like a hacker, the more advanced the media industry makes things, the better the hacks will be. The iPhone is super advanced, which means a jailbreak of the iPhone gives you a great device. Same thing with Despotify, the software that made it possible to save tracks from Spotify, the music industry streaming service.

Really, I don't think recuperation is such a big problem. It's good if it happens, because then you can advance one more step. The worst that can happen is if you are stuck in the same problem, repeating the same conflicts. And given that innovation happens at the edges of the network, the more the complex hierarchical organisations of the industry try to move in the direction of the network, the better it is. Because the internet will always be faster and further than what they do. If they try to recuperate what we do it only means that we have a better platform to work on and that the problem becomes more advanced, that is, filled with more potentiality.

I am also simplifying things here by talking about us and them, systems and mainstreams. Lately, we have instead been thinking in terms of tunnels. Large and small, temporary or reinforced, with connections to each other. This is what the internet is, a system of tunnels, there is no surface or centre. And you can extend this logic to things outside the net as well. For example, in the last years, we stopped considering the EU to be a system which sends out laws, and instead a system of bureaucratic, legal, communication systems and discursive tunnels that are surprisingly open. Sometimes you have to dig a bit, but it is completely possible to enter into these processes and start working on them instead of seeing it as an abstraction that you can only be for or against. This should be done with the cultural industries as well, by whoever has the means and time, to discover that they are in fact assembled as societies with different parts that can be disconnected and modulated. In relation to what we do, some activities amplify the effect of it, some neutralise it, some straightforwardly try to attack it, but they can also be turned against one another.

We don't feel that we have to protect our ideas and activities from recuperation because the essence of what we are is not a position but a movement. A way of moving and traversing different political issues.

All projects are events and movement. So the question is how these events interact with different parts of activist, capitalist and cultural logics. This can only be answered by experimentation.

1. kopimi (pronounced, and sometimes also spelled *copyme*) is the opposite of copyright, specifically encouraging that the work be copied-for any purpose, commercial or non-commercial.

Piratbyrån** (The Bureau of Piracy) **describes itself as a 'conversation' about the technological, the artistic to the political.
www.piratbyran.org

CIRCULAR LOGIC

/

SOME THOUGHTS AROUND CRAFTIVISM

GLENN ADAMSON

Craft + Activism = Craftivism
Concept Store invited Glenn Adamson and Ele Carpenter to offer their opinions on the recent Craftivism trend.

In 2004, a group operating under the name Cast Off – described by one journalist as a "coalition of militant knitters" – congregated on the Circle Line on London's underground, equipped with needles and balls of yarn.[1] To the bemusement of fellow riders they settled in and started to work, swapping tips and gossip as their socks and mittens and scarves took form, stitch by stitch.

As its name implies, the Circle Line is without terminal points. It goes round and round the city until the tube closes for the night. It was a pragmatic choice – people could join in or depart as was geographically convenient – but also a symbolically apt one. Like many contemporary DIY groups, the question lurking behind Cast Off's activities is well expressed by the title of the old American hymn: 'Will The Circle Be Unbroken?'[2] The instinct that lies behind an activity like this one is tacitly political (Cast Off sometimes engage in more overtly activist projects, carrying banners with slogans like 'drop stitches, not bombs') but also historical. In their simple act of knitting, there is an attempt to disconnect from the confusions and conflicts of the present. Even when sitting on the rumbling modern machinery of London's transport system, craft provides a connection to something remote, small-scale and reassuringly slow. For each knitter this yearning to touch the past may well have a biographical aspect. (Many crafters have a story about learning from an older relation – ideally a grandmother.)[3] But the maneuver is also easily understood according to the calculus of 'retro' hipness. Much like a musical style, a hairdo, or a trouser leg cut, it is only when a skill has gone way out of fashion that adopting it can seem cool again.[4]

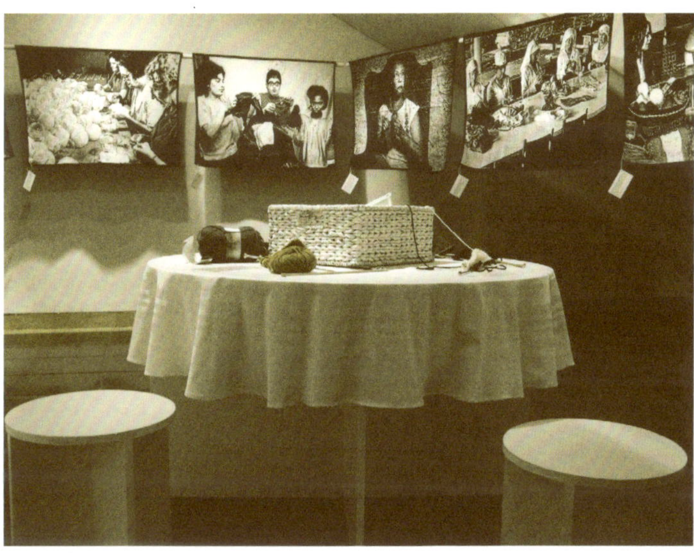

Wartime Knitting Circle, Sabrina Gschwandtner, 2007
Courtesy Sabrina Gschwandtner and the Museum of Arts & Design, New York
Photograph Alan Klein

The knitting circle has another symbolic meaning too, for craft and enclosure seem to go together. Both imply continuity, and also self-sufficiency. One thinks of the covered wagons of the American frontier, circling for protection at night, or (in a more pointed mode) the monumental triangular palisade of craft that is Judy Chicago's *Dinner Party*. Both of these examples are about creating a safe space to inhabit by keeping something else out: hostile Native Americans, narratives of masculine dominance. For Cast Off and their many kindred organisations in the contemporary DIY movement, what is held at bay, seemingly, is the otherwise pervasive rush of mass-produced capitalist commodities.

This is at best a provisional tactic, though: there are many ways to puncture the knitting circle's seeming independence and authenticity. Let's start, as crafters themselves might, with the question of materiality. Those needles, that yarn: where do they come from? Some DIYers actually do fashion their tools from a sustainable grove of backyard

bamboo, and source yarns locally (some even clip, card, and spin their wool themselves). But for most people who do it, DIY is not so pure. Knitting a jumper by hand rather than buying one at Gap may seem a way of dropping out, but in reality it is simply a shift from one commodity framework to another. The craft industry is a vast capitalist enterprise in its own right, which profits not only through the sale of tools and 'raw' materials (which, needless to say, are often very much processed), but also 'how-to' instructional kits, patterns, magazines, books, videos, and innumerable other aids to the hobbyist. And it's not just the physical accoutrements of DIY that are furnished by the corporations that crafters so dislike. Even the grandmotherly, homespun rhetoric of the scene is arguably modelled on sales techniques developed and mastered by yarn companies long ago.

Things become more complex when we look at political protest art in the DIY mode, or 'craftivism', of which there is an increasing amount. We are experiencing the return of explicit political ideology to craft, not seen since the days of hippies and the *Whole Earth Catalogue*. I have been particularly struck by one motif that runs through much of this work: pink yarn. An iconic example is the collaborative work led by the Danish artist Marianne Jørgensen, in which a network of knitters were asked to contribute small pink squares which the artist then fashioned into what can only be called a tank cosy. Similarly, for her MFA show at the California College of Art, the young queer crafter Lacey Jane Roberts used the material to cover a barbed wire fence, while Canadian artist Barb Hunt employs pink yarn to create a knitted landscape of antipersonnel ordnance as a protest against unexploded land mines around the world. We might understand such art projects as a new spin on a familiar story: the appropriation of marginalised craft to raise the voice of protest. It's another joining of a circle. Pink yarn, a product once confined mainly to the shelves of DIY stores, has been repurposed. It now speaks not of suburban sentimentality, but rather Feminist conviction, ironic chic and childlike delight. It is our moment's macramé, the expression of our very own 21st Century folk revival.

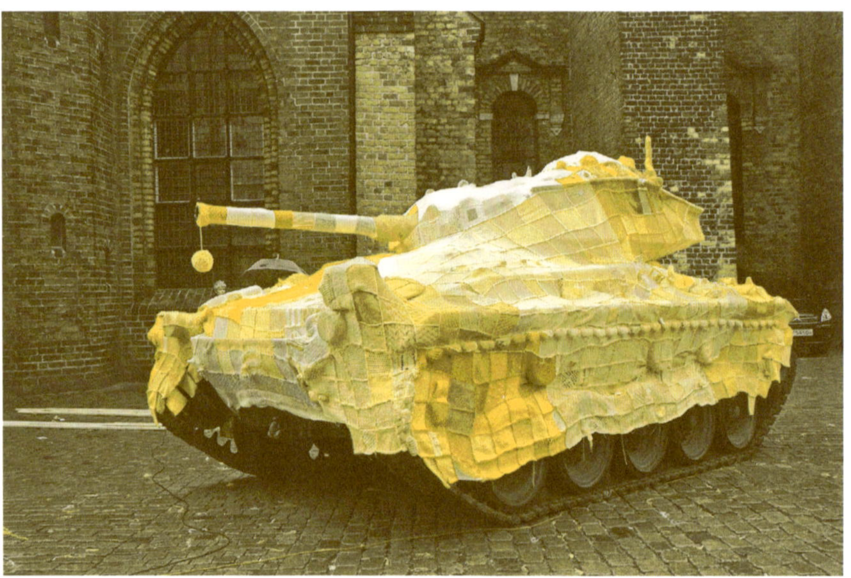

Pink M.24 Chaffee, Marianne Jørgenson, Copenhagen, 2006
Courtesy the artist

Should we object to political artworks made from pink yarn (or other currently fashionable media such as low-fired clay, sequins and such), which tend to operate on the assumption that colour and material are adequate signifiers of women's (or queer) identity and authentic political expression? There is something worryingly retrograde about such ideas. But we might come to a different conclusion if we lift our eyes from

the clicking needles, and instead meet the gaze of the people sitting across from us. This is essentially what all these artists are trying to do, each in their own way, and the same is true of many of their 'craftivist' peers.

Sabrina Gschwandtner's 2007 installation *Wartime Knitting Circle* is particularly explicit and effective in this regard. Gschwandtner is practically a craft industry in her own right: author of a book called *KnitKnit*, based on an occasional journal that she edits of the same title, she also makes films, writes penetrating critical analyses of DIY, and keeps up an active online presence.[5] What distinguishes her *Wartime Knitting Circle* from its often-hectoring counterparts in the craftivist art movement is its lack of dogmatism. The idea is simple: people sit around a table, knitting useful military equipment such as balaclavas and squares for blankets, much as women on the home front were encouraged to do during the First and Second World Wars. The perimeter of the installation is defined by a set of blankets, machine-knitted, based on archival photos of people doing just that. In these charged surroundings, participants are encouraged, gently, to talk about war. Gschwandtner prescribed no political position. People could choose to make mittens to a pattern devised by artist Lisa Anne Auerbach, in which the current body count of the Iraq War is used as a decorative feature; or they could actually support the war effort, perhaps by making slippers to be sent to naval personnel in the Middle East. In effect, she invited people to express their own position through their knitting. She was tacitly exploiting the fact that crafting is always a commitment of sorts.

Gschwandtner's work suggests what craft-based art could be if it is conceived in sufficiently open terms – if the figure of the knitting circle is rendered permeable, as it were, rather than closed. Another way of putting this is that, if 'craftivism' is sometimes negligible as art, and naïve as politics, maybe that's OK. The real value of craft in the DIY circle, as in any social configuration in which craft appears, is its power to bind people together for a time, and simultaneously act as a physical articulation of this binding. And for that purpose, the circle is again a perfect emblem: for that is a project that will never end.

1. Campbell, J. "It's A Knit-in." *The Independent Review* 23 March (2004): 6. Cast Off was founded by Rachael Matthews and Amy Plant in 2000.
2. Written in 1907 by Charles Gabriel and Ada Habershon.
3. For a typical example of such an origin story, see Stoller, D. *Stitch'n'Bitch: The Knitter's Handbook*. New York: Workman Publishing Company, 2004.
4. Guffey, E. *Retro: The Culture of Revival*. London: Reaktion Foci, 2006.
5. Gschwandnter, S. *KnitKnit: Profiles and Projects from Knitting's New Wave*. New York: Stewart, Tabori and Chang, 2007; "Let 'Em Eat Cake." *American Craft* Aug/Sept (2008); "Knitting is ...," *The Journal of Modern Craft* July (2008): 271–278.

Glenn Adamson is Head of Graduate Studies in the Research Department at the Victoria and Albert Museum.

ACTIVIST TENDENCIES IN CRAFT

ELE CARPENTER

Is the Craftivism movement really activist? And what are the woolly threads that unravel the argument?

Many are sceptical of the political claims of the DIY and craft movement, but the search for an authentic object can be misplaced in a contemporary networked and decentralised field of production. At the same time critical enquiry has to negotiate the hazards of knitted cakes!

Notions of craft and activism are continually readdressed through visual art such as David Medalla's 1960s collectively darned *Stitch in Time*, and Germaine Koh's extended *Knitwork* performance started in 1992. These works raise issues of collective production, experiential and durational performance, valuing the production process as a meditation on making and a focus for dialogue. Artists often turn to folk or craft culture for both metaphorical and tactile exploration of social and hand-made production, situating art practice within the everyday.

Each generation has its radical crafters. In the 1980s, the publication *The Subversive Stitch: Embroidery and the Making of the Feminine* was inspired by the exhibition of the same name curated by Pennina Barnett, and the AIDS Memorial Quilt gained global media coverage.[1] But it took the 1990s generation for the DIY and Craft movements to be aligned with socially engaged art, and the 2000s for craft to be thoroughly subsumed within popular culture. The Calgary Revolutionary Knitting Circle (est. 2000) carries out Knit-In's and Peace-Knit's as public protest within the peace and anti-capitalist movements. In a more gentle reclamation of public space for creative action, London's Cast Off Knitting Club (est. 2000),[2] organises public knitting in locations such as the Circle Line.[3] But the most iconic symbol of activist craft is a protest against Denmark's involvement in the Gulf War by Danish artist Marianna Jørgensen. She coordinated the collective production of a pink knitted cover for a M.24 Chaffee tank exhibited in *Time* at Kunsthallen Nikolaj, 2006.[4]

In these practices the social, performative and critical discourse around the work is central to its production and dissemination. Here craft is not simply a luddite desire for the localised handmade, but a social process of collective empowerment, action, expression and negotiation. In the *Craftivism* exhibition at Arnolfini (2010) art-activist craft practice is increasingly performative and interventionist, although its efficacy is subdued by the aesthetics of the gallery context, where works become a symbolic model of themselves more akin to a design proposal, rather than transformative of a social or political space.

At the same time the massive resurgence in contemporary craft online (stitch 'n' bitch, *www.ravelry.com*) has been made possible through the social connectivity of the web and it's use by communities of interest and practice. Here the stitches aren't perfect, the patterns are circulating, the politics evolving, but the correlation between craft and free libre open source culture is not always apparent.

Will knitting spark revolution? Or are Molotov cocktails the answer?

This often-gendered polemic offers military violence as an effective political tool, whilst undermining non-violence as woolly activism. It's important to take on this challenge within a cultural as well as a political framework for political change, identifying the misnomers, and revisiting the activist history of women's Non-Violent Direct Action.

Firstly, the complex and multiple approaches to Craftivism are as diverse as approaches to art and activism. Individual commitment to follow through political ideals waxes and wanes with the economy and socio-environmental fears, and can be trapped

in the impotency of neo-liberal political normalism where capitalism is seen as natural, and therefore the only way of organising labour and value.[5] But whilst it might seem trite to claim to be saving the world by sewing a button on your shirt, it becomes a political act when thousands of shirts are thrown into landfill simply because they are missing the very same button. Making and mending by both men and women is an expression of material and environmental care and often a necessity, regularly perceived as too specialist and time consuming. Even DIY culture reveres the creation of new products over repair of the old.

But mixed up in the revolutionary fervour is a passion for domestic making epitomised by the fashion for knitted cakes.[6] Rather than a call for social reform, nostalgic creativity mimicking 1950s feminine ideals seems to intentionally confuse attempts at criticality. Instead of acknowledging the feminist politics of knitting to reclaim public space, knitted cakes attempt to re-value domestic skills and re-glamorise motherhood, snapped up by the 'yummy mummy' phenomena of older mothers with disposable incomes. In other words, knitted cakes symbolise capitalist recuperation of feminist critique. The cupcake is nearly synonymous with chocolate as the answer to 'what women really want?' further commercialising women's desires as bodily sustenance and nurture without nutrition or subjective choice. Unlike the 1950s post-war advertising of labour saving devices enticing women back into the home, the knitted cupcake is a uniquely female celebration of domestic space and work. But the nostalgia for wartime 'make and mend' where women were often in charge of a household economy in the old-fashioned sense, has been translated into a contemporary shopping extravaganza consuming brands such as Nigella Lawson and Cath Kidston. As Charlotte Raven writes in her article 'Strike a Pose: How the 'new feminism' went wrong: from pole-dancing lessons to baking cupcakes, modern woman thinks she can do it all':

> The Madonna-ised woman views femininity as a tool for getting what she wants, whatever that might be. In this moment it is more or less compulsory for intelligent women to reveal a passion for baking cupcakes. The domestic goddess is a pose, not a reversion to old-style femininity. Now that 'attitude' is out, and old-fashioned feminine virtues are 'in', so Madonna-ised woman is ready to reveal that cake-making is her number one 'guilty pleasure'.[8]

Craftivism sells itself short when it attempts to identify itself with the frivolous and non-essential activities of baking cakes, knitting cakes, and eating chocolate. Moore and Prain's book *Yarn Bombing* (2009) adopts military terminology to give a 'cool' edge to knitted interventions in public space.[9] This flirting with opposite materials, network models, and gender stereotypes, lacks self-critique of its use of language. It's no coincidence that Moore and Prain acknowledge the "never-ending supply of chocolate" to enable them to write *Yarn Bombing*. [10]

Knitted cakes are also an irritatingly joyful distraction from the important history of craft as Non-Violent Direct Action (NVDA), from Ghandi's handspun fabric to the Greenham Common Women's woven-web blockades,[11] and AWE Aldermarston Women's knitting actions.[12] NVDA is direct form of activism which works at the point of power transaction. The action seeks to prevent an exercise or an abuse of power by disrupting, interrupting or transforming it. NVDA, like much socially-engaged art, functions as both gesture and agency. Here the simplest action is carefully planned to take or reveal responsibility for a socio-political convention, explored through collective creativity and individual volition. It is active resistance and transformation.

The 'pink wool' phenomena in contemporary knitting culture was used to maximum effect in Jørgensen's *Pink M.24 Chaffee*. Whilst a seemingly fleeting gesture, the image of the pink shrouded tank circulating on the Internet can be understood as part of the effect of the work itself. This symbolic transformation of military hardware into an object of comic irony seeks too disarm the offensive stance of a machine justified by its defensive capability. Whilst the sinister Trojan undertones of disguising a real weapon as soft and fluffy lead us to review the deaths from 'friendly' fire, as well as the women and children who suffer the largest percentage of deaths in most conflicts. Activist craft has many forms of symbolism and disguise. I remember weaving bracken into the fence at Greenham to disguise a hole in the perimeter fence cut by peace-women on their way to dance on the cruise missile silos. The web was a powerful symbol of networked participation at Greenham before the Internet was in public use. Meters of patchwork wrapped the airbase whilst others wove webs of wool across the bodies of women lying in the road blockading the gates.[13]

The Greenham women put into practice the concept of conflict transformation rather than conflict resolution, using fabric, metaphor, song and physically obstructing the British-American Nuclear Weapons programme. In 2006 the pink tank is also an effective Craftivist gesture transforming the hardware through soft-wear. The tank is a manifestation of military expansionism traded and paraded globally, but its pink outfit proposes an alternative of care, compassion, or conflict transformation. But most importantly the *Pink M.24 Chaffee* enables, or should enable, an alternative critical discourse about global militarism. If the cover prevented the use of a tank in conflict, it would be an effective direct action.

Does Craftivism reinforce gender stereotypes?

Craftivism, when muddled up with the retro feminine fashion for knitted cakes can be seen to reinforce gender stereotypes.[14] However, as the *Craftivism* exhibition demonstrates, the issues of openness, economy, ecology and reverse engineering are consistent across all kinds of creativity including electronics, engineering, poetry and baking.[15] The hybrid tech-craft culture is also evolving through Maker Faires which include all kinds of programming, electronics and knitting, providing opportunities for cross fertilisation of ideas and practices, experimenting with wearable technologies and increasingly including women's tech groups.[16]

However, the commercialisation of knitting blurred by those darned cakes, confuses the political intention of activist craft. The work is too often promoted as cool, daydreaming, 'stupendous feats',[17] but we urgently need a more critical vocabulary for unravelling the relentless media support of war and its 'heroic' deaths, and an intellectual feminist critique of engendered militarism.[18] This invites a rethinking of female relationships to technology beyond a softening of military hardware. In the Open Source Movement, women are creating spaces for peer2peer learning of technical processes both in hardware and software.[19]

The popularity of DIY is a modern response to the separation of labour and domestic skills, and the legal restrictions on making and mending anything, but specifically electronics. Using the hacker language of reverse-engineering as a learning process – taking apart your jumper or video player to learn how to fix or reuse it – is very different from buying a knitted cupcake complete with strawberry frosting, even if it is locally made. Womens' networks such as MzTek.org in London takes a playfully serious approach to developing spaces for women to learn technical skills, balls of wool and knitting needles are replaced with arduinos and a soldering iron.

Here women are learning the craft of electronics, de-black-boxing their Casio along with their wardrobe. The culture of DIY is applied to coding and knowledge production, as well as developing practical skills and resources.

Alongside the cutesy approach to selling craft back to women as a form of artificial liberation, another form of capitalist recuperation is taking place in the word of DIY. The commercial adoption of low-tech, DIY aesthetic by mainstream advertising for globalised mass production has led to the mass production of non-ironic artificially distressed new products (think pre-scuffed shoes, distressed furniture and jeans).[20] At this point the more reified production of contemporary visual art has the opportunity to reclaim its stake in critiquing visual expression through complex and problematic forms. The Open Source Embroidery project examines the moment at which craft gives up its aspirations to join the fine art market, and engages with contemporary visual art discourse on participation, production and distribution. Instead Open Source Embroidery invests in process, dialogue and social relations that transform the very idea of culture, reclaiming making and thinking from the cultural industries, and situating it at the heart of social and technical communications networks.

There are many cultural, political and aesthetic arguments for creative practice that engage in cultural shifts and transformations for a political project. In part these practices keep a window of activity in the encroaching private control of public space, but at their best they equip practitioners with skills, confidence, networks and working methodologies for direct action wherever it might be needed.

1. Parker, R. *The Subversive Stitch: Embroidery and the making of the Feminine.* London: Women's Press Ltd, 1984.
2. Cast off <http://www.castoff.info>.
3. Campbell, J. "It's a knit-in". *The Independent* 23 Mar. 2004.
4. *Pink M.24 Chaffee*, Marianna Jørgensen, 2006. Exhibited in *Time*, Kunstallen Nikolaj, Copenhagen, 2006.
5. Fisher, M. *Capitalist Realism: Is there No Alternative?.* UK: Zero Books, 2009.
6. Penny, S. *Knitted Cakes.* Kent: Search Press Ltd., 2008.
7. Power, N. *One Dimensional Woman.* UK: Zero Books, 2009.
8. Raven, C. "How the 'new feminism' went wrong: From pole-dancing lessons to baking cupcakes, modern woman thinks she can do it all." *The Guardian* 6 Mar. 2010 <http://www.guardian.co.uk/books/2010/mar/06/charlotte-raven-feminism-madonna-price>.
9. Moore, M and Prain, L. *Yarn Bombing: The Art of Crochet and Knit Graffiti.* Vancouver: Arsenal Pulp Press, 2009.
10. Ibid. 11.
11. Kidron, B. and Poulton, L. *Your Greenham.* 2006 <http://www.yourgreenham.co.uk/#fabric>.
12. McDonald, D. "Nuclear Information Service (NIS) Annual Report, 2007." *Nuclear Information Service.* 2007 <http://nuclearinfo.org/view/publications_%2526_media/NIS_annual_reports>.
13. Fairhall, D. *Common Ground: The Story of Greenham.* London: IB Tauris, 2006.
14. Raven, C. "How the 'new feminism' went wrong: From pole-dancing lessons to baking cupcakes, modern woman thinks she can do it all." *The Guardian* 6 Mar. 2010 <http://www.guardian.co.uk/books/2010/mar/06/charlotte-raven-feminism-madonna-price>.
15. Rackham, M. "Coders, Crafters and Cooks: Melinda Rackham, Craftivism, Arnolfini, Bristol." *RealTime* Feb–Mar. 2010: 51 < http://www.realtimearts.net/article/95/9771>.
16. Maker Faire <http://www.makerfaire.com/newcastle/2010>.
17. Moore, M and Prain, L. *Yarn Bombing: The Art of Crochet and Knit Graffiti.* Vancouver: Arsenal Pulp Press, 2009.
18. Cockburn, C. *From Where We Stand: War, Women's Activism and Feminist Analysis.* London and New York: Zed Books, 2007.
19. Derieg, A. "Things Can Break: Tech Women Crashing Computer and Preconceptions." *eipcp.* 2007 <http://eipcp.net/transversal/0707/derieg/en>.
20. Heath, J and Potter, A. *The Rebel Sell: Why the Culture Can't be Jammed.* Mankato: Capstone, 2004.

Ele Carpenter is an independent curator and researcher. She is currently Research Fellow at HUMlab in affiliation with the BildMuseet at the University of Umeå, Sweden, and a lecturer at Goldsmiths College, London.

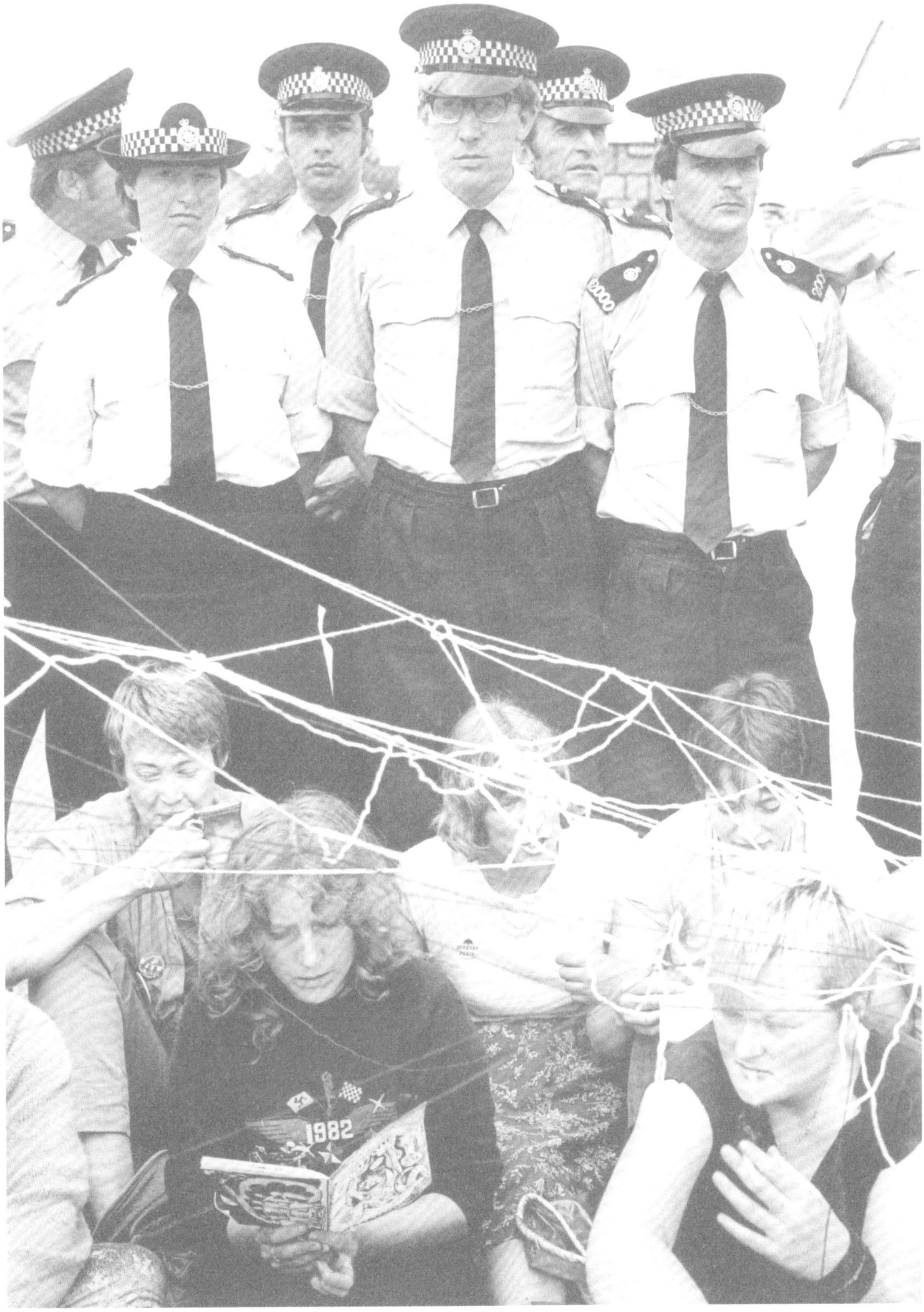

Greenham Common Women's Peace Camp,
international blockade, July 1993
Courtesy Lesley McIntyre

ANALYSIS OF THREE EVENTS

The forcible denial of my right to proceed with my ideas, whether by Exxonmobil in 2000, or by Emschergenossenschaft at the behest of Fraunhofer Institute for Applied Information Technology in 2009, or by the BND regarding our Chernobyl investigation in 1986, results from a misunderstanding of the new concepts with which I have worked. Such is normal with the 'new' that is art. The misunderstanding has led, in each case, to a denial of, or revocation of, the property rights of me and my colleagues.

In the Exxonmobil case, the right was to pursue a research project with a grant from The Lilly Foundation, for $2 million. The research was for sustainable removal of hydraulic and biological vigour within catchments. Exxonmobil thought I was trying to find a new source of energy, and they acted pre-emptively, not unlike a Mafia hit squad. The action was devastating (not just to me and my colleagues, but also to the offeror – he had a heart attack). Exxonmobil did not notice that I was actually trying to find a sustainable way of working with an entire ecosystem. Exxonmobil cannot grasp this idea. We can see this with their current algae-to-energy schemes, which are commodity oriented and monocultural, not ecosystemic. Thus, a 'good idea' was thwarted.

In the BND case, wherein the agents said I was "not qualified" to make analyses of satellite data which my company had purchased, they think that the issue is one of scientific credentials as mandated by politically-approved entities, like universities or the State. But for me, the issue was one of my right, and even duty, to exercise the US Constitution's Bill of Rights: namely, to act in a well-organised civilian organisation to 'bear arms', or military technology, as appropriate to public defence (Second Amendment), and to publish what I know, letting the public decide (First Amendment). My rights were fortified by a technical fact: any scientist or institute, or rival entity, could purchase the same satellite data and conduct similar or different algorithmic analyses, to confirm or contradict my published conclusions; whatever I did was fully open to public review and correction. This indeed occurred: the London Times article about the findings of my company was prompted by disclosures to the Times from another scientist, who purchased the same data and proved my findings to be correct. The BND did not understand my commercial and citizen's rights, being fixated on the notion that such satellite data must be handled only by 'professionals'.

In the Emschergenossenschaft case, the issue was how to efficiently harvest a wide range of biomass sources for seasonal production of biogas, with challenges including where and how to cut, what boats to use, what wagons to use, what silage to set up, where and when to collect, and with what people, and at what level of expertise. This cluster of challenges was interpreted by Fraunhofer as chiefly a question of adapting a 'mini-fermenter' designed for a very different digestion task. I had an ecosystem-wide query, involving a river basin and its dammed or stilled waters, and the scientists had – as their own report declares – a commodity query.

But with the Emschergenossenschaft case, a much-more serious violation of rights occurred than in the other two cases. Whereas Exxonmobil and the BND had intervened from the outside, the Emschergenossenschaft intervened from within. I was invited to enter into a close consultation with them, and I was encouraged to give them 'my best'. I did. I gave them the best ideas and proposals I could muster. I poured months of time, energy, goodwill, contacts and money into the submission. I did so with the understanding that if the project were 'machtbar', or do-able, then I could proceed with it. But the Emschergenossenschaft, probably most due to an administrator there, decided that any project I proposed could only be do-able by third parties, other than me, and could only be done if I had no property rights, research and development role, or other practical relation to what I proposed. From within the confidentiality of a full disclosure by me to a trusted entity, the Emschergenossenschaft, I was to be stripped of any future role with my own ideas. If I were to proceed with the EmscherKunst show as they planned,

I would not be able to ever say, to investors or buyers or the general public, that I had any property rights or reputation, any ability to do business, in what I had proposed to do.

A relation of trust, essential to conducting any project, was systematically violated. Even at the end, I was expected to have zero stake in any 'Technik' that would be conducted, but then asked to spend hours in discussion, hence consultation, with one of the suppliers of equipment for the 'Technik'. In effect, I was asked to give away all that I know and am, assuming photo and video documentation, to a third party.

In the Emschergenossenschaft case, I was repeatedly and systematically denied any chance to continue with the work I had started to do in preparation for the EmscherKunst show. The Emschergenossenschaft caved in to demands by the Fraunhofer Institute to let them, not the artist, be the main researcher, developer and author, together with a few local staff scientists, of what the artist had proposed.

Damage to the artist has probably already been done, in that now, all that he had pioneered and risked his reputation to develop is being researched and developed, with deep pockets of State funding, in a way the artist can never access.

The German Constitution may have also been violated. The Constitution, in Article 5, declares that art, like literature, journalism, scholarship, science, is 'free'. That is, it is not subject to State control. But what is the handing over of an artist's initiative to a State-funded entity by another state funded organisation for the benefit and authorship rights solely of that State-funded entity and related state assignees, but a subordination of the artist's work to State control?

In the Exxonmobil case, the artist lost a possible $2 million, and the initiative for a project in New Zealand, as in Indiana, was lost – for about a decade.

In the BND case, the government managed to appropriate all the data tapes left in Munich, such that regaining the property purchased by the company, and then reprocessing that property to yield similar-quality images, could cost around 40,000 Euro.

In the Emschergenossenschaft case, the danger was that two decades of work, built on three decades of publication, always featuring the 'sehr gute Idee' of harvesting waterplants, not land plants, to yield biofuels, would be permanently lost. All the public credit for such an idea would be taken from the artist, if the project went ahead as the Emschergenossenschaft planned, never to be regained.

It is commonly thought that in the 21st Century we people of the civilized world would behave better than we had in previous centuries. But humanity doesn't change. The battles of the 20th Century over access to petroleum will be replaced by battles in the 21st, with the same brutalities, over access to renewables.

PETER FEND

Peter Fend is an artist, and co-founder of Ocean Earth Development Corporation in 1980.

CELE
BRATING
THE
FREE
DOM
TO
FLY...

JAMES PANTON

In August of 2007, at the high point of the British summer holiday season, flights out of Heathrow were delayed and disrupted by environmental campaigners demonstrating against the environmental impact of our ever increasing love of cheap flight.

The television news images were revealing. The television news images were illustrative: on the one hand environmental anti-flight protestors camping out near the airport predicting environmental destruction, and holding wanton flight as an unnecessary and guilty activity which is destroying the world we live in, for now and the future. On the other hand: families in their shorts and flip-flops with their screaming toddlers, queued up like cattle to pass through airport security, desperately hoping to get their two weeks of sunshine before they have to come home to work for the rest of the year.

The latter looked mostly despondent and annoyed – at flights delayed and hold-ups which were coming at the end of long months spent looking forward to two weeks of (almost) guaranteed sun and relaxation. But they also looked a little sheepish: guilty, perhaps uncomfortable, at the thought that their holiday could have become the focus of such national media attention. The former looked inspired and utopian: ready to party to save the world from the needless, selfish, destructive hubris of those who would seek relaxation and sunshine without a care for their environmental footprint.

For me, these combined images – of sheepish, uncomfortable holiday-makers who had never considered their holiday as anything other than a right; and anti-flight campaigners, optimistic, themselves in holiday-mood, cheered by the attention they were receiving, and chastened by the over-determining importance of their cause – revealed a number of aspects of the contemporary narrative on environmentalism.

> The first and clearest aspect of the anti-flight campaign was its demand that holiday-makers should be made to feel guilty: guilty for their carefree abandon of daily responsibility, guilty for the damage they would bring to the environment, and guilty that they had not even considered any of this before booking their flights online. The anti-Heathrow protestors had arrived to offer moral salvation.
>
> The second, and somewhat ironic, aspect was the seriousness with which the campaign of these would-be radicals – purposefully taking up a position as outsiders (outside the airport, outside the mainstream, outside the guilty masses) – was discussed by news reporters and media commentators. Despite their outsider image, the anti-flight, anti-Heathrow, anti-holiday protestors were a major mainstream force in political discussion.
>
> The third, and rather disillusioning, aspect was the depressing message that was being expressed behind the appearance of revolutionary utopianism: that the onward march of human development, technology and leisure is unnecessary and destructive. For all their apparent optimism about the possibility of a better world, the world they seemed to propose would involve none of the ease, abundance and guiltless consumption that was once the very essence of utopia.

In response to these contradictory elements of the environmentalist narrative, the Manifesto Club, an organisation of which I am the co-founder, launched a campaign to *Celebrate the Freedom of Flight*. We argued that the vast expansion of flight over the past few years – particularly cheap flight – has been experienced as liberation for millions of people. The achievement of flight, dreamed of for millennia, is a great

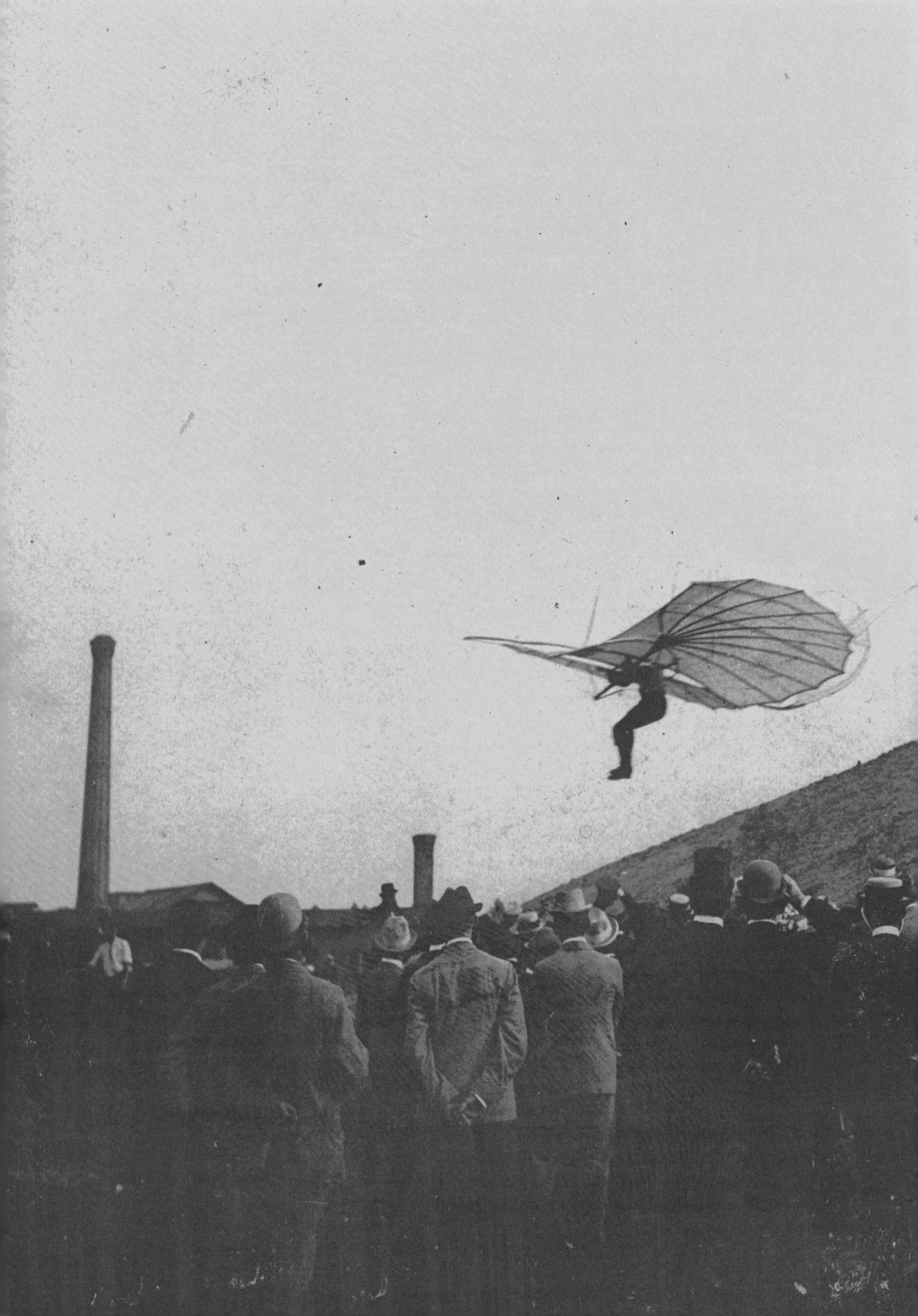

human achievement, and its effects over the past 50 years have been hugely positive: to bring the world closer together, to allow people to visit and experience new cultures and see the wonders of the world up close, to allow people to form relationships across borders, to have lovers in far-flung places, and to move, to work, to earn money, to support their families in the developing world. We further argued that the more recent vast expansion of low-cost air travel was a profoundly democratising moment: because it meant that the kind of travel that was once reserved for the über-rich was now something that we could all benefit from. And we said that we shouldn't feel guilty about that – on the contrary, we should celebrate it.

Flight, in my view, and the moralised discussion around it, is one of the most illustrative examples of the profoundly anti-humanistic underpinnings of the environmentalist narrative. Flight is often viewed as an 'addiction' pursued for wanton, selfish ends. Mark Ellington, founder of Rough Guide, argued that we suffer from Binge Flying; and the think-tank the IPPR recently proposed the introduction of health warnings at airports, much like those now put on cigarette packets, to help cure people of their addiction to cheap flights.

The environmental campaigner Geroge Monbiot explains this logic thus:

> Many of the things we have until now understood to be good – even morally necessary – must now be seen as bad. Perhaps the most intractable cause of Global Warming is 'love miles': the distance you must travel to visit your friends and partners and relatives on the other side of the world. The world could be destroyed by love.

What I think we see here is that a broad-based concern about modernity: its productive, consumptive, perhaps meaningless, industrial, polluting activity comes to be located at the level of individual morality and individual action: so it is by changes at the level of individual action that pollution can be tackled and consciences can be cleared.

Leo Hickman, the Guardian's Eco-Man, expressed the underlying sentiment well in his *Life Stripped Bare*: "Everything we do (from the mangetout we eat that is flown from Kenya, the TV we watch, the cosmetics we use, the newly painted nursery for the children we are expecting to be born) has a negative knock-on effect – we should try to reduce our impact on the world wherever we can."

The underlying logic of this environmental narrative is that of recognising that human action in the world causes harm, human activity has an impact, and the less our actions, the less our impact, the better the world will be. Ultimately, we have a moral script and ethical code of conduct, which starts from the assumption that human actions are bad, and moves to the conclusion that therefore the less we act, the better the world will be.

The problem, I think, is not just the anti-humanist nature of this structure of thinking; it's not just the symbolic and gestural nature of this underlying logic, but it's that it ultimately leads to a celebration of inaction – and I suspect, therefore, a decreased capacity to resolve the problems the environment throws at us, as well as a diminished aspiration for the kinds of social organisation and action that we will have to pursue if we actually want a world of greater equality, of greater well being, and of greater social justice.

As the environmental narrative demands that we should feel guilty for the ever greater ease by which we live our lives, it seems perfectly fitted to fill the vacuum left by our broad-based disaffection from organised religion – it provides a moral script for virtuous living, a clear contrast between good and evil, and a step by step guide to individual salvation. It is perhaps for this reason that the environmentalist narrative, for all its radical outsider self-image, and all its dreams of a better tomorrow,

Previous page: Otto Lilienthal with *Normalsegelapparat* (Normal soaring apparatus)
Courtesy archives Otto-Lilienthal-Museum (lilienthal-museum.de)
Photograph Alex Krajewsky, 1895. On "Mount Flight" (artificial hill erected by Lilienthal at Lichterfelde, near Berlin)

has been so easily adopted by the mainstream. Politicians of every shade of gray, church leaders, money-making capitalists and business interests, as well as local councils and daily workplaces, have all been easily able to adopt a language and ritualistic practice demanded by the environmental narrative.

The current public discussion about flying fails to recognise the role that flight plays in our daily lives. Up to 1.5 million of us pass through Heathrow every week in the summer months, but we are being asked to limit our travel or atone for our emissions with carbon offsets.

However many environmentalists ask us to feel guilty for every flight we take, the reality is that we continue to fly – more often, for longer, and further. The possibility of a cleaner, faster and more efficient system of air travel is well within our grasp. The truly radical counter-cultural, anti-establishment, humanist act, might be to recognise and then to celebrate that fact.

James Panton is a politics tutor at St John's College, University of Oxford, and co-founder of the radical civil liberties campaigning group the Manifesto Club.

DECLARATIONS \ THE POLEMICS OF ART ENGAGED WITH CONFLICT

NAV HAQ

There are few things more topical than war, and the art-world loves to reflect on the topical. The proliferation of biennials – global platforms very often themed around 'globalism' and other global issues – around the world is one of the main structures perpetuating this trend, which subsequently filters down to museums and galleries. For me, the question is not about the legitimacy of conflict as a thematic for art, but more about the nature and legitimacy of the intention in presenting work about such subject matter, the specific strategies employed by artists and institutions to engage with the issues, and the relationship to audiences. The UK, like any other nation (but perhaps as we've been more implicated in it over recent years), has had a fair amount of exhibitions and discussion events on this subject.

An exhibition that I've often found to be a good example for discussion is the ICA's *Memorial to the Iraq War*, 2007. This group show presented a number of proposals by an international selection of artists invited to produce a memorial (as opposed to a monument) for the war in Iraq. Some of the proposals were incredibly interesting and thoughtful in terms of their political engagement and response to such an invitation. Yet there were two things that struck me as being truly limiting. Firstly, looking around at all the other visitors, I was reminded that a very specific kind of demographic visits the ICA and because of this, the exhibition felt like it was ultimately only preaching to the converted. And secondly, the exhibition really was about its own potential – for the possibility of some of the proposed memorials being realised and sited within the public realm, thus offering a whole different type of encounter with the work and the issues. To date this hasn't happened, though I understand it has been investigated. Somehow, the subject matter of the exhibition made the relationship with its audience seem absolutely essential.

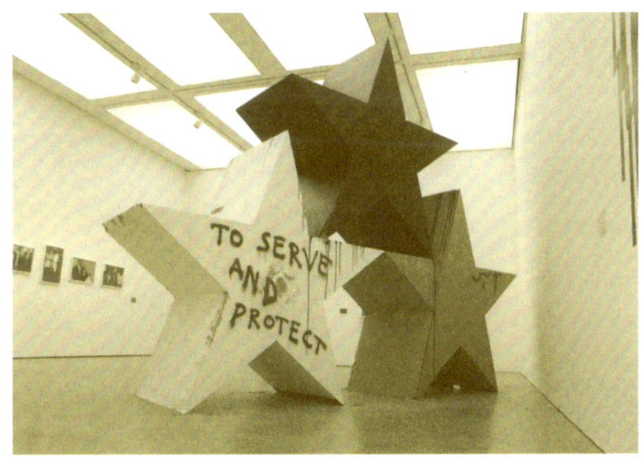

Memorial to Iraq War, ICA, 2007
Courtesy of the ICA
Photograph Steve White

Memorial to the Iraq War was very much a straight-to-the-point kind of exhibition. It looked head-on at a major geo-political issue that still continues to unfold, situated within the capital of a nation implicated in the offensive. But is this kind of direct critical-engagement always the most affective way of producing political art and exhibitions? Curator Maria Lind's essay from 2004 entitled 'This Is Going To Be Really Funny: Notes on Art, Its Institutions And Their Presumed Criticality ' discusses the issues involved with 'political' or so-called 'critical' art, and the intentions behind its production.[1] She eloquently creates an analogy between the act of telling a joke and the declarations inherent in much political art. It basically goes: if when you're about to tell a joke, and before you tell the joke you make the declaration: "This is going to be really funny", then in all likelihood the listener is probably not going to find the joke funny. There's just something about the initial declaration that diffuses the humour – the surprise factor is removed, and you can prepare in advance for something coming up that

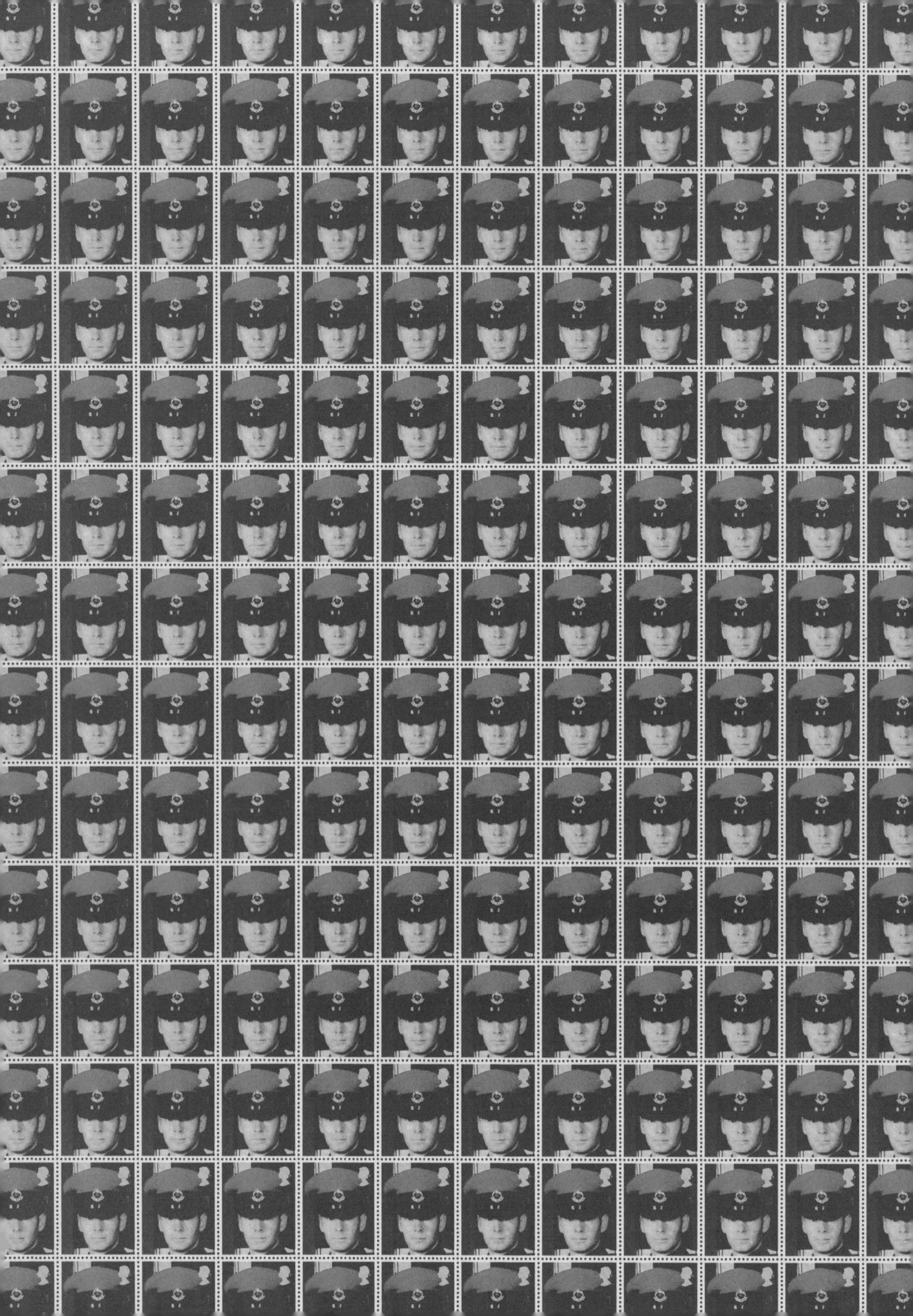

Left: *For Queen and Country, Lance Corporal Benjamin Hyde, Adjutant General's Corps (Royal Military Police), Died 24 June 2003, aged 23*, Steve McQueen, 2007
Courtesy the artist

might be funny. A similar thing could be said for critical art. If you initially make the declaration that your work is going to be highly critical, it is likely to lose its criticality straightaway. You pre-empt the impact of your own practice. I tend to agree with Lind's thoughts, and wonder whether a certain ambiguity with your intentions can lead in the end to a more potent criticality.

Take for example, artist Steve McQueen's project *For Queen and Country* (2007), which the artist produced as a result of his position as the UK's official war artist. The work is a proposal for a series of 98 postage stamps each depicting a different member of the armed forces killed in Iraq. There was, and still is, much resistance to the stamps from the Ministry of Defence, and the Royal Mail have turned down the proposal. Curiously, the public response to the work – exhibited at the Great Hall at Manchester's Central Library – was overwhelmingly positive, whether or not individuals were for or against the war. But McQueen's stated intention for the work is decidedly ambiguous, neither pro nor anti-war. The absence of such a declaration of clear opinion has left a space for interpretation that allows for a much more discursive response, as well as a more direct level of engagement with the issues.[2]

Video art is a ubiquitous medium in relation to this discussion. Video appears a lot in biennials because it is considered a kind of 'lingua franca' – an international intermediary language, and is often used by artists to (re-) present crisis and conflict. Ursula Biemann is an example of a practitioner who yields the camera in pursuit of an array of issues of geo-political concern, everything from trans-Mediterranean migration to the oil industry's path of destruction. In works such as *Sahara Chronicles* (2007) and *Black Sea Files* (2005), Biemann documents the plight of individuals affected directly by imposed hardship and injustice. In contrast, Renzo Martens' mildly controversial video *Episode 3: Enjoy Poverty* (2009) critiques both the neutrality and reality captured by the camera lens, as well as suggesting that a lot of art merely postures as an agent of social change purely for cultural capital. The work documents the poverty journalism industry in the Congo, where Western journalists sell their images of extreme hardship resultant from the apathy of corporations or ineffective aid to the Western media. Proposing to the affected Congolese that they capitalise through self-exploitation, by cutting out the intermediary and taking images of themselves, Martens' interventionist approach sets up a situation that brings to light the futility in reversing the hegemonic space between the subject and the gaze. This futility also

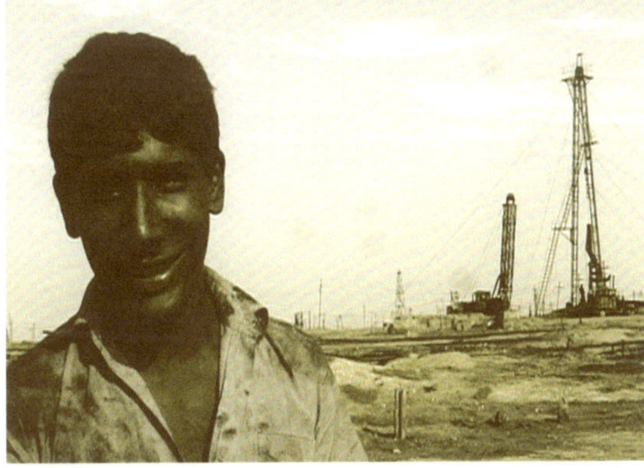

Black Sea Files, Ursula Biemann, 2005
Courtesy the artist

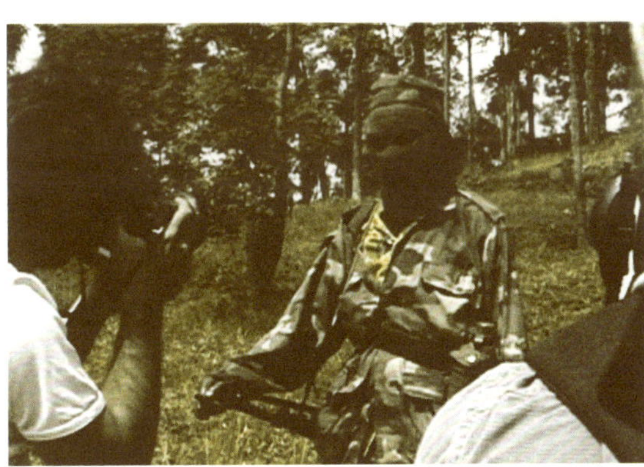

Episode 3: Enjoy Poverty, Renzo Martens, 2009
Courtesy the Artist, Wilkinson Gallery, Galerie Fons Welters

in turn creates a provocative comparison between the lens of the poverty journalist and the lens of the pseudo-documentary video artist. It's very rare that either form genuinely helps the individuals they are portraying, and in real terms they only help those in control of representation, whether for financial or cultural progress. Don't they both exploit the exploited?

The spontaneity in responding to conflict or impending crisis, has also become a polemic in itself. A few years ago I was invited to participate in a workshop in Amman organised by the European Cultural Foundation (ECF). It brought together a number of practitioners from around Europe and the Middle East region, temporarily forming a 'Mediterranean Reflection Group' for discussion of a range of issues intended to inform policy decisions by the ECF. The most memorable discussion was about the artist's role in times of crisis, and included presentations by the Beirut-based musician and artist Tarek Atoui, and the Istanbul-based writer, curator and self-confessed 'neo-anarchist' Erden Kosova. Between the two of them they managed to form an extremely insightful and useful polemic on crisis and conflict, and their affects on artistic practice. Atoui discussed the impulse he and other Lebanese artists experienced to produce work during and immediately after the 2006 Israeli invasion of Lebanon. The work, generally speaking, was highly politically orientated – mostly reflecting on the trauma of the crisis – and in hindsight, many of the artists considered these particular works to be among the worst of their careers. They were embarrassed that they had reacted in such strange, irrational and 'expressive' ways and suffice to say, most of these works will never see the light of day.

Kosova on the other hand, discussed some of the work produced around the time of the assassination in early 2007 of the high-profile Istanbul-based Armenian intellectual Hrant Dink, in a politically motivated attack. Some artists responded to the specificity of this situation in ways that were very public, and very sensitively 'inserted' into the aftermath of an event of such national significance. Before his death, Dink asserted that in the event of his assassination (which he could clearly imagine happening), he would prefer the public not to protest vocally or through large banners, urging instead a silent, more thoughtful response. His funeral was also the largest public march in Istanbul for nearly 20 years. (This was an occasion by chance I happened to have witnessed, as it took place on the same day as the opening of an exhibition I co-curated at Platform Garanti artspace was meant to happen. In the end we chose to cancel the opening and decided to go and join the procession, along with most of the Istanbul art community.) One image from this day, that I subsequently

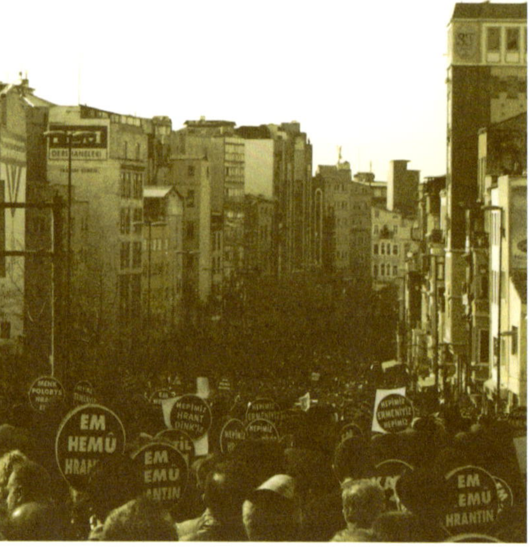

Istanbul Protest
Courtesy Onder Ozkalipci

Next Page: Episode 3: Enjoy Poverty,
Renzo Martens, 2009
Courtesy the Artist, Wilkinson Gallery,
Galerie Fons Welters

learned through Kosova's talk was actually an artistic project, was particularly memorable. This was the abundance of small, round table-tennis-bat-sized placards that numerous people seemed to be holding that read simply "We are all Armenians". They could only have been produced at very short notice, but they had been distributed widely. The message was clear, and it was an example of how a simple insertion in the public realm that countless people participated in collectively, could give a quiet yet clear message to the Turkish authorities. Here, Kosova provided an example of a specific political situation that created an opportunity for an artist to respond in a way that would have been impossible under 'normal' circumstances.

The two issues here – the dichotomy between the traditional spaces for art and the wider public realm, and the specific strategies employed in declaring such critical engagement – seem to me to be the essential considerations in the presentation of such politically engaged art. Imagine the scale of the discussion that might ensue if Steve McQueen's proposed stamps were ever produced and issued. Politically engaged art is always somehow a responsive act, and the level of engagement and control in this response also seems to have a major affect, artistically speaking, on the art produced. It's clearly not easy to negotiate all these factors, the conditions of which are often determined by the nature of violence, crisis and conflict. The fog of war indeed.

1. Lind, M. "This Is Going To Be Really Funny: Notes on Art, Its Institutions And Their Presumed Criticality." *Spin Cycle*. Bristol: Spike Island and Systemisch, 2004: 33–4.
2. The campaign to have the stamps produced by the Royal Mail is ongoing with an online petition <www.artfund.org/queenandcountry>.

Nav Haq is Exhibitions Curator at Arnolfini.

An earlier version of this text was originally commissioned and published by Axis in the Dialogue webzine: www.axisweb.org/artandconflict

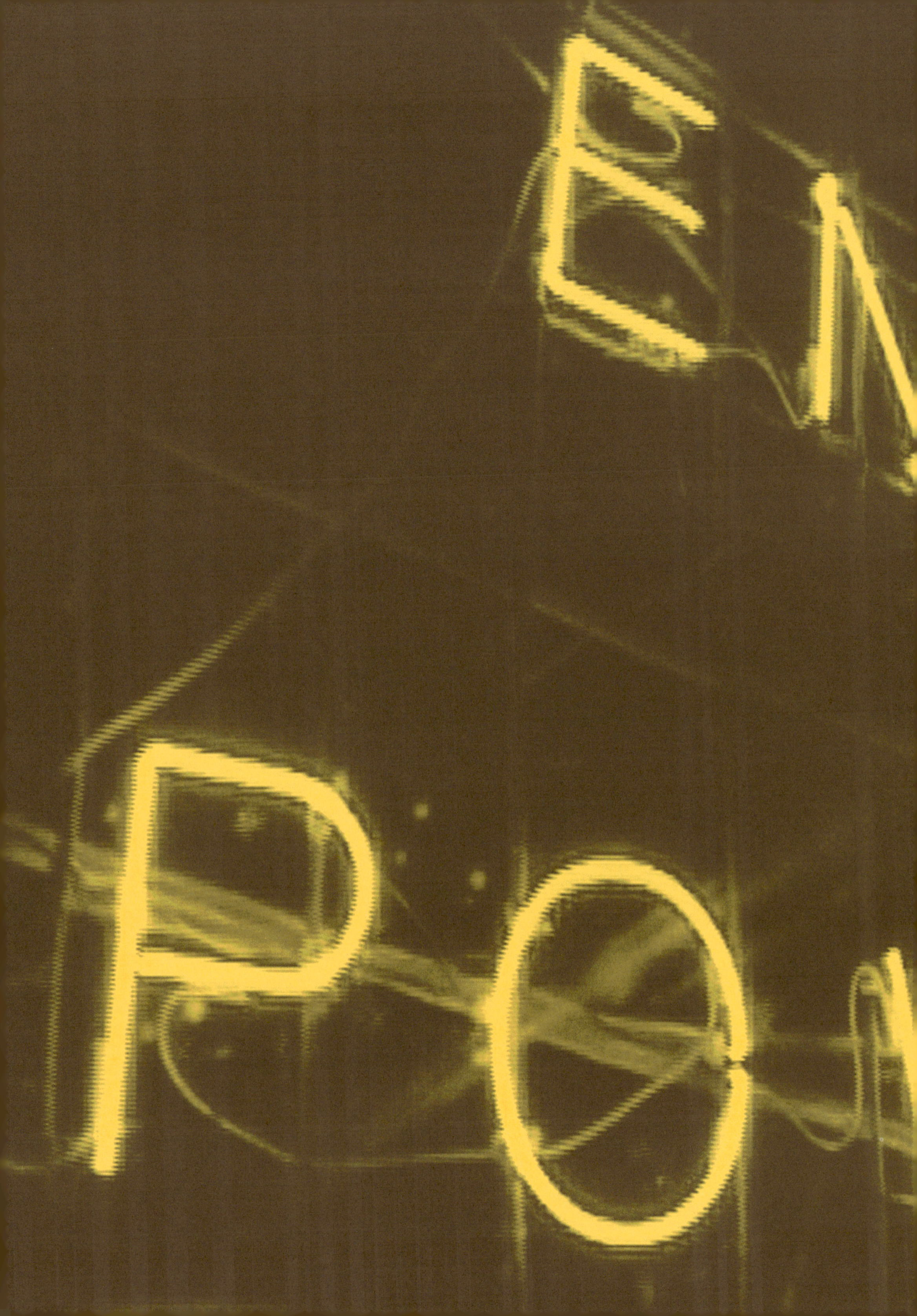

JOY
PLEASE
ERTY

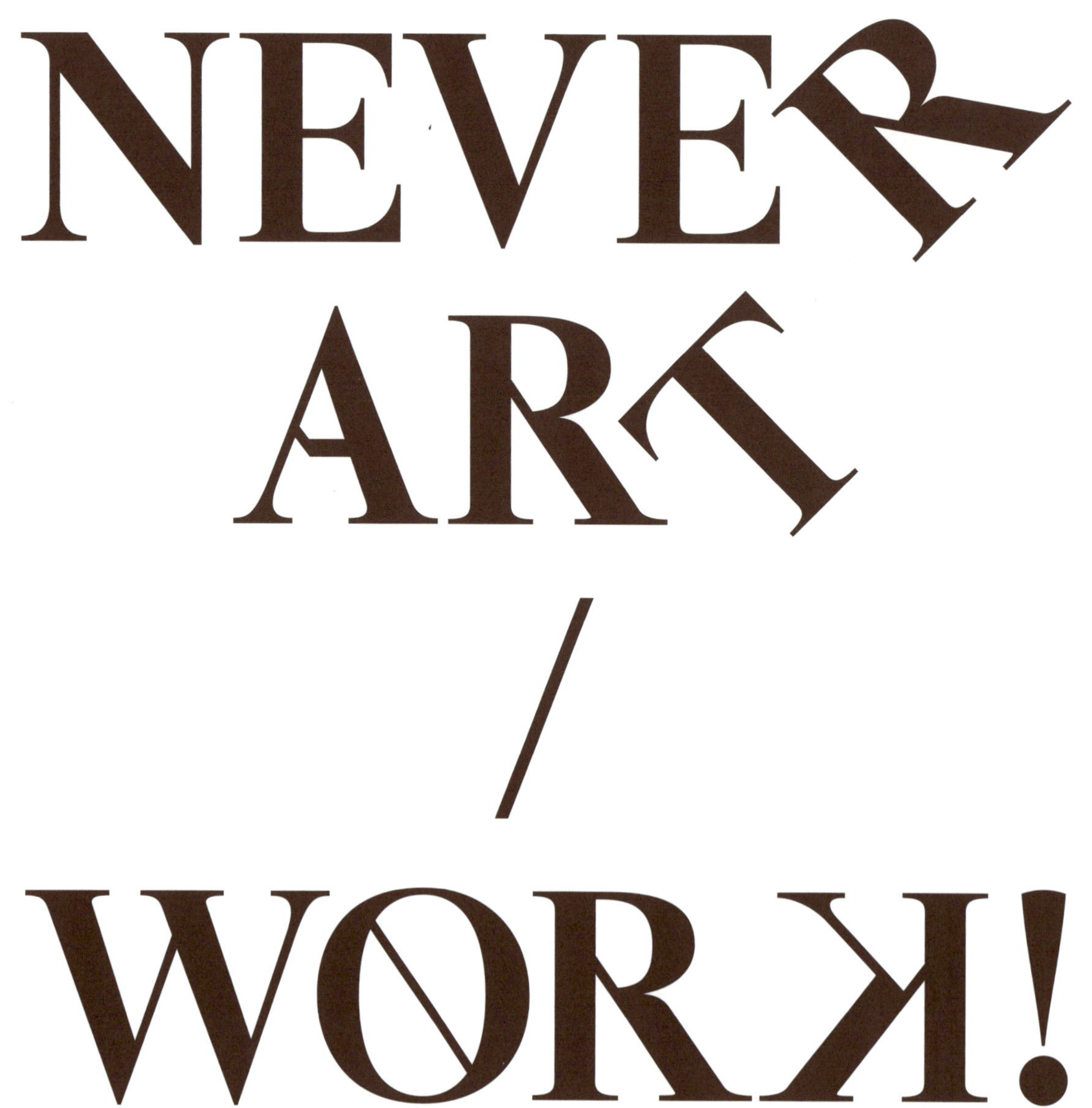

STEVPHEN SHUKAITIS
& ERICA BIDDLE

Everyone is an artist. This would seem a simple enough place to begin; with a statement connecting directly to Joseph Beuys, and more generally to the historic avant-garde's aesthetic politics aiming to break down barriers between artistic production and everyday life. It invokes an artistic politics that runs through Dada to the Situationists, and meanders and dérives through various rivulets in the history of radical politics and social movement organising. But let's pause for a second. While seemingly simple, there is much more to this one statement than presents itself. It is a statement that contains within it two notions of time and the potentials of artistic and cultural production, albeit notions that are often conflated, mixed, or confused. By teasing out these two notions and creatively recombining them, perhaps there might be something to be gained in rethinking the antagonistic and movement-building potential of cultural production: to reconsider its compositional potential.

The first notion alludes to a kind of potentiality present but unrealised through artistic work; the creativity that everyone could exercise if they realised and developed potentials that have been held back and stunted by capital and unrealistic conceptions of artistic production through mystified notions of creative genius. Let's call this the 'not-yet' potential of everyone becoming an artist through the horizontal sublation of art into daily life. The second understanding of the phrase forms around the argument that everyone *already* is an artist and embodies creative action and production within their life and being. Duchamp's notion of the readymade gestures towards this, as he proclaims art as the recombination of previously existing forms. The painter creates by recombining the pre-given readymades of paints and canvas; the baker creates by recombining the readymade elements of flour, yeast, etc. In other words, it is not that everyone will become an artist, but that everyone already is immersed in myriad forms of creative production, or artistic production, given a more general notion of art.

These two notions, how they collide and overlap, move towards an important focal point: if there has been an end of the avant-garde, it is not its death but rather a monstrous multiplication and expansion of artistic production in zombified forms. The avant-garde has not died, the creativity contained within the future oriented potential of *the becoming-artistic* has lapsed precisely because it has perversely been realised in existing forms of diffuse cultural production. 'Everyone is an artist' as a utopian possibility is realised, just as 'everyone is a worker'. This condition has reached a new degree of concentration and intensity within the basins of cultural production; the post-Fordist participation-based economy where the multitudes are sent to work in the metropolitan factory, recombining ideas and images through social networks and technologically mediated forms of communication. We don't often think of all these activities as either work or art. Consequently it becomes difficult to think through the politics of labour around them, whether as artistic labour or just labour itself.

The notion of the Art Strike, its reconsideration and socialisation within the post-Fordist economy, becomes more interesting and productive (or perhaps anti-productive) precisely as labour changes articulation in relation to the current composition of artistic and cultural work. The Art Strike starts with Gustav Metzger and the Art Worker Coalition and their call to withdraw their labour for a minimum of three years from 1977–1980. Metzger's formulation of the Art Strike is directed against the problems of the gallery system. Metzger's conception was picked up by Stewart Home and various others within the Neoist milieu who called upon artists to cease artistic work entirely for the years 1990–1993. In this version, the strike moves beyond a focus on the gallery system to a more general consideration of artistic production and a questioning of the role of the artist. In the most recent iteration, Redas Dirzys and a Temporary Art Strike Committee called for an Art Strike as a response to Vilnius, the capital of Lithuania, becoming a European Capital of Culture for 2009. The designation of a city as a capital of culture is part of a process of metropolitan branding and a strategy of capitalist valorisation through the circulation of cultural and artistic heritage. (In Vilnius this has played out through figures like Jonas Mekas, George Maciunas, the legacy of Fluxus, and the Uzupis arts district.) In Vilnius we see the broadening of the Art Strike from a focus on the gallery system to artistic production more generally, and finally to the ways in which artistic and cultural production are infused throughout daily life and embedded within the production of the metropolis.

The Art Strike emerges as a nodal point for finding ways to work critically between the two compositional modes contained within the statement "everyone is an artist." An autonomist politics focuses on class composition, or the relation between the technical arrangement of economic production and the political composition activated by forms of social insurgency and resistance. Capital evolves by turning emerging political compositions into technical compositions of surplus value production. Similarly, the aesthetic politics of the avant-garde find the political compositions they animate turned into new forms of value production and circulation. The Art Strike becomes a tactic for working between the utopian not-yet promise of unleashed creativity and the always-already but compromised forms of artistic labour we're enmeshed in. In the space between forms of creative recombination currently in motion, and the potential of what could be if they were not continually rendered into forms more palatable to capitalist production, something new emerges. To re-propose an Art Strike at this juncture, when artistic labour is both everywhere and nowhere, is to force that issue. It becomes not a concern of solely the one who identifies (or is identified) as the artist, but a method to withdraw the labour of imagination and recombination involved in what we're already doing to hint towards the potential of what we could be doing.

Bob Black, in his critique of the Art Strike, argues that far from going on a strike by withdrawing forms of artistic labour, the Art Strike formed as the ultimate realisation of art, where even the act of not making art becomes part of an artistic process. While Black might have meant to point out a hypocrisy or contradiction, if we recall the overlapping compositional modes of everyone being an artist, this no longer appears as an antinomy but rather a shifting back and forth between different compositional modes. While Stewart Home has argued repeatedly that the importance of the Art Strike lies not in its feasibility but rather in the ability to expand the terrain of class struggle, Black objects to this on the grounds that most artistic workers operate as independent contractors and therefore strikes do not make sense for them. While this is indeed a concern, it is also very much the condition encountered by forms of labour in a precarious post-Fordist economy. The Art Strike moves from being a proposal for social action by artists to a form of social action potentially of use to all who find their creativity and imagination exploited within existing productive networks.

But, ask the sceptics: how can we enact this form of strike? And, as comrades and allies inquire, how can this subsumption of creativity and imagination and creativity by capital

be undone? That is precisely the problem, for as artistic and cultural production become more ubiquitous and spread throughout the social field, they are rendered all the more apparently imperceptible. The avant-garde focus on shaping relationality (for instance in Beuys' notion of social sculpture), or in creative recombination and detournément, exists all around us flowing through the net economy. Relational Aesthetics recapitulates avant-garde ideas and practices into a capital-friendly, service economy aesthetics. This does not mean that they are useless or that they should be discarded. Rather, by teasing out the compositional modes contained within them they can be considered and reworked. How can we struggle around or organise diffuse forms of cultural and artistic labour? This is precisely the kind of question explored by groups such as the Carrotworkers' Collective, a group from London who are formulating ways to organise around labour involved in unpaid forms of cultural production, such as all the unpaid internships sustaining the workings of artistic and cultural institutions.

In 1953, Guy Debord painted on the wall of the rue de Seine the slogan "Ne travaillez jamais", or "Never Work". The history of the avant-garde is filled with calls to "never artwork", but the dissolution of the artistic object and insurgent energies of labour refusal have become rendered into the workings of semiocapitalism and the metropolitan factory. To renew and rebuild a politics and form of social movement adequate to the current composition does not start from romanticising the potentiality of becoming creative through artistic production or working from the creative production that already is, but rather by working in the nexus between the two. In other words, to start from how the refusal of work is re-infused into work, and by understanding that imposition and rendering, and struggling within, against and through it.

Art Strike Biennial. <http://www.alytusbiennial.com>.
Carrotworkers' Collective. <http://carrotworkers.wordpress.com>.
Home, S. *The Neoist Manifestos/The Art Strike Papers*. Stirling: AK Press, 1991.

Stevphen Shukaitis is an editor at Autonomedia and lecturer at the University of Essex.

Erika Biddle is a PhD candidate in Communication and Culture at York University, Toronto.

CONCEPT STORE #3: Art, Activism and Recuperation
SPRING 2010

Concept Store is a biannual journal published by Arnolfini, focusing on critical issues of contemporary art and their relationship to wider cultural, social and political contexts. While Concept Store reflects upon ideas explored within Arnolfini's artistic programme as well as future research projects, it is intended to be a critical platform in its own right, operating as a discursive space for commissioned texts, artists' contributions, interviews and other experimental forms. It aims to challenge the conventions of the exhibition catalogue and the inter-relations of artistic production, critical writing and cultural theory. The journal also continues Arnolfini's engagement with contemporary design practice, with each issue guest-designed by a different practitioner.

Editors: Geoff Cox, Nav Haq and Tom Trevor
Advisory Group: Shumon Basar, Binna Choi, Neil Cummings, Maria Lind, Carol Yinghua Lu
Assistant Editor: Lucy Badrocke
Picture Research: Laura Beadell
#3 designed by Ryan Ras | Message and Meaning
(Message and Meaning nominated by Europa, designers of #2)
Typeset in Franklin Gothic, Prestige Elite and Courier

ISBN: 9780 907738 97 8

ARNOLFINI
16 Narrow Quay
Bristol BS1 4QA, UK
info@arnolfini.org.uk
www.arnolfini.org.uk/journal

Thanks to the Digital Urban Living research centre, partly funded by the Danish Council for Strategic Research grant number 2128-07-0011

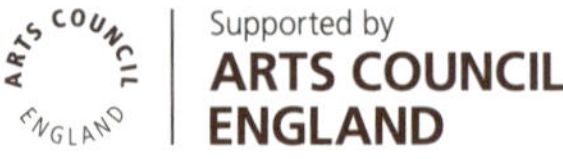

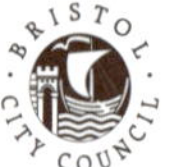

ARTIST/ACTIVIST SERIES
Devised by Tom Trevor

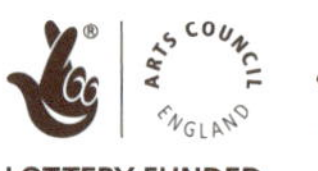

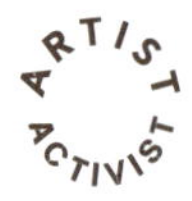

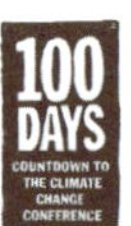

URSULA BIEMANN
Black Sea Files
12 September–8 November 2009

PLATFORM
C Words: Carbon, Climate, Capital, Culture
3 October–29 November 2009
African Writers Abroad, Ackroyd & Harvey, Institute for the Art & Practice of Dissent at Home, Laboratory of Insurrectionary Imagination, Hollington & Kyprianou with Tamasin Cave & Spinwatch, Trapese Collective and Virtual Migrants
Curated by PLATFORM
www.platformlondon.org

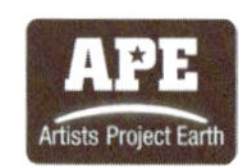

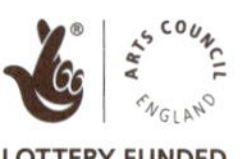

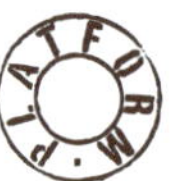

OCEAN EARTH
Peter Fend, Kevin Gannon, Catherine Griffiths, Heidi Mardon and Eve Vaterlaus
Situation Room: Technology Change/Climate Stability
21 November 2009–17 January 2010

BARBARA STEVENI
Beyond the Acid Free: Artist Placement Group Revisited
21 November 2009–17 January 2010

CRAFTIVISM
12 December 2009–14 February 2010
Kayle Brandon & Heath Bunting, Rhiannon Chaloner & Manuel Vason, glorious ninth, GOTO10, Rui Guerra, Household, Christine & Irene Hohenbüchler, JODI, Mandy McIntosh, Gloria Ojulari Sule, Trevor Pitt & Kate Pemberton, Janek Simon, Stephanie Syjuco and Clare Thornton
An Arnolfini/Relational project, curated by Zoe Shearman with Geoff Cox and Anne Coxon
www.craftivism.net, www.relational.org.uk

relational

Adam Mickiewicz Institute
CULTURE.PL

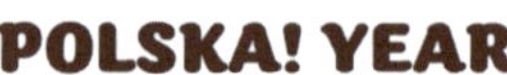

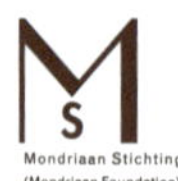

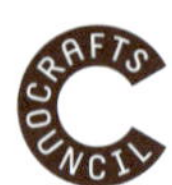

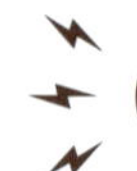

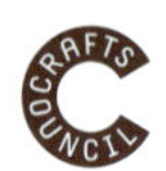

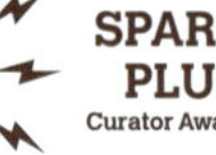

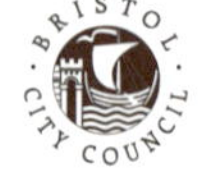

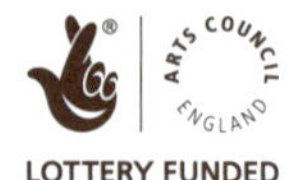

Seminar:
Who's Recuperating Who?
26 November 2009
Gustav Metzger, Ursula Biemann, Peter Fend, Janna Graham/Ultra-Red, Brian Holmes, Esther Leslie, PLATFORM and Tom Trevor. Moderated by Geoff Cox and Nav Haq